OCCASIONAL CONTRIBUTIONS FROM THE MUSEUM OF ANTHROPOLOGY OF THE UNIVERSITY OF MICHIGAN

No. 16

THE ARZBERGER SITE

HUGHES COUNTY, SOUTH DAKOTA

BY

ALBERT C. SPAULDING

ANN ARBOR

MUSEUM OF ANTHROPOLOGY,
UNIVERSITY OF MICHIGAN

1956

ISBN (print): 978-1-949098-49-5
ISBN (ebook): 978-1-951538-47-7

Browse all of our books at
sites.lsa.umich.edu/archaeology-books.

Order our books from the University of Michigan
Press at www.press.umich.edu.

For permissions, questions, or manuscript queries,
contact Museum publications by email at umma-
pubs@umich.edu or visit the Museum website at
lsa.umich.edu/ummaa.

CONTENTS

ILLUSTRATIONS

PLATES

(Plates I–XVII follow page 173)

FIGURES IN THE TEXT

MAPS

INTRODUCTION

THE work at the Arzberger site described here represents the major part of the second season of excavation in the Dakotas by Columbia University parties. In the first season (1938) excavations in co-operation with the North Dakota Historical Society were conducted on a historic Mandan village and a protohistoric Cheyenne site, with additional testing at several other North Dakota sites. It was decided to devote the 1939 season to South Dakota, with particular emphasis on the problem of Arikara prehistory, and an arrangement was made for a Works Projects Administration investigation jointly sponsored by Columbia and the University of South Dakota Museum. The entire program, which also included ethnographic research, was a continuation of the long-maintained interest of William Duncan Strong, Professor of Anthropology, Columbia University, in central and northern Plains culture history.

The 1939 party consisted of five Columbia University students: Robert B. Cumming, Jr., Dorothy E. Fraser, Joan Howson, Joseph Jablow, and Albert C. Spaulding. Excavations at the Arzberger site were directed by Spaulding, field cataloguing and other laboratory work was done by Fraser and Howson, and Cumming and Jablow acted as field assistants. The group was under the general direction of Professor Strong, although circumstances combined to prevent him from visiting the field party during the summer. Excavation at the Arzberger site extended from June 6 to August 19, 1939, the rest of the summer being occupied with excavation at the Buffalo Pasture site in Stanley County. The working force other than the Columbia students consisted of a WPA crew averaging eight men.

The problem of choosing a site for excavation was comparatively easy owing to the extremely helpful advice given us by W. H. Over, at that time director of the University of South

Dakota Museum. Mr. Over placed at our disposal his extensive survey notes on the sites along the entire length of the Missouri River in South Dakota and recommended to our attention several sites in the vicinity of Pierre, among them the Arzberger site. We were very much impressed by the surface features of the latter site, its position was within the area traditionally ascribed to the Arikara in the mid-eighteenth century, and, finally, permission to excavate was readily granted by Charles Arzberger, the owner of part of the site. At a later stage in our work one house on the property of John Holts was excavated with his permission.

We are indebted not only to Mr. Over and the owners of the site for their indispensable aid, but also to several other people for help of various kinds. These include Frank Kerley, who at that time rented the Arzberger property, Lawrence K. Fox of the South Dakota Historical Society, and several residents of Pierre and Fort Pierre who volunteered information about local archaeology and helped to make our stay pleasant. Bob Butts, state director of the Research and Records Division of the Professional and Service Division, WPA, was very helpful, not only from the standpoint of WPA administrative procedures, but also in obtaining permission to excavate. Local WPA officials were equally co-operative, and the members of the crew were competent workmen. A large part of the laboratory work was done at the University of South Dakota Museum (now the W. H. Over Museum); the facilities of the Museum and the assistance of the staff greatly increased the efficiency of our work.

SURFACE FEATURES

THE Arzberger site is in Hughes County, South Dakota, approximately 7.5 miles east-southeast of Pierre. It occupies most of the southwest quarter of sec. 10, Twp. 110 N., R. 78 W. Its general situation with relation to topography and drainage is shown in Map 1 and in Plate I A. The site can be described briefly as a fortified village on the essentially level top of a precipitous terrace which is presumably a remnant of a flood plain made by the Missouri River at an earlier stage in its history. The river, the general course of which is here slightly south of east, has at the present time cut to more than 100 feet below the level of the terrace top and is about a half mile to the south of the terrace. On the south the foot of the terrace is separated from the river bottom by a gently sloping apron of detritus, but to the north it is almost completely cut off from the higher level of the glaciated plains by steep-sided creek valleys. Immediately to the west of the terrace is the small valley of an intermittent stream known as Mush Creek, and on the east and northeast is the rough topography of the glaciated plains and the fronting apron of sediment derived from their erosion. The top of the terrace is bisected by a draw which heads near its north edge and runs to the south. At the mouth of this draw, on the south side of the terrace, is a knoll which is at about the same level as the terrace top (Pl. I A) and is obviously an isolated remnant of the terrace formed by the downward cutting of the draw.

This situation was very favorable for a horticultural group needing a village site adapted to fortification. Easily tilled fields were available on the river and creek bottoms in the immediate vicinity, there was timber on Mush Creek and along the river, and springs seep out of the terrace itself at the point of contact of the underlying Pierre shale and the overburden of sediment. The steep sides and almost complete isolation of the terrace make it a natural fort, and the scarcity or absence

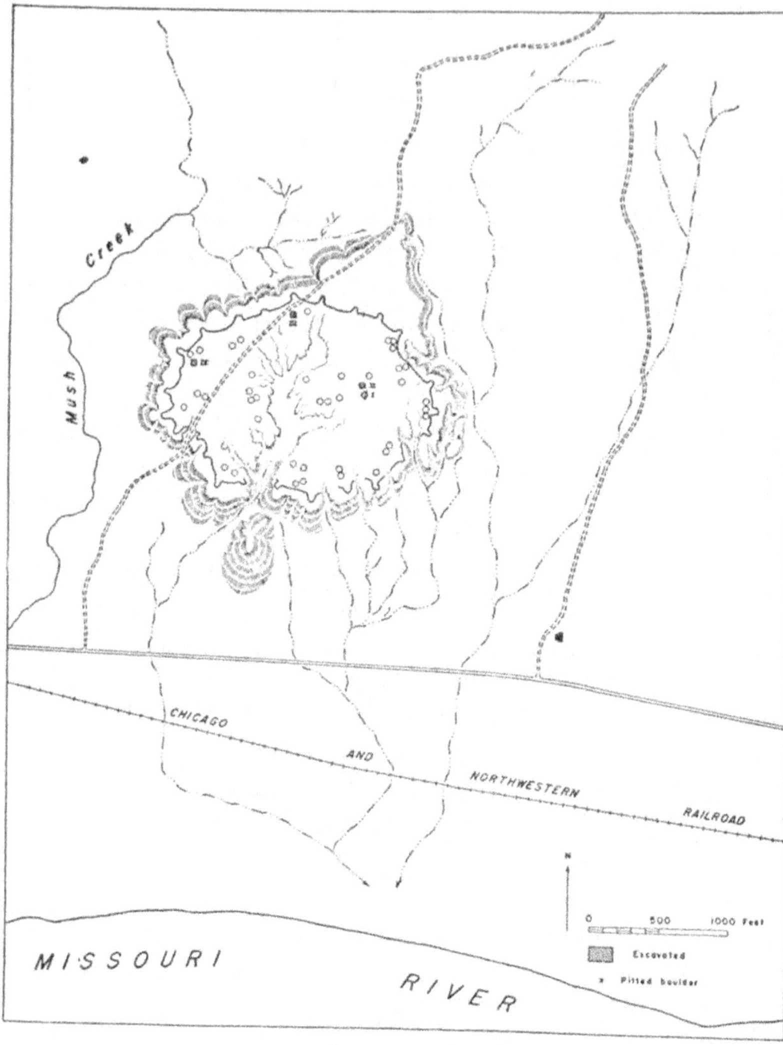

MAP 1. The Arzberger site, SW. ¼, sec. 10, T. 110 N., R. 78 W., Hughes County, South Dakota.

of other terraces of this type for miles up and down the river would almost ensure its choice by a large group looking for an easily defended position.

The most striking cultural feature of the site is an enclosing ditch which follows the edge of the terrace closely for most of its length and juts out to form a bastion at intervals of 50 to 100 yards (indicated by a heavy line in Map 1). There are 24 bastions on the perimeter of about 1.5 miles. Most of them are closely adapted to the natural contours of the terrace, occupying points bounded by the numerous small gullies which have scalloped the terrace edge. On the northeast side of the site the ditch does not follow the terrace edge for a distance of 800 feet; here the terrace extends to form a point, but the ditch cuts across the base of this point and regains the terrace edge. In general form the figure enclosed by the ditch is a rather regular ellipse with axes of about 2,000 and 1,300 feet and an area of about 44 acres. There are only two extensive breaks in the ditch, one near the center of the south edge of the site where the large draw mentioned above interrupts its course, and the other at the eastern end where another unusually well-developed ravine extends headward into the terrace top. In a few other places the ditch is either obliterated or very obscure, but for the most part its course can be traced easily, both on the ground and on a vertical aerial photograph. The average depth of the ditch is about a foot, and in most places its width is 10 feet or more. In some places, and particularly at the bastions, the inner border is higher, indicating that most of the dirt removed in excavating was thrown to the inside. The two breaks mentioned above are probably original features, as the close relationship between the bastions and the smaller draws suggests that no great amount of erosion has taken place since the site was occupied. In 1939 the site was in native grass and probably had never been plowed.

Thirty-seven house rings were observed on the site, and seven more were identified on a large-scale vertical aerial photograph. Most of the rings were indistinct and were detected most easily by the greener and taller grass growing in the central depression. The largest and best-defined ring, that of House III, was about 0.8 foot in depth and had a diameter of about 50 feet; few of the others approached these dimensions. More representative figures would be a depth of about

0.4 foot with a diameter of from 35 to 40 feet or even less. It is highly probable that many house sites were not observed because of their obscure rings. As is indicated in Map 1, no house sites were found outside the fortification, and there appears to be a tendency for the houses to be placed near the line of fortification and the large central draw. Occasional examples elsewhere, however, and the prevailing obscurity of house rings do not permit any detailed discussion of village plan. Certainly, the number of house sites observed, amounting to no more than one to an acre, is surprisingly low for as large a site. It is possible to argue, however, that the position of the fortification was dictated by topographic considerations and that there were comparatively few houses because a small group strained its manpower resources to the utmost to take advantage of a convenient defensive position. If this is the correct explanation, the military situation must indeed have been desperate. A final explanation, assuming again that the total house count given is substantially correct, is that the fort was a refuge for other villages in the neighborhood of the terrace. In the absence of direct evidence for the presence of such groups, it seems futile to carry this line of thought further.

No undoubted refuse mounds were found on the site, and surface material was practically absent. This scarcity of refuse might be interpreted as an indication of a short occupation, but it might also be in part the result of a practice of throwing refuse over the edge of the terrace or into the large draw, where it would be washed away. In addition, there has been no plowing to expose the topsoil material.

Another cultural feature of interest is a large rock (Pl. I B) having a maximum diameter of about 3 feet which is situated immediately outside the ditch on a small isolated ridge at the east end of the site (the position is indicated by an X in Map 1). It is covered with round pits an inch or more in diameter and perhaps a half inch or less in depth. The pits were produced by pecking and are quite uniform in size. The rock is an igneous glacial erratic and presumably was transported to its present position by natural agencies. There is no direct evidence other than its position to link it with the fortification and houses.

To the south of the terrace, on the river bottom, are other house depressions and some surface material. A small collection of surface sherds made here does not show any of the characteristic Arzberger types, and it was concluded that the site had no particular relationship to the Arzberger site proper. DeLand (1906: 553–54) reported evidences of villages above and below Mush Creek on the river bottom.

An earlier description of the site (DeLand, 1906: 553–58) does not appear to differ in essential features from our observations, although there are some discrepancies in minor matters. It should be noted that the basic data of Map 1 were obtained by means of a plane table and stadia survey controlled by a taped base line with some details added from a Department of Agriculture vertical aerial photograph. The United States Geological Survey's Canning Quadrangle topographic map shows the general topographic situation of the area: contour interpolation on the 1937 edition indicates that the approximate elevation of the Missouri River bank is 1,420 feet above sea level, an average elevation for the site is 1,550 feet, and the general level of the plains to the north of the river is a little over 1,700 feet.

EXCAVATIONS

THE excavations can be divided into six major units, of which four were individual houses, one was a cross section and exploratory trench of the ditch, and one was an irregular pit in a burial area on the top of the knoll at the south side of the site. In addition to these excavations of features, several small test pits were dug in very low rises surmised to be refuse mounds (the results were negative) to obtain normal soil profiles. The positions of the excavation units other than the burial area are indicated on Map 1 by hatching.

HOUSES

Four house sites were selected for excavation. Two of these (Houses I and II) lay close together in the east-central part of the site, the third (House III) was close to the fortification in the north-central area, and the fourth (House IV) was close to the fortification at the western edge of the site. These houses were chosen because of their relatively distinct rings and their scattered position in the enclosed area.

The same basic technique was followed in the excavation of each house. The first step consisted of excavating a pit 1 m. square in the center of the ring to determine, if possible, the depth of the floor and the position of the fireplace. Following this initial digging, trenches a meter in width were run through the house site in north-south and east-west directions to determine the horizontal extent of the floor. The resulting quadrants were then excavated by horizontal slicing with shovel and trowel. The house fill was not screened. After the floor was exposed, all post molds were dug out, special features such as cache pits were excavated, and a cross section of the fireplace was made. As a final step, a trench was dug through the floor to undisturbed soil to check on the possibility of superposition of structures. Post molds and other features were plotted on the excavation plan by means of the plane table and alidade.

House I. The site of House I was marked on the surface by a depression a little more distinct than most of those on the eastern part of the site. It was approximately circular with a diameter of 40 feet and a depth of about 0.7 foot. There was no surface material in the vicinity. The excavation technique outlined above was followed, but no definite fireplace, post molds, or other architectural features were found. The fill within the depression was composed of a fine, sandy loam which everywhere covers the site. In a vertical section through the middle of the depression, a dark lens was visible which was about 1.1 feet thick in the center. The upper edge of this lens joined the thin top humus zone, but its lower border sloped up from the center and pinched out at the surface humus zone at the edges of the depression. This dark central lens was noted at all of the houses excavated on the site and is probably the result of comparatively heavy humus accumulation because of the more abundant vegetation in the depression and because of deeper penetration of water in the less compact house fill. Another factor of possible significance in producing the dark lens is the fact that the fill was largely composed of roof material with its heavy topsoil content.

Occasional sherds, flint chips, and bone scraps were collected from the fill to a depth of about 1.5 feet, but most of the refuse, including bits of charcoal and numerous cracked rocks, was around the periphery of the depression at a depth of 0.2 to 0.7 foot. Perhaps three-quarters of the material found, excluding cache pit contents, came from this peripheral area. In the approximate center of the depression at a depth of 0.7 to 1.0 foot, some unworked angular rock fragments were found. They covered a horizontal area having dimensions of about 3 by 8 feet, but no traces of ash or burned earth were associated. Near the edge of the depression at a depth of 0.4 to 0.8 foot were two other groups of rock fragments, one arranged in an arc vaguely suggestive of a fireplace, but there was no trace of ash or charcoal in the area. No explanation other than the vagaries of refuse disposal is apparent for these features.

Nine other features were noted in the excavation; three of these (Features 5, 7, and 11) were shallow basins with dark loose fill, and the remainder (Features 3, 4, 6, 9, and 10) were large cache pits with neck and expanded bottom. The position of these features is indicated in Figure 1, and a detailed description is given immediately below.

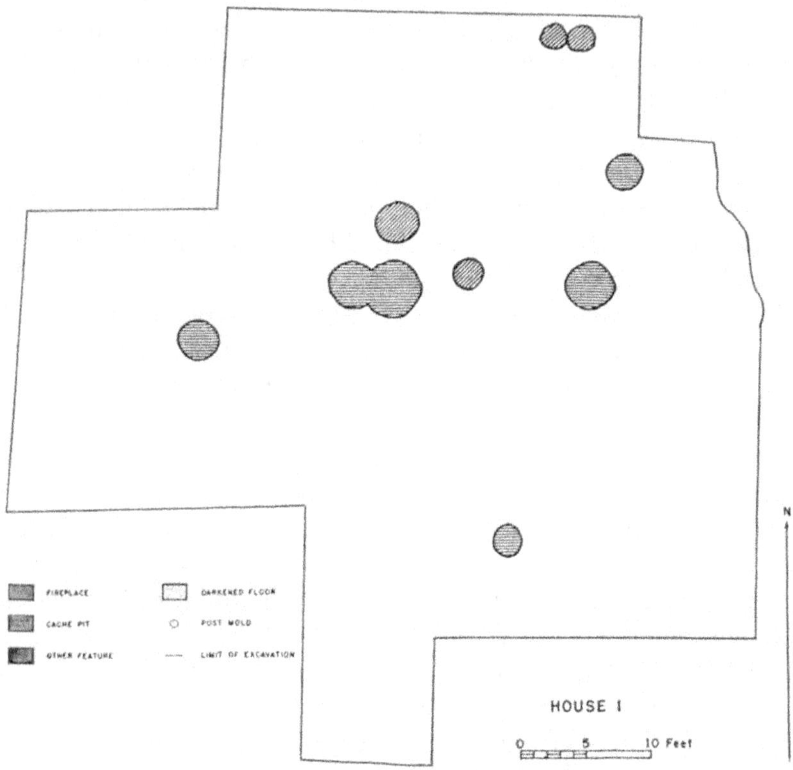

FIG. 1. Plan, House I.

Feature 5 was a round basin 2.5 feet in diameter and about 0.4 foot in depth. Its center was about 6 feet north-northeast of the approximate center of the excavation, which was also very close to the center of the surface depression. Its top was discovered 2.1 feet below the surface. The fill was darker and softer than the surrounding soil and contained scraps of bone, sherds, and a small deposit of flint chips.

Feature 7 is the designation given to the two contiguous basins at the north edge of the excavation. Each was roughly circular with a diameter of about 2.0 feet and a depth of 0.3 foot. The tops of these pits were first seen at a depth of 1.3 feet below the surface. As the pits lay outside of the surface depression, it is probable that their tops were close to the present surface and that their apparent depth was the result of our failure to see them until the humus-stained topsoil was dug away. The fill was mixed ash and dark earth and contained in its upper part a small deposit of flint chips and a fragment of a vein chalcedony knife.

Feature 3 was a definite cache pit lying 18.5 feet west of the center of the excavation, a location within but close to the western edge of the surface depression. Its top was at a depth of 1.5 feet, where it showed plainly as a circular dark stain in the lighter surrounding soil. The fill was much looser in texture than the undisturbed earth and could be excavated by troweling from the side walls. The observed depth of the pit was 2.4 feet and the diameter at the top was 3.2 feet. At the point of maximum expansion 1.2 feet below the top, the diameter was 5.3 feet. The pit expanded sharply, the shoulders beginning about 0.3 foot below the observed top. This extremely short neck suggests that a part of the pit was cut away before its presence was suspected. The fill contained scraps of bone and flint, unworked rocks, fragments of charcoal, sherds, a mussel shell, and other refuse; artifacts found include a hammerstone, a sandstone abrader, two flint end scrapers, two bone chipping tools, an apparently polished fragment of bison rib, and a bison scapula hoe.

Feature 4 was 13 feet east-northeast of the center of the excavation, a position about 6 feet from the eastern edge of the surface depression. The top of the pit appeared as a very definite black circle 3.4 feet in diameter. It was first noted at a depth of 2.3 feet below the surface. From the observed top the sides slanted outward and downward evenly to the bottom of the pit, where the maximum diameter of 5.7 feet occurred. The depth at which the top was encountered and the absence of a neck indicate strongly that the upper part of the pit was not seen. The total depth was 3.1 feet. Near the top of the fill was an irregular mass of hard orange-buff earth containing flakes of charcoal and one sherd. The interior of this mass was a powdery white material, which seems to have resulted from the hard burning of a mixture of earth and ash, perhaps as a consequence of a fire built at the top of the pit. On the bottom of the pit lay a number of bison ribs, two worn bison scapula hoes, and a part of an unworked scapula. Scattered through the fill were bone scraps, sherds, and flints, including two end scrapers.

Feature 6 was near the edge of the excavation (20 feet northeast of the excavation center) and barely outside the edge of the surface depression. Its top was seen at a depth of 1.4 feet, immediately below the deepest penetration of humus strain. The mouth was practically round with a diameter of 2.9 feet. The side walls were nearly vertical for about 0.2 foot and then slanted out evenly to the maximum diameter of 6.1 feet, which occurred at the bottom. The observed depth of the cache pit was 3.3 feet. Both form and dimensions are very close to those described for Feature 4. Specimens were scattered throughout the fill but were more plentiful in the upper 2 feet. Sherds, bone awls, a bone fishhook, a worn mussel shell, various flint and chalcedony knives and points, a grooved granite maul, and many fragments of bone were found. An unusual feature was an irregular ring of 20 unworked rocks around the edge of the pit at a depth of 1.7 feet from its top. The rocks seemed to be waterworn pebbles with an average maximum diameter of 0.4 foot. Some were broken, and there was some ash associated. The walls did not show any sign of burning, and it was inferred that the rock and ash were fireplace debris which had been disposed of in the pit. A few more rocks were found below this level. As was the case with the other pits, the fill was much darker and softer than the surrounding earth.

Features 8 and 9 are discussed together as they were intersecting cache pits. The center of Feature 8 lay 6 feet north-northwest of the center of the excavation, and the center of

Feature 9 was about 3 feet west of that of Feature 8. As was true for Feature 4, their tops were at a depth of 2.3 feet. Because of their intersecting tops, the pits were excavated by a vertical sectioning technique in order to determine the original order of digging and to segregate the artifacts of each. Feature 9 was the first pit dug, and a part of its fill was removed in subsequent excavation of Feature 8 by the Indians.

The diameter of Feature 9 at its mouth was about 3.6 feet. From the mouth the sides extended down almost vertically for a few inches and then flared out to a maximum diameter of 5.4 feet at a depth of 2.3 feet below the top. The pit fill was distinctly stratified; five irregular but definite layers were noted. At the top was a stratum on the order of 1.5 feet thick of light colored earth with occasional dark lenses. This layer contained many sherds and scraps of bone. The next stratum was composed of about 0.3 foot of harder and much darker fill and contained many fragments of bone. Resting on the top of this stratum was a nearly complete bison skull. The third layer was an almost sterile stratum of light soil with a maximum thickness of 0.5 foot. It pinched out about 1.3 feet from the east side of the pit. The fourth layer was a very productive and relatively thick (about 1.0 foot) zone of soft dark earth. The last layer was from 1.3 to 1.8 feet thick and was composed of mixed sandy loam and gravel. Much scrap bone, some small pieces of charcoal, and a few sherds were found. Curiously, the material of this bottom layer was very similar to a gravel stratum in the undisturbed soil at this depth, although it seems difficult to explain the implication that the Indians dug the pit and promptly threw back some of the material removed. Specimens in the pit as a whole represented practically all the types of artifacts found at the site—sherds, scapula hoes, flint arrow points, knives, end scrapers, grooved mauls, rib "shaft straighteners," grooved sandstone abraders, bone awls, and other material were collected. The stratified fill was clearly the result of deliberate filling by the inhabitants of the site, the strata representing refuse collected from various sources. This inference is also supported by the bison skull which was placed in the pit when it was nearly full.

Feature 8 had a roughly circular mouth with the large diameter of 4.3 feet, although the depth at which it was discovered (2.3 feet) makes it quite possible that there was originally a restricted neck above the observed position of the top. In shape Feature 8 differed from the other cache pits of House I in being nearly cylindrical, which again suggests that its upper part was not seen. The bottom of the pit was 3.8 feet below the observed top and was 5.1 feet in maximum diameter. The sides bulged outward very slightly so that the maximum diameter of the pit occurred about midway between bottom and top. For the first 1.0 foot from the top the fill was almost entirely composed of a dome of burned earth and ash. Around the edge of this burned plug was a deposit of dark earth similar to the dark fill in other pits. Below the burned earth and ash was a rather uniform fill of light earth and pebbles extending to the bottom of the pit; it appeared to be identical with the bottom stratum of Feature 9. This distinctive light fill clearly cut the stratified fill of Feature 9. Sherds and scrap bone were scattered through the fill, and a few other specimens, including scapula hoe fragments, bone awls, flint points, and flint scrapers, were found.

Feature 10 lay about 15.5 feet south-southeast of the excavation center, a position about 6.5 feet inside the surface depression. Its top was first observed at 1.6 feet below the surface, where it showed clearly as a circular dark stain 2.3 feet in diameter. From the top the side walls ran down vertically for about 0.7 foot and then flared out sharply into definite shoulders. The bottom of the pit was 3.0 feet below the top, and the maximum diameter of 5.1 feet occurred about 0.6 foot above the bottom. A north-south section showed that the shape was decidedly asymmetrical, with the side wall bulging considerably more on the south and west than it did in the opposite direction. The fill was soft dark earth together with a little light ash. Many scraps of bone and sherds were found, and other specimens were scattered through the fill. Among the latter were fragments of worked scapulae, flint end scrapers, flint arrow points, and several mussel shells.

The assemblage of features included under the label "House I" is difficult to interpret. The surface depression was similar to that of the undoubted house sites described below, and the cross section exhibited the same general characteristics noted in the excavation of the remaining houses. The five cache pits inside the limits of the surface depression and the concentration of refuse around its edges also suggest a house site. Despite these positive indications, however, no clear trace of any structural feature was discovered. A few vague black spots were noted, but neither their shape nor their horizontal relationship to one another suggested post molds. No trace of a fireplace was seen in the central area unless the few scattered rocks seen are to be so interpreted, but such an interpretation seems very dubious because they were not accompanied by ash or burned earth. Excavation in the central area was carried to plainly undisturbed earth (a layer of gravel), and on the periphery the presence of various cache pits indicated that the floor level had been reached or more than reached. The general absence of well-defined necks on the cache pits can be taken to mean that the level from which they were dug was not recognized in the course of the excavation and consequently that the floor level was also unwittingly destroyed. An alternative explanation, that the surface depression was entirely the result of a concentration of outdoor cache pits rather than a house site, has the attractive feature of containing no implication of technical deficiency, but the preponderance of evidence seems to favor the house theory.

House II. The south edge of this house site lay about 25 feet north of House I. The depression was shallow (about 0.8 foot maximum depth), approximately circular, and of about the same diameter as House I. There was no surface material in or around the depression, although refuse was found in considerable quantity in the excavation of the fill.

The fill was a dark sandy loam and exhibited in cross section a dark lens like that of House I. Refuse and artifacts were rarely found in the central part of the fill, but they were abundant around the edges. Two small deposits of flint chips were 14.7 feet to the northeast of the fireplace at a depth of 0.3 to 0.6 foot, and several small fragments of charcoal were noted 15.4 feet east of the fireplace, at a depth of 0.4 foot. A few small streaks of ash and charcoal were in various parts of the fill from 0.3 to 0.8 foot below the surface.

In gratifying contrast to the situation at House I, the floor features were easily discerned, and the basic structural plan and other details can be described with considerable accuracy (Pl. II A and Fig. 2). The house was a nearly circular earth lodge with four central posts, a central fireplace, and an entrance passageway extending to the southeast. The diameter was approximately 43 feet, and the floor depth averaged about 1.1 feet. The original excavation could hardly have been more than a thorough removal of sod. The outer post molds were on the order of 0.3 foot higher than the surface of the fireplace, but the central post molds were not seen clearly until excavation had proceeded from 0.2 to 0.4 foot below the fireplace. These levels seem to indicate a slightly basin-shaped floor, but the differences are so small that they are probably of little significance, since as much as 0.3 foot of variation occurred in the levels of the outer posts alone. The floor was somewhat darker than the surrounding soil but was not noticeably harder.

The figure formed by the outer posts can best be described as a slightly modified circle. Using a point 1.1 feet northwest of the middle of the fireplace as a center, a circle 43 feet in diameter cuts the outer posts quite regularly on the northeast, northwest, and southwest sides at, or within a few inches of, their centers. On the southeast side the situation is obscure, probably because of special arrangements in connection with the entrance. The postholes of the north, south, east, and west segments lie outside this circle. In the north and west segments, where the situation is clearest, the curve is fairly regular, with a maximum departure from the basic circle of about 1.6 feet. These "corners" are less definite and less regular on the east and south, again possibly because of a wall modification related to the entrance. On the south it would appear that some of the molds of the outer ring were not discovered, and the situation is further complicated by several post molds inside what has been taken to be the outer ring, but a corner can be made out by selecting the outer molds. On the east, however, a defi-

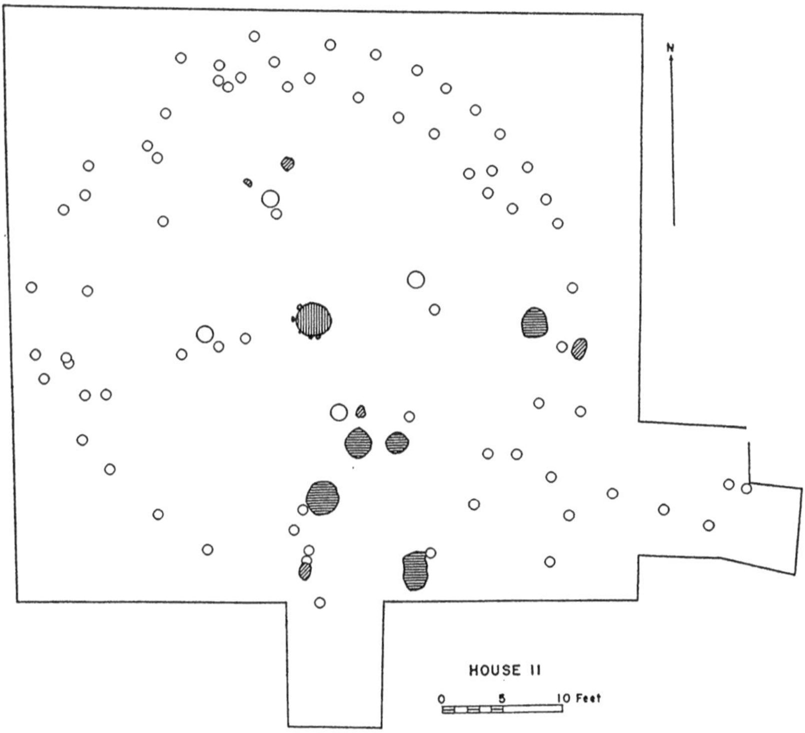

FIG. 2. Plan, House II. See Fig. 1 for explanation of symbols.

nite bulge occurs, although its maximum departure from the 43-foot circle is no more than 0.7 foot. Assuming that the southern segment has been interpreted correctly, it is difficult to avoid describing the basic shape of the house as a four-cornered circle, a notable solecism. On the east side of the house the molds are spaced quite regularly at intervals averaging slightly less than a yard, but on the west the spacing is both wider and less uniform. In addition to the molds representing the outer wall of the house, the northern quadrant shows an inner arc of molds approximately parallel to, and about 3 feet from, the main circle. The other parts of the wall area also show interior molds, and a few exterior molds are present, but no particular pattern of placement is evident. Possible functions for the inner molds might include bracing for shaky outer posts or support for beds or other domestic gear.

Seven molds of the entrance posts were found. Their position indicates an entrance passage extending to the southeast for slightly over 16 feet beyond the southeastern wall of the house. The width is rather uncertain because of a scarcity of molds on the northeast side of the passage, but it was probably a little less than 4 feet. On the southwest side the pattern of molds appears to be reasonably complete; here there are four quite evenly spaced molds with an interval of about 4 feet. The entrance is aligned so that an extension of its long axis intersects the fireplace and meets the southeast side of the square formed by the central posts at an angle close to 90°. This alignment is by no means mathematically exact, however. The depth at which the entrance molds were found did not differ appreciably from that of the outer posts.

The central posts formed an approximately square figure about 13 feet on a side with the corners as defined by the posts rotated some 12° counterclockwise from the cardinal directions according to our compass observations. The position of the post on the north was slightly irregular (about a foot out of place) with relation to the other three posts, and the center of the fireplace failed to coincide with the center of the square which fell within, but close to, the north edge of the fireplace. Associated with the main center post were five smaller posts which may have been braces.

A clearly conceived structural pattern is implied by the basic regularity of the post mold positions. It seems justifiable to infer that some sort of surveying technique was used in laying out the house, although placement of structural features can hardly be considered precise. The fundamental construction figure was a circle about 43 feet in diameter, presumably defined by a simple peg and thong method. Cardinal directions with the center of the circle as a point of origin were established, and the position of the outer wall corners, the entrance passage, and the center posts determined. Center posts and corners were established approximately on the cardinal radii by direct or indirect methods, and the long axis of the entrance was laid out at right angles to the southeast side of the central post square. The observed irregularities are of the order which might be expected with paced distances and estimated right angles. Our excavations did not provide any information on the manner in which the entrance passage floor rose to the ground surface, nor did we observe any trace of leaner posts outside of the exterior wall posts.

The outer post molds ranged from 0.3 to 0.7 foot in diameter, the majority falling in the 0.4 to 0.5 foot range. Their shape in horizontal section was usually round, although a few examples were definitely elliptical. Depths ranged from 0.4 to 0.7 foot with much variation between these limits; the depths given are undoubtedly minimums, as it is highly probable that some of the top was pared off in every case before the mold was observed. The fill of the molds was a soft dark loam which contrasted well with the lighter surrounding soil and made it possible to excavate the fill with confidence. Charcoal fragments were frequently present in the fill, and occasionally bits of decayed wood were found. In a few molds there were sherds, bone fragments, or flint chips. All of the molds appeared to be vertical or nearly vertical. The entrance passage molds were much like those of the outer wall in diameter and depth; one contained four stones and a fragment of bone which had evidently been wedged around the post to make it more stable. The main central posts were both greater in diameter and deeper than those from the entrance and the exterior wall. All exceeded 0.5 foot in diameter and two were more than 0.7 foot. Their range in depth was from 0.7 foot to 1.5 feet, three being more than 1.0 foot. The auxiliary central posts were also rather large and varied from 0.3 foot to 1.6 feet in depth. All of the post molds in the central area were approximately vertical, and their fill was like that of the outer molds. Traces of charcoal and bone fragments were observed in both main and auxiliary central molds.

Floor features of the house other than post molds consisted of the fireplace, an unworked rock, the broken remains of a pottery vessel, three small pits of unknown function, a small lens of burned clay, and four cache pits. A fifth cache pit was immediately outside the outer posts. The unworked rock (its greatest diameter was about 0.7 foot) lay about 12 feet northwest of the center of the fireplace. The smashed vessel was spread over an area of several square feet about 10 feet southeast of the fireplace. It was not complete but was clearly a vessel like that represented by the large sherd illustrated as Plate XI A. The first of the three small pits (Feature 1) was a conoidal excavation in the house floor about a foot in diameter and 1.5 feet deep lying about 2 feet east of the south main central post. Its fill contained soft black earth with much scrap bone, a few sherds, an end scraper, and a sandstone abrader. Its position and general shape suggest a large central post, but the fill was very much like that of the cache pits. It might also be considered a small cache or perhaps the site of a wooden mortar for pounding corn. The second small pit (Feature 7) was a basin 1.3 feet by 1.0 foot in diameter and 0.9 foot deep. It lay directly south of the fireplace on or slightly inside the outer wall and had a dark, quite soft fill containing a few sherds and an arrow point. The third small pit (Feature 8) was a similar basin immediately outside the outer posts on the east side of the house. Its top was oval with axes of 1.1 feet and 1.0 foot and an interior depth of 0.8 foot. A few scraps of bone were found in its fill. A final minor feature (Feature 9) was a small lens of burned earth 0.2 foot thick and 1.1 by 1.3 feet in major horizontal dimensions.

As was mentioned above, the center of the fireplace was about a foot southeast of what seemed to be the architectural center of the house. The fireplace was somewhat oval with diameters of 3.1 and 2.7 feet. Five unworked pebbles were placed around the south and west sides with their tops projecting an inch or two above the ash fill. A vertical section showed a layer of fluffy wood ash from 0.3 to 0.5 foot in thickness, and on the east side this ash was underlaid by a shallow lens of hard-burned earth. The sides were practically vertical with little evidence of burning.

No particular arrangement of the cache pits is evident other than that all are in the front (entrance) half of the house and outside the square formed by the center posts. Feature 2 was directly east of the fireplace and slightly less than 3 feet inside the eastern corner; Features 4, 5, and 6 formed a group between the south center post and the south corner (these features are respectively 14 feet south, 12 feet southeast, and 11 feet south-southeast of the center of the fireplace); and Feature 3 was immediately outside of the south corner and even in part underneath the projected line of the outer posts. If the outer posts served as supports for leaning wall posts, however, the pit was within the outer wall of the house.

Feature 2 showed plainly as a darker area at the level of the outer post molds. Its top was roughly a truncated oval with diameters of 3.1 and 2.8 feet. From the top, the sides extended down quite symmetrically to a maximum diameter of 4.6 feet a few inches above the floor, which was 2.2 feet below the top. The floor was practically flat. Soft dark earth mixed with some ash was the chief ingredient of the fill. A harder lens of nearly white ash about 0.3 foot thick was noted 0.3 foot below the top of the pit, and some cracked, unworked pebbles were present in the lower part of the fill. Scrap bones, sherds, a fragment of a chalcedony knife, and a flint scraper were scattered through the fill. The absence of a neck on this pit is puzzling, as the general clarity of floor features in the house does not give reason to think that much of the top was removed inadvertently. Unless the pit was dug after the collapse of the house or before its construction, it seems necessary to assume that the description as given represents the complete form.

Feature 3, like all of the cache pits, was discovered at floor level about a foot below the surface. Its top was an irregular ellipse with a long axis of 2.6 feet. From the top downward, the sides expanded irregularly; the west side showed a regular bulge from a point a few inches below the top to the bottom of the pit, 2.3 feet below the top, but the east side sloped downward and outward in a nearly straight line to a maximum extension about 1.3 feet below the top and then curved back slightly to meet the flat bottom. The maximum diameter of the pit was 3.8 feet. The fill contained many pieces of angular rock around the sides in the upper part of the pit, and scattered rocks were present elsewhere. Scrap bone was plentiful, and a number of artifacts, including sherds, bone awls, a fragment of a rib arrow-shaft straightener, and a fragment of a scapula hoe, were found.

Feature 4 differed from most cache pits at the site in having a nearly cylindrical shape. The top was essentially circular with a diameter of about 2.0 feet. The depth from the observed top was also 2.0 feet, and the bottom had the same diameter as the top. The east wall of the pit bulged slightly, forming a faint shoulder at about 0.8 foot below the top, but elsewhere the walls were practically vertical. The fill produced scrap bone, sherds, two bone awls, an end scraper, and a vein chalcedony knife.

Feature 5 conformed more closely to the conventional Plains cache in shape. The mouth was approximately circular with a diameter of about 1.7 feet, and its sides descended almost vertically for a little more than 0.3 foot and then expanded in a smooth curve to a maximum diameter of 3.9 feet about 0.3 foot below the bottom. The depth of the pit was 2.2 feet. Extending down 1.3 feet from the bottom of the main pit was a smaller, cylindrical hole with a diameter of 1.0 foot. The fill of the main pit was soft and black in the central part but somewhat harder near the walls. It contained many fragments of bone and flecks of charcoal and a few scattered stones. Many objects were found in the fill; the most important were five scapula hoes, a grooved maul, a charred corncob, and a large part of a miniature pottery vessel. Sherds, flint chips, a hammerstone, and two end scrapers were also present. The cylindrical hole had a fill like that of the main pit and contained a number of bone fragments.

The final cache pit, Feature 6, was regularly shaped in vertical section. It had a short, practically straight-sided neck below which the sides bulged symmetrically to a maximum diameter of 2.8 feet at a depth of 1.2 feet and then curved back to the bottom of the pit, which was 1.8 feet below the mouth. The fill was dark and was somewhat harder in the bottom of the pit. Comparatively few specimens were found, the total being a few bone scraps, a sherd, and a leaf-shaped flint knife.

House III. This house was situated in the extreme north-central part of the site about 130 feet inside the line of the ditch (Map 1). Its position was marked by the largest and most impressive depression observed on the site. The depression was a little less than 50 feet in diameter, was approximately circular in shape, and had a maximum depth of about 0.7 foot. A small pit dug by an unidentified collector in the center of the ring fortunately proved to be too shallow to do any damage to the underlying floor features. There was no refuse on the surface or in the vicinity of the depression. Excavation proceeded without serious difficulty; the fireplace appeared in the original test pit, and the floor was exposed by horizontal slicing to the indicated depth.

The fill was much like that of House II in composition and also showed a similar dark lens above the floor and a concentration of refuse around the edges of the depression. A small piece of charcoal was found 11.5 feet north and 14.1 feet west of the fireplace at a depth of 0.3 foot, but no other features except occasional sherds and other refuse were noted during the fill removal.

The major structural characteristics and the orientation of the house were clear and were in their essential details very much like those of House II (Pl. III A, Fig. 3). The ground plan might equally well be described as a modified circle or a square with very deeply rounded corners. There were four center posts, or more accurately, four groups of center posts and an entrance passage extending to the southeast from the center of the southeast wall. The fireplace was in the approximate center. The plan is regular enough to suggest that it was the result of the same sort of surveying technique postulated for House II. The major dimensions were 40.7 feet for the northwest-southeast diameter and 41.7 for the northeast-

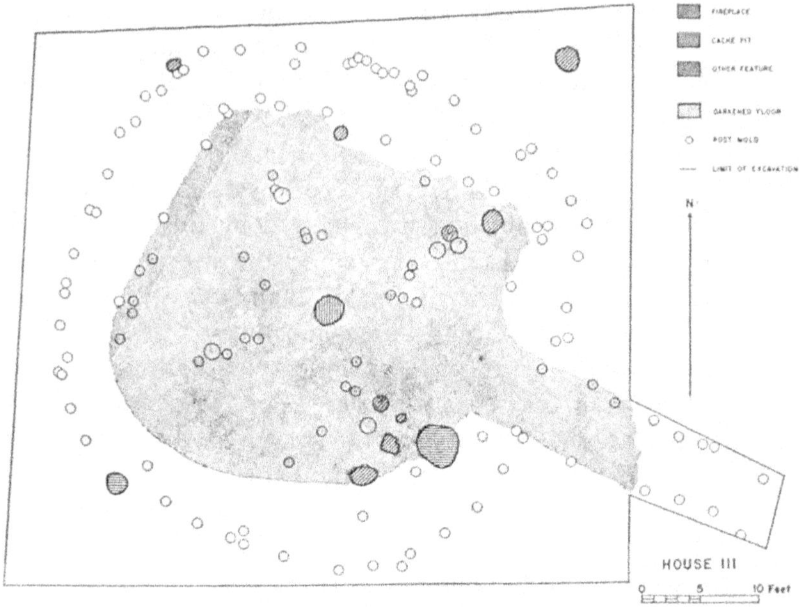

Fig. 3. Plan, House III.

southwest diameter. The observed depth of the floor varied from 0.95 foot at the fireplace to about 0.8 foot at the outer molds on the edges of the house. The floor tilted downward slightly to the south, as did the surface of the ground. A slightly basin-shaped floor is suggested by the levels of the fireplace and central posts in relation to the outer posts, the former being about 0.9 foot lower than would be expected if the floor were flat. Although some of this variation can be attributed to obscurity of features and lack of precision in excavative technique, the relatively large difference would indicate that the basin shape was a genuine feature of the original floor.

Two series of outer post molds can be seen on the floor plan, an outer group defining the edge of the house and an inner group roughly paralleling the outer wall and from 3 to 5 feet away from it. The outer series was exceptionally complete, with post molds closely spaced and in some cases nearly touching. The maximum interval between outer molds was 5 feet, but the average spacing was considerably less than 3 feet. On the southeast side a quite regular interval of about 3 feet occurred. The more thickly placed posts in other parts of the outer wall were probably the result of repairs. This was particularly true on the northeast side, where for several feet the molds were almost contiguous and were not carefully aligned with the original wall. The inner row was less regular both in the spacing of posts and in its general outline. On the southwest corner it failed completely, and no clear trace of it was found for several feet on either side of the doorway. For the most part, however, the inner molds also seem to have been originally a fairly regular series of posts which was obscured by subsequent additions in the form of braces or replacements.

The outer rows of molds varied in maximum diameter from 0.4 to 0.7 foot. Most were clearly round or elliptical in horizontal section, but a few examples had irregular shape. The fill of the molds was a loose dark loam, and frequent traces of rotten wood and charcoal were observed. Less commonly sherds, fragments of bone, or flint chips occurred in the fill. Depths ranged from 0.4 foot to 2.1 feet with an average of about 0.8 foot.

The entrance molds define a passage extending to the southeast from the center of the southeastern wall. The length of this passage was 21 feet, and its width varied from 6 feet near the house wall to about 5 feet at the outer end. In both alignment and spacing the molds were rather irregular. The dimensions and character of the fill of the entrance molds were like those of the outer series, and one still contained a sizable piece of wood.

The main central post molds were noticeably larger in cross section than those of the outer wall. Their positions defined the corners of a square measuring about 15 feet on a side. Three were accurately placed, but the fourth (on the east) was somewhat out of position. The orientation of this square corresponded with that of the outer wall, i.e., the sides were approximately northeast, northwest, southwest, and southeast. As was true of House II, the plan is rotated several degrees counterclockwise from the cardinal directions. In addition to the large molds, several smaller molds were clustered inside the square near each corner. These were presumably braces. Other molds, some of large size, lay close to the corners on the exterior of the square. The fill of the central post molds was dark and soft like that of the other post molds. One contained a stone, probably tamped into the hole to brace the post, and most had small fragments of charcoal. In one, scraps of bone were also noted. The four primary center posts averaged nearly 0.7 foot in diameter, and three were 1.8 feet or more in depth.

Floor features other than the post molds include a darkening of the floor itself, the fireplace, two cache pits, a large flat rock, and six small basins containing ash, charcoal, and other refuse. The position and extent of the darkened floor area are indicated by the dotted area on the floor plan (Fig. 3); it will be noted that it stops at the first of the two outer rows of posts and extends from the house out the entrance passage for some distance. The darker color seems to indicate the area of intensive use, which further suggests that the inner row of wall posts formed supports for beds or storage racks. The floor was not noticeably harder than the surrounding soil. The flat rock mentioned above lay about 2 feet southeast of the south-central post (Fig. 3 and Pl. III A). It showed no clear evidence of working or use, but its shape was well adapted for use as an anvil or grinding stone. A few cracked rocks lay near it. Occasional cracked rocks were also found at other points on the floor.

The fireplace was easily recognized, as its upper fill consisted primarily of fluffy, light-colored wood ash. It lay approximately in the center of the square defined by the central posts and consequently at the center of the house. Its shape was roughly circular with an average diameter of about 3 feet (the edges were rather poorly defined at floor level). A vertical section showed a lenticular shape with a maximum depth of 1.0 foot near the center, and at the bottom the underlying earth had been burned to yellow and red shades. The fireplace fill was mixed wood ash and dark earth with a much higher proportion of ash in the upper 0.3 foot. A few streaks of dark earth were noted immediately above the burned earth at the bottom of the basin.

In addition to the central fireplace, three small lenses of ashes and burned earth were present at the floor level. These were circular or elliptical basins from about 1.6 to 2.3 feet in maximum diameter and a few inches deep. Two were situated inside the house, the first near the inner row of wall posts at the south corner of the house about 4 feet south of the south-central post and the second in a corresponding position about 5 feet northeast of the east-central post. The third was completely outside the house, being some 8 feet beyond the outer row of posts on the northeast side. It was at a slightly higher level than the outer posts and was not much over 0.6 foot below the surface.

Three small pits having a different sort of fill were found. The first almost touched two posts of the outer row at the northern corner of the house. Its top was elliptical with dimensions of 1.2 feet by 1.0 foot, and its interior depth was 0.7 foot. The sides were nearly vertical for a short distance and then curved in to an almost flat bottom, and the fill was soft brown earth with fragments of charcoal, bone, and one stone. A second pit of this type, immediately inside the inner row of wall posts on the northeast side of the house, was cylindrical, with a diameter of 1.1 feet and a depth of 1.0 foot. The fill was black at the extreme top and brown below. A few pieces of charcoal and a bone fragment were found in the fill. The third pit lay about 3 feet to the east of the south-central post. Its major horizontal dimensions were about 1.5 by 1.3 feet, and its depth was 1.1 feet. The sides converged slightly to a rounded bottom. At the top the fill showed a layer of charcoal less than 0.1 foot thick, but below this was rather lumpy earth containing a number of stones and a few scraps of bone. Finally, there were two small basins, which were originally thought to be central post molds, containing charcoal, a small amount of scrap bone, and two sherds. They were only a few inches deep. The first of these is the northernmost of the cluster of three posts on the east corner of the central square; the second is about 2 feet to the east-northeast of the south-central post.

The two cache pits, Features 3 and 4, were situated, respectively, on the line of inner wall posts a short distance southwest of the entrance and immediately outside of the outer wall on the southwest corner of the house. Feature 3 was a large pit with a constricted neck. Its horizontal dimensions at floor level were 3.7 by 3.3 feet and its depth was 2.8 feet. The side walls ran down nearly vertically for about 0.5 foot and then expanded evenly to meet the nearly flat bottom, which had a diameter of 4.9 feet. Layers of soft dark earth, powdery ash, and harder brown material were noted, but the bulk of the fill was composed chiefly of white powdery ash. Many specimens and bone scraps were in the fill, including a number of worked scapulae, bone awls, vein chalcedony knives, chipped scrapers, and a large number of sherds. Some fragments of clam shells were also present. Feature 4 (Pl. III B) had a comparatively small, circular top 2.1 feet in diameter. From the top the sides contracted to form a distinct neck at a depth of 1.1 feet and then expanded, finally curving in to meet the flat bottom 3.8 feet below the top. The diameter of the bottom was 4.2 feet. The fill was a compact dark loam and was quite uniform. It contained sherds, a small hammerstone, chipped scrapers, and about 0.4 foot above the bottom a bison skull and a number of scapula hoes.

House IV. The site of this house was marked by the most distinct depression in the extreme western part of the site. Its diameter was about 36 feet, but its depth was no more than about 0.4 foot. The fill had no unusual characteristics and contrasted well with the lighter subsoil; in fact, its color was an important guide in the excavation, as the regular floor features were poorly marked. Specimens occurred in about the same quantity as in the other houses. The fireplace was found at a depth of 1.6 feet below the surface, the central posts were at a slightly higher level, and the outer posts averaged about 0.4 foot higher than the fireplace. The approximate depth of the outer posts below the surface was 1.0 foot.

A satisfactory delineation of the architectural pattern of the house was not possible owing to obscurity and absence of floor features. Enough evidence remained, however, to suggest that the structure had been an approximately circular earth lodge with four central posts and a central fireplace (Pl. II B, Fig. 4). No clear evidence of an entrance was seen, but floor discoloration suggested that a passageway ran to the east. The general arrangement appears to have been much like that of Houses II and III, although it is not possible to assert whether or not the same tendency toward corners was present. To judge by incomplete arcs of post molds, there was an outer circle of posts with a diameter of about 23 feet. Both circles center on the fireplace. A number of post molds did not fall on either arc, and the interpretation advanced here can hardly be considered certain. The central part of the floor was considerably darker than the surrounding soil, and the edge of the darkened area followed the inferred inner row of wall posts quite closely, as it did in House III. The central posts defined an approximate square about 7.9 feet on a side with corners roughly northeast, northwest, southeast, and southwest of the fireplace. All of these dimensions indicate a house which was somewhat smaller than Houses II and III.

The outer post molds averaged about 0.4 foot in diameter and about the same in depth. In many of them the fill was light in color and difficult to distinguish from the surrounding earth. A number of molds contained bits of rotten wood or charcoal, and occasional bracing stones, scrap bones, and sherds were found. Molds of the central posts were somewhat larger, varying from 0.5 to 0.9 foot in diameter and having a maximum depth of 1.5 feet. It should be emphasized that it was difficult to distinguish post molds, and it is quite possible that some were missed and that some of those mapped should have been omitted.

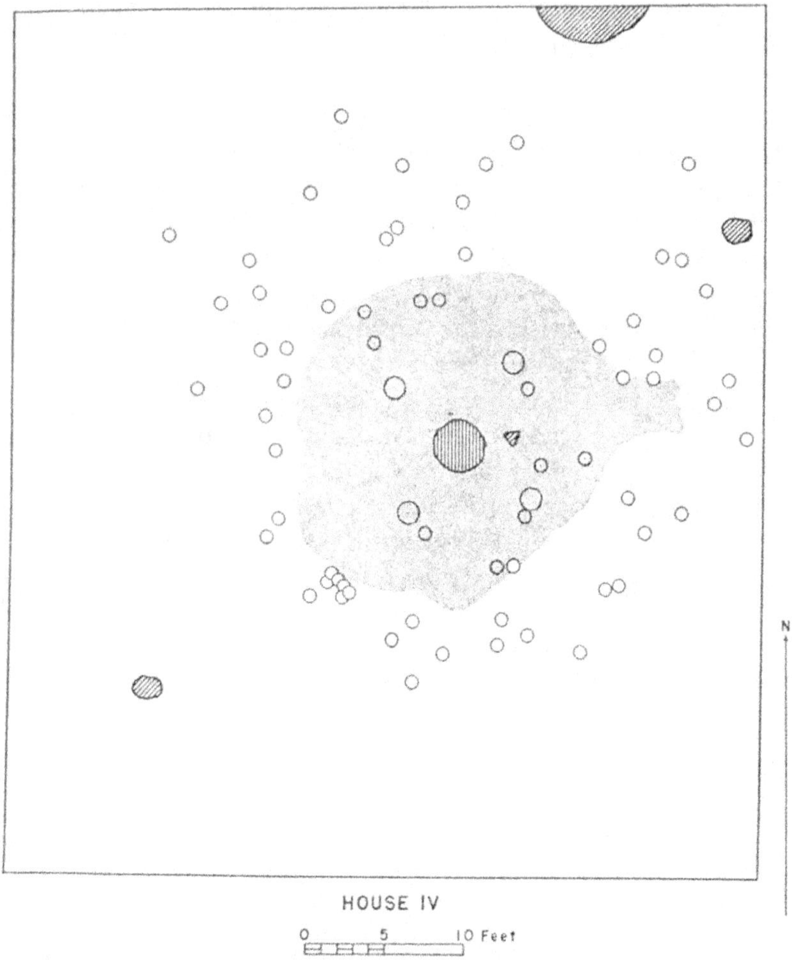

FIG. 4. Plan, House IV. See Fig. 1 for explanation of symbols.

Floor features other than the post molds were nearly lacking, the only two being the fireplace and a flat rock about 3 feet to the east of it. The fireplace was merely a darker area in the center of the structure with little evidence of use. It was roughly circular and had a diameter of about 3 feet. The flat rock lay at the same level; it showed no sign of working or use, but perhaps could have been an anvil. The darkening of the floor area has been mentioned above. The complete absence of cache pits seems strange in view of the ease with which they were detected at the other house excavations. This general vagueness and scarcity of floor features can best be explained, perhaps, by the assumption that the house was occupied for a very short time.

Three features were encountered in the excavation outside the house. The first was a lens of white ash which was about 3 feet from the outer wall on the northeast side of the house. It had a diameter of 1.6 feet, a thickness of 0.7 foot, and a depth below the surface of 0.7 foot. The second feature was a shallow basin-shaped pit about 10 feet outside the floor on the southwest side of the house. It had a loose dark fill containing a number of bone scraps. Its bottom was slightly below floor level. The total thickness was 0.5 foot and the diameter was 1.6 feet. The final feature noted was a larger pit with a fill of dark earth containing some ash and a considerable amount of scrap bone and specimens. It was situated about 10 feet to the north of the house, and only its south half fell within the limit of our excavation. Its top probably began at the surface, as it was well defined at a depth of 0.5 foot. The diameter was estimated at about 7 feet, and the observed depth was 1.8 feet. It was not possible to excavate the north part of this pit owing to lack of time.

DITCH AND STOCKADE

Two excavations were made in the fortification, the first a trench at right angles to the course of the ditch to obtain data on its depth and configuration as seen in transverse section and the second a long, shallow exploratory trench to search for stockade post molds. Both excavations were on the north side of the site in the section of the fortification immediately to the east of House III (Map 1).

The cross section was obtained by excavating a trench 1 by 10 meters (3.3 by 32.8 feet) in an approximately north-south direction, the ditch here having a general east-west course. The troweled side walls of the excavation showed the original profile of the ditch fairly well, although not as clearly as had been anticipated. A very dark humus stain was observed in the upper part of the ditch fill which contrasted with a lighter natural humus zone on either side, but the lower part of the fill was only slightly darker than the undisturbed earth surrounding it. Sharp delineation of the ditch fill was made more difficult by the presence of irregular dark stains in the undisturbed soil. A few sherds were found in the fill. As originally dug, the ditch seems to have been about 3.8 feet in depth and about 10 to 12 feet wide at the top. The bottom was rounded with the maximum depth approximately in the center. At the present time fill has accumulated to such an extent that the average depth is no more than a foot. The width is considerably greater than it was in the original condition, of course, because of the washing of material from the sides and immediate vicinity into the deeper part of the ditch. Little evidence of an embankment is now present except at the bastions. Presumably, the greater part of the earth removed in the original excavation has washed back to form most of the fill. The profiles obtained and observations at other points suggest, however, that most, if not all, of the excavated earth was piled on the inner side of the ditch to form an embankment for additional protection. Definite mounds of earth were present inside the bastions, where the material removed from a long section of ditch was concentrated.

The exploratory excavation was a shallow trench from about 4 feet to over 13 feet in width (Fig. 5, Pl. III). It paralleled the course of the ditch for approximately 325 feet, usually about 10 feet inside the center line, covering the relatively straight section between two bastions and following completely around one (Map 1). The position of the trench was governed by the course of a stockade which was first discovered in a preliminary pit at the eastern end of the excavation, the rest of the trench being merely the result of our attempt to follow the line of post molds. For the first 130 feet from the east the stockade was plain, with post molds regularly spaced at an interval averaging a little less than 3 feet. About 25 feet before the turn to form the eastern part of the bastion, the molds failed except for sporadic examples and did not appear again in quantity until the trench reached the outer end of the bastion. On the end of the bastion and on the western side a large number of molds appeared, but on the curve between the western side and the straight ditch to the west only a few were present. The stockade molds were distinguishable by their loose texture, or more rarely, by their darker color. All were dug out, and a series of 11 were sectioned vertically. Occasionally, bits of charcoal and rotten wood were found in their fill. Diameters ranged from 0.3 to 0.7 foot, with the majority from 0.4 to 0.5 foot. Most of the molds were from 0.3 to 0.6 foot in depth, but extremes of less than 0.3 foot and more than 1.2 feet were recorded. No particular concentration of large or deep molds was noted. The tops of the molds were observed at a depth of about 0.8 foot except on the bastion, where as much as 1.5 feet of embankment covered them. This means that they were only a few inches above the bottom of the ditch in its present condition or about 3 feet above the original bottom. A few sherds were found in the trench, including some of the post molds.

The large number and systematic position of the post molds seem safe ground for inferring the presence of a stockade from 6 to 15 feet inside of, and approximately parallel to, the ditch. The shallowness and irregular shape of many of the molds suggest that their tops have been destroyed by erosion and that the original situation was a stockade with its base placed in an inner embankment. Subsequent erosion would have washed most of the embankment into the ditch, leaving preserved only the bottoms of the post molds which had penetrated into undisturbed earth. Unfortunately for this theory, the deep embankment in the bastion did not show post molds rising to the present surface, but it seems possible that the

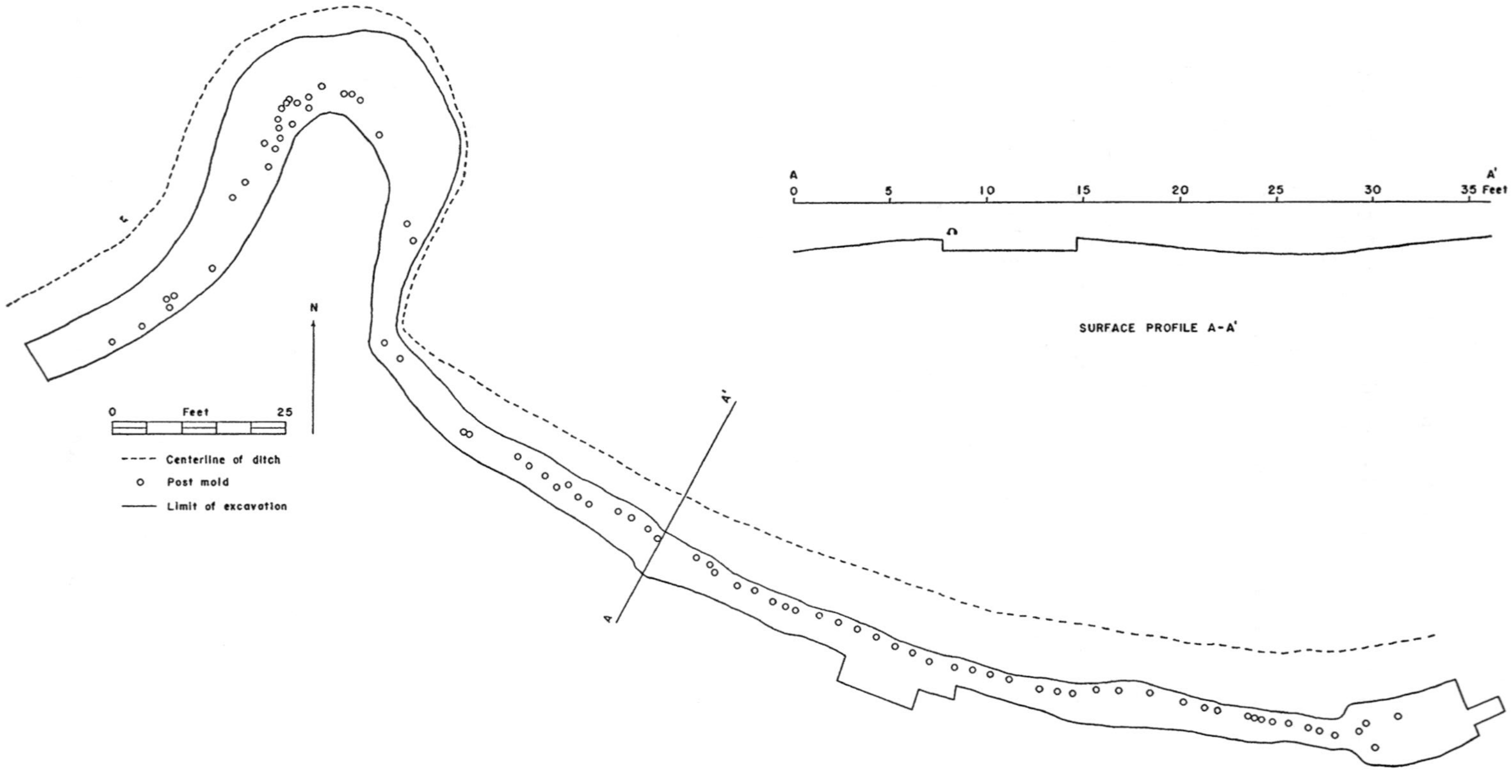

FIG. 5. Plan and surface profile, ditch and stockade excavation.

looser texture of the earth used in the fill permitted greater penetration of ground water and obliteration of the upper part of the mold without actual removal of material. The comparatively wide spacing of molds, even where a regular pattern is present, indicates that the stockade must have had supplementary horizontal poles or other screening if it offered effective protection from projectiles.

BURIALS

Burials representing six individuals were excavated. All were in the top of the knoll on the south side of the site at the mouth of the large central draw. The total area in which the burials were found was only 10 by 15 feet. Irregular holes and scattered fragments of human bone on the surface indicated that some recent disturbance had taken place. All of the burials were very shallow; the skull of Burial 1 was actually exposed, and the deepest burial was covered by only 2.0 feet of the loose sand and gravel of which the top of the knoll is composed. The casual pitting and disturbance so prevalent made even these observations of doubtful significance. Practically all that can be said of the original depth of the burials is that it was somewhat greater than that observed, as the loose material of this high point must have suffered some erosion since the time of aboriginal occupation. No indication of the shape and size of the burial pits was observed. Moreover, a complete absence of grave goods makes it impossible to show that the burials were associated with the site—they may well be the work of the inhabitants of the lower village or of the still later horse-using population of the area. Two of the better preserved burials are illustrated as Plate IV A. The data obtained will be summarized by individual burial. Sex designations are those given in the field and consequently are subject to revision by more expert opinion.

Burial 1 was a very tightly flexed adult male. Apparently, the body had been placed in a small pit in a squatting position and then compressed as much as possible. The top of the skull protruded from the ground. Nearly all the bones were present, and preservation was good.

Burial 2 was an adult male in a semiflexed position. The body had been placed in a prone position with the legs flexed to the left at the knees. The head was to the south. The skull, cervical vertebrae, and most of the right side of the skeleton were missing, including the right arm bones, femur, ribs, clavicle, and innominate. Two large rocks had been placed on the body, one on the left hip and the other on the feet. It should be added that waterworn rocks are plentiful in the soil of the knoll. Depth from the surface to the highest part of the burial was 0.5 foot. The missing bones undoubtedly had been removed by casual digging. Preservation of the remaining bones was fair.

Burial 3 was a semiflexed adult, probably female, The body had been placed in an almost supine position with legs and arms flexed to the right. The long axis of the skeleton was approximately east-west with the skull to the east. Preservation was only fair, and some of the smaller bones were missing. The grave fill included a rock near the left hip and others by the feet (Pl. IV A). Depth below the surface was about 0.7 foot.

Burial 4 (Pl. IV B) was a semiflexed child. The skeleton lay on its right side with the legs flexed. The head was to the south. Preservation was poor, with many small bones missing. The skull was smashed, and all of the bones were somewhat rotten. A large rock was placed above the body, and others were immediately to the east of it. Depth below the surface was only about 0.4 foot.

Burial 5 was a semiflexed child whose body had been laid in a supine position with the knees flexed upward. The lower legs were crossed, and the arms were extended downward with the hands resting on the pelvis. The head was to the east. Rocks had been placed at the side of the head, over the pelvis and lower arms, and over the knees. About 2.0 feet of earth covered the skeleton. The bones were rather fragile, and a number were broken.

Burial 6 consisted of the bones of a left foot at a depth of 0.8 foot. Traces of red ocher were visible on the bones. In the vicinity, on and under the surface, were other fragments of bone, and it seems clear that the foot bones were the undisturbed remnant of a formerly complete burial.

ARTIFACTS, FAUNAL REMAINS, AND VEGETAL MATERIAL

GROUND STONE

SOME of the stone artifacts are not available for direct description, but the completeness and excellence of a preliminary analysis made by Dorothy E. Fraser in 1939 make possible an accurate characterization. Mineral identifications and notes on the sources of material are largely based on information given Fraser by Dr. E. P. Rothrock, state geologist of South Dakota, during the course of her laboratory investigation at Vermillion.

Pipes. Four fragments of objects which are almost certainly pipes were found. All were made of mottled and streaked catlinite which was undoubtedly obtained from the well-known Minnesota quarry. The first specimen (Pl. V N, P) seems to be a part of the anteriorly projecting stem of a disk or elbow pipe of classic type. It was broken squarely across so far forward that no part of the bowl or the mouthpiece end of the stem is present. In cross section at the proximal end its shape is subrectangular with the following measurements (in cm.): the sides about 1.6, the top 1.2, and the bottom 1.1. The length of the fragment is 5.9 cm., and when viewed from above (Pl. V N) it tapers evenly to its prowlike distal end. Ornamentation consists of two sinuous flanges which project about 2 mm. from the sides of the stem; they are cut so that they stand out boldly except at the extreme distal end, where they merge into the prow. The flanges are from 2 to 3 mm. wide and are nearly identical on both sides of the stem, i.e., the stem is bilaterally symmetrical. On the top of the stem, and to a lesser extent on the bottom also, is a series of transverse scratches which are grouped into units of parallel lines. The scratches were apparently made with a multitoothed implement of some sort. As the surface on which they were made is very smooth, it may well be that they are decorative in purpose rather than an incidental feature of the smoothing process. Shallow scraping striations are visible above and below the decorative flanges, but the specimen as a whole exhibits skillful workmanship.

The second pipe fragment (Pl. V Q) is part of the proximal end of a subrectangular stem 2.9 cm. in length. In cross section it is slightly smaller than the specimen described in the preceding paragraph, and its sides are more rounded. It is pierced longitudinally by a cylindrical or slightly tapering hole estimated to be a little less than a centimeter in diameter at the mouthpiece end. The fragment is broken so that no part of the bowl is visible, but enough of the mouthpiece end is present to show that it was neatly cut off at right angles to the long axis of the stem. On one side of the stem, probably the top, half of a carved loop projects about 6 mm. (it appears on the bottom in the illustration); it presumably served for the attachment of some ornament or a wooden stem. It is pierced by a biconical hole parallel to the stem hole. Again, workmanship is good, although very fine smoothing scratches can be observed. The stem hole shows faint longitudinal striations, as if it had been subjected to some sort of reaming process.

The next specimen (Pl. V O) is apparently a short tube open at both ends instead of a conventional pipe bowl. Its total length is 3.1 cm. At the larger end it has an exterior diameter of about 1.9 cm., from which it tapers to a diameter of about 1.5 cm. at the smaller end. The interior diameters taper still more, with a maximum at the larger end of about 1.5 cm. and at the smaller end of 1.0 cm. Both the exterior wall and the interior aperture are approximately round in transverse section. Faint longitudinal scratches are present on the exterior, which is otherwise well smoothed. A shallow groove extends part of the way around the tube close to the small end. The interior has a less polished appearance, and again there are longitudinal scratches. The larger end is cut off squarely, but the smaller end, although cut off at right angles to the long axis of the piece, has more irregular, beveled edges. Workmanship is quite good on the whole—the piece is thin walled, the aperture is well centered, and the lip at the larger end is squared off regularly.

A final catlinite specimen from the House III fill, probably also a pipe fragment, is no more than a sliver from bowl or stem. The original specimen seems to have been round in cross section, and the perforation is estimated to have about the same diameter as has that of the second pipe fragment discussed.

Sharpening Stones. A flat piece of catlinite (Pl. V Y) has been classified as a sharpening stone, even though this material would not appear to be particularly suitable for such a function. It is a tabular piece of irregular outline with a quite uniform thickness of about 9 mm. The edges are shaped and have a somewhat worn and polished appearance. One edge is broken, but even here some polish is visible on the fractured surface, presumably from handling and use after the fracture occurred. The other edges have scratches in their polished surfaces, suggesting that they were used for rubbing with the stone in a vertical position. The major evidence of usage, however, appears on both of the flat surfaces in the form of innumerable fine scratches running in various directions. All tend to intersect at the center of the piece, with the result that there is a shallow depression there. The only use which comes readily to mind for this artifact is that of imparting a final polish and sharpening to the points of bone needles or awls.

A second piece of flat catlinite is essentially similar but lacks the surface striations. Like the first, its edges are shaped and smoothed, although they have a less rounded and worn appearance. This piece is somewhat thicker and smaller than the first. Both probably represent utilized by-products of pipe making.

Grooved Abrading Stones. Two complete sandstone shaft polishers with longitudinal polishing grooves are illustrated as Plate V F and M. In addition to these, fragments of nine other specimens were found. These implements are roughly rectangular in cross section, although usually with rounded corners and bulging sides. In a few cases the form is more nearly that of a semicylinder with a single polishing groove on the flat side. As can be seen on the illustrated specimens, when viewed from above one end tends to be rounded and the other more or less rectangular. Four of the polishers, including the illustrated examples, have polishing grooves on top and bottom faces, and one even has a trace of a third groove on the side. The others have a single groove, and several show ungrooved facets which suggest that they were used for abrading objects other than shafts. The dimensions of the illustrated specimens seem to be characteristic; they are about 9 cm. long, 2.5 to 3 cm. wide, and 1.5 to 2 cm. thick.

One fragment of a grooved abrader was made of the reddish scoria commonly called "float rock."

Grooved Mauls. Grooved mauls are represented by seven essentially complete specimens and one fragment. The most common type is a granite cobble, undoubtedly of glacial origin, which is unworked except for an encircling groove. One maul was made from an elongated quartzite pebble, and another was of basalt. On one rather rectangular maul, grooves on the corners replaced the more usual completely encircling groove. One very large specimen was distinctive in having a triangular cross section and evidence of deliberate pecking to form a more regular shape. Weights of the complete specimens clustered very closely around 3.5 pounds with the exception of the large, carefully finished maul, which weighed about 9 pounds.

Hoes. An unusual type, represented by only one specimen, is a roughly flaked and ground granite hoe or spade. This is a large specimen (19 by 20.5 cm. over-all) shaped by chipping, but with ground grooves for hafting. The basic shape may be described as trapezoidal with the narrower end notched for hafting. All of the corners are roughly rounded, and the blade has a convex edge. The hafting notches are broad, shallow indentations beginning about 2 cm. below the upper edge. At the upper end the hoe is 5.5 cm. thick. It weighs slightly less than 8 pounds.

Hammerstones. Ten flattened waterworn pebbles show by

their battered edges that they served as hammerstones, and five other pebbles also have traces of battering on their edges. A broken cylindrical concretion having a diameter of 2.5 cm. also has a battered appearance and may belong in this category.

Paint Stones. Ten small lumps of hematite (4 cm. maximum diameter) were found. Several of these have one or more flat faces and were presumably rubbed to obtain red pigment. Two unworked pebbles of chalky white material and a fragment of yellow ocher were also collected and may represent a source of pigment.

CHIPPED STONE

Stone chipping was an important industrial process, to judge by the 623 specimens which are considered to be artifacts. Major types are illustrated in Plates IV and V; they include small, mostly triangular projectile points, end scrapers, retouched flakes of various forms, ribbon flakes, a number of larger blades of several forms, and a special series of knifelike forms made from a distinctive tabular vein chalcedony. In addition to the artifacts, there were many flakes representing either incidental refuse products of artifact manufacture or, in the case of some deposits in pits, perhaps stocks of raw materials.

Several varieties of chalcedony, quartzite, and other materials were used for chipped tools, and most were probably obtained from local gravels of glacial origin. Some materials, however, came from more distant sources. The vein chalcedony mentioned above is native to the White River Beds so well exposed in the Badlands of southwestern South Dakota and extreme northwestern Nebraska. It is a translucent milky or sometimes faintly pinkish stone which occurs in flat pieces with a uniform thickness of 4 to 8 mm. This tabular character makes it possible to produce a serviceable-edged tool by simple flaking of the characteristic square edges. Most of the fragments have a rough, weathered crust on the flat surfaces, but a few have a fresh appearance as if they had been quarried from their original source. A more striking example of material from a distant source is a flake of black obsidian, which was probably obtained from the well-known deposit in Yellowstone Park. Quartzites of several kinds were also utilized, including faintly green and purple varieties thought to be from the Bijou Hills in southern Brule County, South Dakota, and their continuation to the westward across the Missouri River, the Iona Hills. A few pieces of quartzite resembled closely the material from the Spanish Diggings of east-central Wyoming and may have been derived from that locality. Flakes and a few artifacts were of a brown chalcedony which is probably Knife River flint from the quarries near the mouth of that stream in North Dakota.

Projectile Points (Pl. V A–E, G–L). Sixty-five projectile points, either whole or fragmentary, were found. With two exceptions discussed below, all are small specimens, the maximum length noted not exceeding 30 mm., which suggests that they were arrow points. Several varieties of quartzite, chalcedony, and chert were used in their manufacture. Nearly all are thin, and a number show a primary flake scar on one face. Probably most were made by secondary chipping of a small detached flake. Final shaping of the edges was usually accomplished by flaking from both sides. Fifty-three points were sufficiently complete to allow form classification, which resulted in the following frequencies: straight sided, straight based, simple triangular, 23 specimens (Pl. V C, J); straight sided, concave based, triangular, with a pair of side notches, 10 specimens; straight sided, concave based, triangular, lacking side notches, 9 specimens; straight sided, straight based, triangular, with a pair of side notches, 7 specimens; convex sided, concave based, triangular, 2 specimens (Pl. V L). The designation for these outlines in Strong's terminology (1935: 87–89) is: NBa, 23 specimens; NBbl, 10 specimens; NBb, 9 specimens; NBal, 7 specimens; NAb3, 2 specimens. Two classifiable points were not included in this listing because they differed in being heavier, broader, and thicker. The first of these is 19 mm. broad and 25 mm. long and is essentially triangular with convex sides, a concave base, and a pair of side notches. The second is a stemmed, corner-notched form with a convex-based stem; it is 23 mm. broad and 28 mm. long.

The exceptional projectile points mentioned above are tip fragments of brown chalcedony and chert. The chalcedony specimen is 46 mm. long and 14 mm. wide at the broken end. It tapers evenly from the broken proximal end to the point. Flaking is neat and rather delicate; it proceeded from both sides on both edges, resulting in a slightly asymmetrical diamond-shaped cross section. No traces of notches or other modification are present in the remaining part of the point. The chert tip is essentially similar in dimensions and in method of production. Both specimens might be considered lance points because of their larger size and thicker cross section, although it is not possible to rule out arrow points or even knives as a functional interpretation.

End Scrapers (Pls. IV L, S, V, W, X; V W). As is true at so many of the later Plains sites, end scrapers made on flakes are a common type of chipped stone artifact. The total collection from the site includes 162 specimens. The basic form here, as elsewhere, seems to be the result of striking a core with a blow aimed slightly inward so as to produce a short flake which, viewed from the side, is considerably thicker at the end opposite to the striking platform and bulb of percussion. Often the flake scar itself shows a pronounced curve downward near the thicker end. When viewed from the top, the flake thus produced tends to have a trapezoidal or pointed oval form with the greatest breadth at or near the thicker end. These tendencies were exaggerated by secondary chipping on the back of the scraper, either on the broader end alone or on the edges also. Apparently, the only retouching considered to be indispensable was that on the broader end, which produced a more or less straight or smoothly curved working edge and a steep face which intersects the flake scar at an angle approaching 90°. Retouching on the sides was presumably intended to produce the proper shape only; it may be absent if the flake already had a suitable form, or it may be present on one side only. Very thick flakes sometimes show a steep and bold retouch with flake scars from both sides meeting in or near the center to form a longitudinal keel. In other implements the back was simply left in its original form, often showing longitudinal facets where previous flakes had been struck off the core. The specimen illustrated as Plate IV X is an example of this. It would appear that the makers were not overly concerned with the method by which the result was obtained so long as a serviceable implement resulted. The smaller specimens of Plate IV are typical in size; most of the scrapers are from 15 to 25 mm. wide at the scraping edge. A few are long and narrow like the specimen shown as Plate IV X and are essentially ribbon flakes with a retouched scraping edge on one end. The specimen illustrated as Plate V X is one of two very large end scrapers. In spite of its unusual size, its form is characteristic. End scrapers are usually made from chalcedony, with a few specimens of quartzite or chert.

Other Scrapers (Pl. V X). The distinction between knives and scrapers is to a certain extent arbitrary, and the criteria adopted here are intended to facilitate descriptive orderliness rather than to express a final judgment on function. Specimens which have one flat side, usually—although not invariably—a primary flake scar, and a single beveled edge produced by secondary flaking from the flat side or primary flake scar have been considered scrapers. Most of the specimens (113) are simply flakes with one or more sides retouched to produce the scraping edge. They vary greatly in size and shape, but a sort of modal form would be an elongated flake about 2 by 7 cm. in major dimensions. Small oval forms also occur, but are not common, and numerous other shapes dependent on the vagaries of flint fracture are present. A few specimens seem to exhibit a more definite shape and include 14 oval scrapers ranging in length from 5 to 8 cm. and two large ovoid scrapers, one of which is illustrated as Plate V X. The other large scraper is made of chert; it is 7.5 cm. broad and 13 cm. long. Its sides have been shaped to a quite regular oval by secondary flaking, but its back was left in a very rough state. The flat side is slightly concave, and it also has been shaped by flaking so that no trace of a primary flake scar is visible. The specimen measures approximately 3 cm. at the point of maximum thickness, which occurs about a third of the distance from the end. In side view it has a humpbacked appearance, and the cutting or scraping edge curves upward like the profile of the top and bottom sides. The illustrated specimen also has its flat side shaped by the removal of flakes. A final scraper, also of large size (6.5 by 13.5 cm.), differs from the others in being made from a roughly triangular fragment of granite; one long side has been crudely chipped to form a scraping edge. Materials used for the manufacture of scrapers seem to represent the entire range at the site of the siliceous minerals suited to chipping; they are described as chalcedonies, quartzites, jaspers, cherts, and flints, but variously colored chalcedonies are by far the most common.

Drills. Only two specimens which appear to be drills were found. Both are of jasper and were made by fine chipping on the narrow end of prismatic flakes.

Knives (Pl. IV Q, AA–HH). The general characteristic of knives, as the term is used here, is the presence of a double-beveled working edge and two flaked faces. Unfortunately, an immediate qualification is necessary because ribbon flakes (prismatic flakes) with or without retouched edges have also been classed as knives in accordance with traditional usage and probable function. Nearly all of the knives from the site can be put into one of four descriptive categories. These are (1) four-edged, alternately beveled, diamond-shaped specimens; (2) elongated vein chalcedony knives; (3) bifaced blades of several forms, most commonly leaf-shaped; and (4) ribbon flakes.

Four-edged, diamond-shaped knives (Pl. IV BB, CC, GG) are represented by seven complete examples and two fragments if a specimen of vein chalcedony, discussed below, is excluded. The illustrated specimens are characteristic of both outline and size. In particular, the slightly modified lenticular outline of the complete specimens of Plate IV CC, GG seems to be far more common than the broader, more angular shape exhibited by the Plate IV BB specimen. The cross section of these knives is basically more or less lenticular, and both sides are flattened by secondary flake removal. Cutting edges have a pronounced, scraper-like bevel produced by skillful pressure flaking from one side, but ordinarily some flakes were removed from the other side also, resulting in a very asymmetrical double-beveled edge. The bevels are so arranged as to alternate around the four edges of the knife, giving a rough parallelogram in cross section. A length of about 8 cm. seems to be typical for the sublenticular specimens, but the two fragments of the more angular type were probably longer. The thickest part of the cross section does not exceed 11 mm. in any example. Six of these knives are made of various types of quartzite; the others are of chert and jasper.

Complete or fragmentary knives of vein chalcedony (Pl. IV AA) total 126 specimens. The finished form was undoubtedly strongly influenced by the peculiar nature of the material. As has been mentioned earlier, vein chalcedony occurs as flat, thin slabs, and a serviceable knife could be manufactured simply by selecting an elongated fragment of the proper size and retouching one or both long sides to form a cutting edge. Practically all cutting edges were double beveled in true knife style. This utilization of fortuitously broken pieces makes typological description particularly difficult because it is often impossible to decide whether a complete or a broken specimen is under consideration. One form which appears with some frequency has a part of one edge and the tip shaped, with the rest of the specimen unworked. The illustrated specimen is probably of this type. Presumably, such a form would be used without any additional hafting. Others have two retouched edges. Still other forms have a more conventional appearance. A few specimens have a symmetrical leaf-shaped point and two convex worked edges, apparently being copies in vein chalcedony of a form of blade more commonly manufactured in other materials. One example of an alternately beveled, four-edged knife was noticed, and there are a few specimens with carefully flaked square bases and convex sides. This reproduction in vein chalcedony of conventional forms is much less common than are the casual forms taking advantage of the special nature of the material. The maximum length of the elongated specimens observed is about 12 cm., but some of the broken specimens may well have been somewhat longer. Breadth ranges between 2.5 and 5.0 cm. Thickness does not vary, of course, except within the natural 4 to 8 mm. limits of the tabular material. The more definitely shaped specimens seem to have about the same size as their counterparts in other materials. All specimens show on the top and bottom traces of the original surface, either a pronounced patina or, rarely, a fresher looking flat surface.

Ribbon flake knives are represented by 42 specimens. The flakes are not large, the maximum dimensions noted being 16 by 64 mm., and they are not particularly well made. Some show the original crust of the pebble from which they were struck, and maximum thickness may be as much as 8 mm. They may have either two or three longitudinal facets. Delicate retouching, perhaps the result of wear, is common; 23 flakes show retouching on both edges, and 10 are retouched on one edge only. Most of the ribbon flakes are made of chalcedony, but a few examples of jasper, quartzite, chert, and silicified limestone also occur. It seems likely that the small size and crudity of the flakes as compared, for example, to the Hopewell specimens of Ohio and the Illinois Valley are the result of more refractory raw materials rather than lack of skill. Ribbon-flake knives are not illustrated here, but the end scraper made on a ribbon flake, as illustrated in Plate IV X, gives some idea of the general type.

The remaining knives are bifacially flaked blades of several forms, some of which are illustrated in Plate IV Q, R, DD–FF, and HH. One of the distinctive forms is a large leaf-shaped blade, either symmetrical (Pl. IV Q) or with one straight or slightly curved edge (Pl. IV EE, HH). Only four complete or nearly complete specimens of this type were found, but several fragments were probably from blades of this general form. One specimen (Pl. IV EE) has a tang placed somewhat to one side of the broader base. Six specimens, all fragmentary, had definite square bases on broad blades with convex edges. There are seven examples of a narrow, more straight-sided form, also with a straight base (Pl. IV DD) and one with a diagonal base (Pl. IV FF). The peculiar form of the latter specimen may be the result of breakage and reshaping. A final form is a small, leaf-shaped knife with a straight or nearly straight base (Pl. IV R). Fourteen specimens having this outline were collected. With regard to dimensions, the large leaf-shaped blades are from about 8 to 10 cm. in length and have a maximum width of about 6 cm., although most are narrower. All are more than 1.5 cm. in thickness, but the other forms are 1 cm. or less. The small straight-based blades are about 3 by 4.5 cm. Chalcedonies, cherts, and quartzites were the favored materials for making knives of these forms. It should be emphasized that some of the vein chalcedony knives also fall into the form categories just described. In addition to the more complete specimens, there are 51 fragments of indeterminate shape which were probably knives. Some are hardly more than retouched flakes, but many were from the more distinctive forms, to judge by the quality of flaking.

BONE AND ANTLER

Bone tools (Pls. IV and V) of a number of types were found in all of the house excavations in considerable quantity. They were particularly abundant in cache pits, but also occurred in the fill of houses. Preservation is good, but many of the specimens have been damaged by breakage. The kinds of artifacts found include scapula hoes, knives, and other tools; scored bison spine paddles and scored ribs; trimmed and perforated ribs of the type often called shaft straighteners; other trimmed and polished ribs, possibly beamers; awls of ribs, split antelope metapodials, bird bones, and splinters of mammal leg bones; pegs or flaking tools of leg bone splinters; polished antler tines; fishhooks; and a few other types. The more complete scapula hoes are not available for direct description, and the comments on them are taken from the Fraser manuscript.

Scapula Hoes. This ubiquitous Plains implement was represented at the Arzberger site by 23 more or less complete specimens and by 10 fragments. The only extensive modification in hoe manufacture was the removal of the spine and posterior border to approximately the level of the fossae to give a flat implement. The working edge may have been trimmed and presumably was sharpened, but it is not possible to observe this on used specimens. On worn specimens the working edge is beveled, deeply scored, and highly polished by soil abrasion. Evidently the hoes were used until they were quite short. No evidence of blade notching or of any extensive modification of the articular end was observed. All of the specimens seem to have been made from bison scapulae.

Other Scapula Tools. Two cleaver-like implements are illustrated in Plate IV K and O. In these tools the articular end was broken off and slightly smoothed to form a handle. The distal end was rounded off and ground, and the infraspinous fossa was ground and polished to a working edge. The spine itself has been partly cut and ground away in the same manner as for the hoes. The working edge is actually somewhat rounded rather than knifelike. Four other fragments may have been parts of tools of this type. The true function of these tools is obscure.

A third type of scapula tool is a simple knife made from a thin plate of bone from the infraspinous fossa (Pl. IV L, P); this is presumably the squash knife of ethnographic literature. The elongated shape and the presence of cutting edges on both sides of the specimen illustrated as Plate IV L are unusual to judge by the six knives of this type found, the shorter and wider outline of the second illustrated specimen being more characteristic. On two specimens a part of the spinous or posterior border area was roughly ground off to form the back of the knife. A seventh specimen consists of a neatly trimmed, roughly ovate plate of bone of the same general size as the knives; however, it lacks a cutting edge and the high degree of use polishing which most of these knives show. It may be an unfinished specimen.

There are, in addition to the specimens discussed above, 13

fragments of scapulae which are worked but cannot be assigned to a definite type. Three of these, however, are more suggestive of the cleaver type of artifact than of any other familiar tool.

Scored Bison Spines and Ribs. Four paddle-like artifacts made of the long dorsal vertebral spines from the hump region of the bison were collected (Pl. IV T, Y). Two are substantially intact and permit full description. The manufacture of these tools, aside from the scoring, was a simple process performed by cutting off the spine well above its point of attachment to the vertebral body in order to form a rounded handle end and similarly cutting or grinding off the rough bone of the distal end. The complete specimens are, respectively, 26 and 21 cm. long. Heavy grooves were incised across the broader distal end and cover slightly less than the upper half of the tool (Pl. IV Y). Only one side of the specimen bears these grooves, the other being plain. The grooves are from 1 to 2 mm. wide and nearly as deep, and their spacing varies from an average of about 6 mm. to an average of about 10 mm. (the extremes are illustrated). The type of wear shown by these implements is indicative of the manner in which they were used. On the three specimens having the grooved area intact, there is a distinct, elliptically shaped area of wear in the center of the grooved part, and the proximal ends show marked polish from use. This sort of wear is entirely consonant with the suggestion of Wedel and Hill (1942) that artifacts of this kind served as pottery-making paddles. A comparison of modeling clay impressions of these paddles with the markings on grooved paddle-stamped vessels from the site further confirms the plausibility of this interpretation.

A second type of scored artifact is represented by two rib fragments, probably bison. The first of these is 9 cm. long and bears transverse incising at 2 to 4 mm. intervals over its entire length. As on the hump spine paddles, the incising is confined to one side of the rib, here the convex outer side. On one end enough of the original tool is preserved to show that the rib was cut across squarely with slightly rounded corners and that the transverse scoring was carried almost to the end. Wear on the grooved side is more pronounced in a strip along the middle of the scored area for the last 2 cm. toward the cut end. The plain back of the specimen shows a generalized polish. The second specimen was made from a flatter, broader rib and shows no trace of cut ends or pronounced wear. It is 12.6 cm. long, and the scoring covers a little less than 5 cm. at one end. The transverse incising is again confined to the convex outer side of the rib. Spacing of the incising is wide and somewhat irregular, the interval between individual grooves ranging from 6 mm. to more than 1 cm. On both of the ribs the scoring appears to be more carelessly placed and more poorly executed than on the hump spine paddles, but there seems no good reason to doubt that they served the same function.

Perforated Ribs. Eight examples of the familiar shaft straightener were found (Pl. IV U, Z). All are made from ribs, probably bison, and five are fragments which have broken at the perforation. The specimen illustrated as Plate IV U is nearly intact, although a part of the broader end, which was probably finished in a flat curve, has broken away. The total length of the complete artifact must have been in the neighborhood of 16 cm. It is atypical in that it possesses two perforations and two transverse incised lines (on one side only), but it is, of course, possible that some of the broken specimens also possessed such features. The second complete specimen is a section of rib 31.5 cm. long, with a single comparatively small (12 mm. diameter) round perforation 12 cm. from one end. The ends of this specimen are somewhat damaged, but appear to have been cut off quite squarely. A third specimen is 18.5 cm. long and has an ovoid perforation approximately equidistant from the ends. On the remaining shaft straighteners only a section from the perforation to one end is preserved (Pl. IV Z). All the perforations are ovoid with long axis parallel to that of the rib, and the distance from the perforation to the slightly rounded end of the specimen varies from 9 to 15 cm., the shorter distances being more common. One specimen bears a rather deep transverse incised line which runs around both sides of the rib about midway between the perforation and the shaped end. Most of the shaft straighteners have a noticeable polish, which is not localized in such a manner as to suggest a possible function. The perforations have beveled and sometimes highly polished margins in the dense outer bone, and this bevel is more pronounced at the ends of the ellipse. If these tools are shaft straighteners or thong dressers, as is commonly supposed, the object to be worked on must have been held with its long axis parallel to that of the tool. The specimen mentioned above with the nearly round perforation does not have this differential beveling and might be regarded as an unused tool, a view which is supported by the general absence of well-developed polish elsewhere.

Other Worked Ribs. Seventeen additional sections of ribs show working in the form of shaped ends or wear polishing on otherwise unworked specimens. One specimen is probably from a deer, but most of them seem to be bison ribs; identification is uncertain, however.

Three specimens have two cut ends and may be regarded as complete. They range in length from 15.5 to 21.2 cm. One from the relatively flat and parallel-sided central part of the rib shows a considerable amount of polish and numerous faint longitudinal striations. One end is cut and broken more or less transversely and the corners are rounded, but the other was formed by intersecting diagonal cuts and is essentially pointed. Another specimen, much less worn, has quite sharply rounded ends and is made from a rib section having a part of the sharp posterior border. The third artifact of this type also bears a part of the sharp posterior border; one end is a point formed by two intersecting diagonal cuts, and the other is the result of a single diagonal cut across the rib. The sharp point formed by the latter process is somewhat rounded and worn, but the rest of the specimen shows little evidence of use.

Eleven of the rib artifacts are no more than a broken section with one worked end. The longest of these measures 30.5 cm., but most of the others do not exceed about 15 cm. One specimen has been cut off nearly squarely, six have rounded to almost pointed ends, and four have pointed ends produced by means of one diagonal cut across the rib. Two of the rounded or, more accurately, ovate ends are polished and evidently were used for some purpose, but the remainder are either too defective for identification or are simply the result of incising and breaking without subsequent wear or polishing. Two of the specimens with diagonally cut ends also have worn points formed by the dense outer bone at the border of the rib. One of these points is quite sharp, but the other is slightly rounded. A third specimen of this type lacks the tip of the point owing to breakage, but a rather high degree of polish over most of the specimen indicates that it was a tool of some sort rather than an industrial by-product. The three remaining worked ribs are simply sections broken at both ends. They show a certain amount of polish.

Functional interpretation of the worked ribs is complicated by the fact that some may be fragments of shaft straighteners or scored rib paddles. Others, however, are probably beamers or had other functions in the removal and dressing of hides, and some may have been digging tools.

Worked Bison Ulnae. A fragment 11 cm. long from the distal part of the shaft of a bison ulna may represent the artifact often called an ulna pick. The tapering distal end has been hacked and ground into a polished, rounded, and beveled point. The proximal end appears to have been rounded off; thus resemblance to the ulna pick is eliminated. It also has a deep V-shaped notch of uncertain origin. Polish is visible over the surface of the implement except on the rough space marking the area of juncture with the radius. If the implement is nearly complete rather than accidentally fractured at the proximal end, it may well be a heavy stone-flaking tool.

Other Worked Long Bones. Three other specimens are made from long bones, two of which are definitely tools. The first of the tools is a part of the longitudinally split shaft of a leg bone of some large animal. It is 16.2 cm. in length. One end is cut, broken, and ground into a roughly rounded shape. The other end is more carefully shaped into a tapering, rounded point which is beveled from the interior toward the surface of the bone. All of the worked surfaces of this point are smoothly polished, and the total effect when viewed from the side showing the cancellous interior bone is not unlike the bottom of the tip of a pointed teaspoon. The general rounding and smoothness of the point strongly suggest that it was used in some function which involved rubbing. The exterior surface of the bone has a shallow diagonal groove about 1.5 cm. below the tip of the point. Its cross section and other characteristics suggest that it was produced by the wear of a lashing rather than by incising. There are very faint traces of another groove parallel to the first and a few millimeters closer to the point. The remainder of the surface of the specimen is somewhat worn, although it cannot be described as highly polished. The second tool consists of the distal end and part of the shaft of a bison tibia. No particular modification other than a small amount of use polishing is visible on the articular end, but a part of the shaft has been cut and broken away in an irregular fashion to form a bluntly pointed implement 20 cm. long. For a distance of 8 cm. the pointed end is a sliver of bone from 1.5 to 2.0 cm. broad; this was the working end of the tool, to judge by the higher degree of polish visible there. The point itself is subrectangular in transverse section and slightly rounded in top or bottom view. It seems likely that the specimen was a heavy stone-flaking tool; certainly, the polish indicates that it was grasped in the narrower part close to the pointed end. The third worked long bone is a section of shaft 4.5 cm. long and a part of a much battered articular end. Evidence of modification consists of polish and longitudinal striations on the shaft and a transversely cut and broken end. Specific identification of the bone is impossible, but it was probably derived from some small mammal or bird.

Fishhooks. One unfinished fishhook and two complete specimens (Pl. V U, V) were found. The completed specimens are of similar shape but markedly different size. The larger specimen is 5.0 cm. long, and the maximum diameter of the shank is slightly less than 1 cm. Corresponding dimensions of the smaller are 4.0 and 0.3 cm. A part of the point of the larger hook has split away, but enough remains to allow reconstruction of its original form; the point was a simple tapering spike, slightly deflected to the right when the hook is viewed from the front, which extended upward for about half the total length of the hook. In maximum breadth (from the tip of the point to the back of the shank) the hook measures 2.4 cm. A deep line groove encircles the shank about 7 mm. below its top. A considerable amount of polish is present over the entire specimen, but a few traces of cancellous bone can be seen on one side at the juncture of point and shank. In its essential characteristics the smaller hook is similar, the chief differences being a much shorter point in relation to the shank and a somewhat angular, rather than rounded, appearance in the area of juncture between point and shank. The tip of the point is missing, but the entire point can hardly have been more than a quarter of the length of the shank, and the greatest breadth was about 9 mm. Two line grooves are present, the lower being about 7 mm. and the upper about 5 mm. below the end of the shank. Neither of the grooves completely encircles the shank, the front quadrant being ungrooved. Raw material and manufacturing techniques are well illustrated by the unfinished specimen, which is a shaft section of a long bone, 4.8 cm. in length, from some animal of the general size of a deer or pronghorn. The bone was split lengthwise, and the split section was cut or broken off to form a piece of the proper length. In its present condition the ends are rounded, and the entire bone, including the inner surafce, is polished. One side has been ground away vertically, but the other is beveled toward one end to allow sufficient bone for the shaping of the point. A slightly diagonal groove marks the beginning of shank and point differentiation. It can be seen that the point was slightly deflected to the left and that the whole hook closely resembled the larger complete specimen.

Antler Tines. Four tine fragments of deer antler are thought to be artifacts. Three show traces of cutting, but the other has been placed in the artifact category solely on the evidence of a slightly polished surface. Range in length is not great, all of the specimens falling within 6 to 8 cm. limits. The uncut specimen is simply a dully polished curved tine which is broken off jaggedly at the base. Very slight traces of battering are visible on the tip. A second specimen has a base which is squarely cut and broken off. The surface is rough, probably from weathering before utilization, but shows considerable polish and small scratches or cuts at the tip. A third specimen is smooth and highly polished, jaggedly broken at the base, and has a shallow cut groove extending from the broken base for 3 cm. toward the point. The final specimen is straight rather than curved and superficially suggests a conical projectile point. It is also highly polished, particularly in the tip region. The tip itself has been ground to a sharper point and has several small transverse cuts or scratches. The basal end is badly broken, but enough remains to indicate that the base was encircled by a deeply incised groove. An obvious use for these artifacts would be as chipping tools. Different interpretations are possible, however; among other conceivable functions, the straight specimen described last could be a projectile point, and the uncut tine may be a fragment from an antler rake.

Flint Flakers. The tools known as flakers or blunt-headed awls are represented at the Arzberger site by 17 whole or fragmentary specimens (Pl. IV B–E). In general form these artifacts are straight, slightly tapering, peglike objects ranging in length from 6.6 to 13.8 cm. and having a triangular transverse section. They seem to have been made from splinters of long bones or perhaps ribs in some instances. On one flat face, often the narrowest, interior cancellous bone is exposed. A very blunt and approximately conical head occurs on the thicker end of the shaft, but the thinner end has a somewhat sharper point formed by beveling from the cancellous bone face or by more or less even grinding of the angles. The sharper end is often rounded rather than truly pointed, and even the sharpest specimens do not appear to be well adapted for use in perforating hides or for similar functions. All of the specimens have a quite well-developed polish over their surface, and many show faint striations produced by abrading during manufacture. The points themselves are smoothly worn and polished and show no clear evidence of cutting or battering.

Awls. Specimens which appear to be unequivocal awls are illustrated as Plate IV F–J, M, and N. Various types can be distinguished, the differences being in the main associated with the sort of bone used in manufacture, but all have in common a working point which is sharp, gently tapered, and more or less round in transverse section.

An easily recognizable type is made by splitting longitudinally the distal end of a pronghorn metapodial between the pulleys and sharpening the attached section of shaft (Pl. IV J). Two examples were found; both have the articular end as a handle and show considerable polish from the sharp end to a point about 2.5 cm. from the articular end. One of the specimens is 7.5 cm. long, the other 8.1 cm. A second type of awl is also made from a long bone and retains a part of the articular surface (Pl. IV F). In this type the head is relatively flat, partly through wear, but chiefly because of the character of the bone used. Of the five complete specimens found, two were probably made from the proximal end of a deer metapodial and three from the bones of some large bird. A sixth specimen is represented by an unidentifiable fragment of the tip part. Range in length is 6.3 to 11.9 cm., with four specimens 10 cm. or more in length. All of the specimens have sharp, gently tapering points and are well polished.

Two very highly polished tip fragments may have been made from simple splinters of long bones or may have originally retained part of an articular process like the types discussed immediately above. Both are very slender and have exceedingly sharp points. One has a darkened point as if it had been subjected to considerable heat.

Four specimens, all having the head broken off, seem to have been made from splinters of the shafts of mammal long bones. Two of these are about 10 cm. long and show unpolished cancellous bone on one side; one has an asymmetrical point which was formed by making a diagonal cut about half through the flat splinter and splitting away the end to leave a 2.5 cm. sliver to be sharpened for the working point. A third specimen is much like the flaking tools, but it has the slender, sharp awl point instead of the rounded flaking point. The last specimen is not definitely classifiable as to function; it is a narrow, flat section of rib (its dimensions are 7.0 by 0.5 cm.) worked on all sides and having a rounded, spoon-shaped tip. The shaft, which is broken at one end, is parallel-sided to within 2.5 cm. of the tip, where its width is increased slightly by two diagonal shoulders. From the shoulders the sides curve gently inward to form the tip. The extreme tip is broken so that it is not possible to determine whether it was sharp or slightly rounded. In any case, it differs considerably from the conventional awl tip.

The remaining specimens consist of five flat awls made from ribs (Pl. IV G, M, N). One complete awl (Pl. IV M) is probably a good representative of a type. It is a large and sturdy tool (its dimensions are 1.8 by 14.1 cm.) with a rounded head and a carefully ground point. A second complete specimen (Pl. IV G) has the same general characteristics, but it is slightly smaller and much more carefully finished. Its sides are neatly smoothed and most of the cancellous interior bone has been ground away. The final complete specimen (Pl. IV N) is a highly polished flat awl with five perforations spaced along its approximate mid-line for a distance of 6 cm. The perforations, made from the flat exterior side of the rib, are conical and have maximum diameters ranging from 3 to 4 mm. The perforation nearest the point is actually biconical because of a slight bevel, perhaps produced by wear, on the inner side. A break passes through the fifth perforation, but the broken end was repolished either deliberately or through subsequent use. If the slight inner bevel of the lowermost perforation was produced by wear, it would follow that only this perforation was functional, the others presumably being in reserve for use as the awl was shortened through use and resharpening. The two remaining flat awls are tip fragments. Both appear to be parts of tools very like the first specimen described, although one has an abruptly tapering, rounded point more like those on the tools considered flint flakers.

SHELL

Fresh-water mussels contributed in a minor way to the industrial resources of the Arzberger people. Five worked specimens (Pl. V R–T) and at least 31 unworked shells were found in the excavations, mostly in cache pits. One type of shell artifact consists simply of a complete valve with shallow notching on the edge opposite the hinge (Pl. V R). The one complete specimen of this type has a part of the hinge area broken away and has a jagged perforation near the hinge, but there is no evidence to suggest that these are anything but accidental breaks. In addition to the complete specimen, two fragments of notched shells were found. The remaining specimens of worked shell (Pl. V S, T) seem to be knives or scrapers; they were shaped by cutting, breaking, and grinding to give a fairly sharp point and edges at one end. Both bear evidence of considerable wear and polishing.

FAUNAL REMAINS

Unworked faunal remains occurred in considerable abundance in the fill and cache pits of the houses. Unfortunately, no quantitative data were obtained, but what was thought to be a representative sample was taken to the University of South Dakota, where specific identifications were made by Dr. Dallas Meyer, at that time of the University of South Dakota. Mammal bones included those of bison, elk, mule deer, antelope, and coyote. One fish bone was found. Dr. W. H. Over, of the University of South Dakota, examined the molluscan material and found it to be comprised of various species of the four genera *Anodonta, Lampsilis, Symphonata,* and *Quadrula.* It was further pointed out by Dr. Over that no shellfish now occur in the Missouri River, although all of the forms represented are found in its tributaries in South Dakota.

VEGETAL MATERIAL

Vegetal material collected from the site consists of one kernel of corn (posthole fill, House II), three fragments of corncobs (Feature 5, House II), a few bits of wood from a posthole of House III, and a small lot of seeds (provenience unknown, but probably a cache pit). The corncobs were submitted to Dr. J. H. Kempton, of the Bureau of Plant Industry, Department of Agriculture, and to Volney H. Jones, of the Ethnobotanical Laboratory of the Museum of Anthropology, University of Michigan. Both reported that the cobs were eight-rowed, but that more exact identification was impossible. Dr. Kempton also reported that the seeds were those of a small-flowered species of sunflower (*Helianthus*), and Dr. Over commented that modern wild sunflowers of the locality have seeds much like the archaeological specimens. The posthole wood fragments were tentatively identified as cottonwood by Mr. Jones.

POTTERY

Numerous fragments of pottery were found during the course of the excavations. They occurred most abundantly in the fill of the houses, particularly around the outer edges, but were in some quantity in cache pits, shallower pits in house floors, and even in postholes. A few sherds were in the excavation of the fortification ditch, but surface pottery was practically absent from the site. The sherds available for description total 5,124, of which the rim sherds are thought to represent about 900 vessels. A detailed analysis of the pottery is presented in Appendix I, and Plates VI to XVII illustrate the various characteristics.

All of the pottery consists of vessel fragments, almost every one of which exhibits a paste made by mixing a tempering material of crushed igneous rock with the clay. The paste is quite uniform so far as hardness, color, and other attributes reflecting the nature of the raw material and firing practices are concerned. Frequent smoke clouding and characteristic tan and buff hues indicate open firing, and a hardness of about 3.5 suggests a fairly hot fire. Most of the sherds have smooth surfaces, but clear or partly obliterated impressions of a grooved, cord-wrapped, or more rarely a checked paddle are common enough to lead to the inference that all of the vessels were constructed with the aid of a paddle. A number of body sherds have a cherry red coating or filming on the interior or less commonly on the exterior; very rarely rim sherds also show this trait. Characteristic of most of the Arzberger vessels is ornamentation of the lip region with short diagonally incised strokes. Finally, almost all of the vessels are basically jar-shaped and are small to medium.

Since the variable features of the Arzberger pottery are considered at length in Appendix I, no more than a general impression will be attempted here. Two important kinds of vessels are present, here designated the Arzberger Group and the Hughes Group. The Arzberger Group is represented by about 300 rims, each of which was judged to have been derived from a separate vessel. A thickened or collared rim formed either by addition of clay to the rim base or by bending the rim into an S-shape is the fundamental distinguishing feature of the vessels of the Arzberger Group. The Hughes Group consists of fragments of about 570 vessels, approximately two-thirds of those obtained from the site. Vessels within the Hughes Group can be separated at once from those of the Arzberger Group on the basis of their unthickened straight or simply curved rims.

Other features of the Arzberger vessels include collar areas decorated with incised coarse crosshatching, opposed diagonal lines, and multiple horizontal lines. About a tenth of the collars are undecorated. Diagonal lip incising and notching or incising on the projecting base of the collar are very common. Appliqué nodes and lugs were observed but are exceedingly rare. Information on body shape and size is scanty, but suggests rounded bases. The vessels might be described as medium in size, with lip diameters from 14 to 30 cm., shoulder diameters slightly larger, and total vessel heights about the same as the lip diameters. Rim and neck are usually smoothed, but occasionally traces of grooved- or cord-wrapped paddle stamping can be seen. In one example nearly obliterated impressions of a checked paddle were observed. There is a slight tendency for details of shape and rim base treatment to be associated with the decorative patterns, and for this reason the Arzberger Group was divided into the four pottery types: Arzberger Plain, Arzberger Horizontal Incised, Arzberger Crosshatched, and Arzberger Diagonal Incised.

A number of features other than the rim forms mentioned above are frequent or fairly common in the Hughes Group and serve to give it a certain distinction and unity. The most striking of these are plain or incised strap handles, shoulder areas decorated by rectilinear incising, and elliptical orifices. Angular shoulders, lugs, and rim projections occur in some quantity, and decorative incising of the inner lip, the lip proper, or both is the rule. A number of rims are decorated on the exterior with a band of horizontal incised lines, a decorative concept recalling that of the Arzberger Horizontal Incised type. In size the Hughes vessels range from small (mouth diameter about 8 by 10 cm.) to large (mouth diameter about 30 cm.), with medium vessels having a mouth diameter about 18 by 20 cm. more common than either of the extremes. The characteristically small rim fragments and absence of restorable vessels make estimates of size and shape difficult and not overly reliable. With a minor exception, there was no marked tendency for the various attributes to cluster into distinctive types of vessels, and as a result only one formal type name was assigned within the Hughes Group. The named type is represented by 16 rims which were segregated as the Hughes Beveled type; these vessels were grouped together chiefly on the basis of the common possession of a slightly everted and rather high rim combined with an outwardly beveled lip.

A few pottery specimens do not fit into the Hughes or Arzberger categories. Two of these are crude miniature vessels; one is a tiny jar, the other a fragment of a very small bowl.

Of great comparative significance are five rim sherds, representing as many vessels, which were ornamented by impressing cords into the rim surface. Since this technique is very unusual at the site, probably the specimens were the result of trade rather than local manufacture. The presence of a few shell-tempered body sherds also hints at trade.

In terms of actual human behavior, it would appear that the Arzberger potter prepared the raw material by a process of mixing crushed granite, perhaps obtained from the fire-cracked cobbles of a sweat lodge, with clay without regard for the type of vessel which she intended to construct. Construction of the vessel also proceeded by a standard technique which was either modeling from a mass or some other method which did not produce recognizable coil fractures. A paddle with roughened face was used to aid in the modeling; the roughening was accomplished by carving the paddle face with transverse grooves, wrapping with cords, or more rarely by carving intersecting sets of grooves to form a checked pattern. Many, and possibly all, of the simple grooved paddles were made from the long hump spines or ribs of the bison. The type of paddle used seems to have been largely a matter of individual preference rather than the result of customary association of a particular sort of paddle with a definite type of vessel. Most vessels were partly or wholly smoothed, especially in the region of the rim, after the basic form had been achieved. Bodies were sometimes treated with a red wash on the interior or much less commonly on the exterior.

Once the basic form of the vessel had been completed, incised or modeled decoration and lugs or handles might be added. The form was definitely associated in the potter's mind with particular kinds of decoration or appendages. Vessels with collared or S-shaped rims were usually decorated by pinching, modeling, or incising on the base of the collar or its equivalent. Rims were sometimes left plain, but were usually decorated with an incised pattern consisting of a band of horizontal lines, coarse crosshatching, or opposed diagonal lines. Very rarely, lugs or appliqué nodes might be added to the rim. On the other hand, vessels with simple straight or everted rims were considered suitable subjects for the application of strap handles (probably two handles in most cases), lugs, and pointed rim projections. No more than a quarter of the simple rims were decorated, and the decoration was almost invariably a band of several horizontal incised lines. Roughly one out of six vessels shows traces of decorative incising on the shoulder area, but this proportion must be viewed with suspicion because of inadequate data on many rims. A few noncollared vessels described as the Hughes Beveled type seem to show a narrower association of attributes; in particular, a combination of a slightly everted and rather high rim with a beveled lip was apparently regarded as a suitable treatment for this sort of vessel. It is quite possible that other consistent combinations of this sort would be detected if a number of substantially complete vessels were available.

CULTURAL AFFILIATIONS AND CHRONOLOGICAL POSITION

THE type of culture inferred from the artifacts and architectural features of the Arzberger site falls completely within an already described pattern of Plains culture characteristic of late prehistoric and historic time, that of the earth lodge-dwelling, horticultural, village Indians of the Missouri River and its tributaries. Individual traits have numerous parallels in the Central and Northern Plains. At this broadly descriptive level definition of cultural affiliation and chronological position offer no difficulty; the site is clearly an unexceptional representative of the Plains variant of the culture of the eastern United States within the time span elsewhere called the Late Woodland or Mississippi period. This period allocation is sufficiently supported by the presence of a bastioned fortification and pottery vessels with strap handles and rectilinear incising on the shoulder, traits which appear only in the Mississippi-Late Woodland period and which are distributed over a wide area of the eastern United States. On the other hand, the absence of trade metal and glass beads indicates an upper terminus in the prehistoric period, probably before *ca.* A.D. 1700 in this area.

Within this generalized pattern, however, since the particular configuration of traits and the combinations of attributes making up the traits are not easily summarized, it will be necessary to present a more detailed comparison with individual sites and groups of sites in order to make a reasonably full and accurate appraisal of the significance of the Arzberger site. The working principles underlying this comparison are (1) the assumption that the presence of demonstrable, extensive similarities to sites in other areas indicates that the Arzberger people participated in the cultural tradition exemplified by those sites and (2) that very close similarity indicates contemporaneity or near contemporaneity. If the conclusion adopted here that the Arzberger site was the product of a culturally homogeneous group over a restricted period of time (Appendix I) is substantially correct and if the comparative principles are sound, then it follows that the assemblage of traits found provides a valuable temporal cross reference for

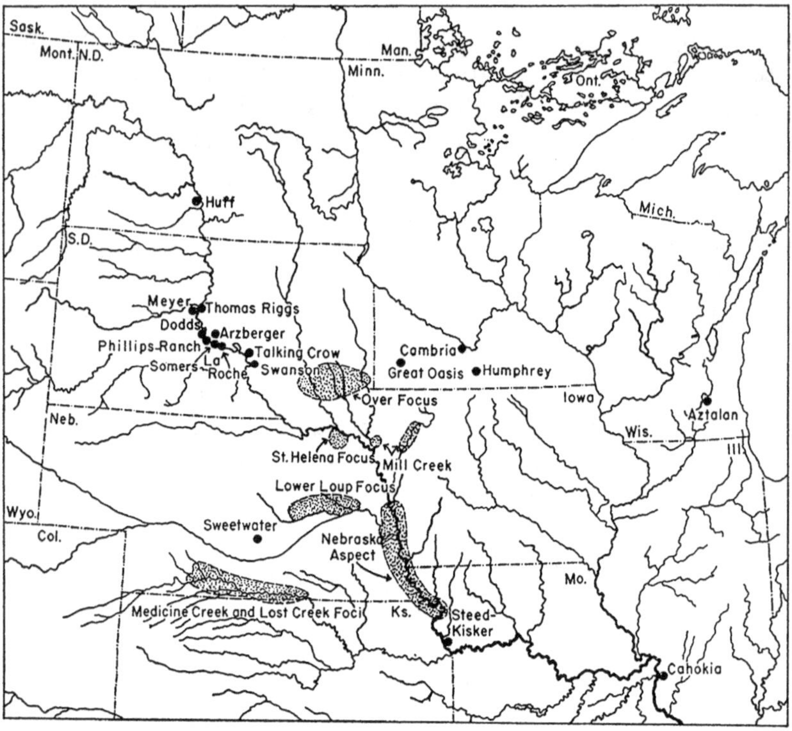

MAP 2. Position of sites and other cultural units in the Plains and adjacent regions.

the several traditions which seem to be represented. The situation at Arzberger may further aid in understanding the place and manner in which the contacts between traditions took place. The discussion following is organized on the basis of the traditions currently recognized. On geographical and historical grounds it would appear that the data from the Central Plains, the Iowa-eastern South Dakota-southern Minnesota area, and the upper Missouri River (in North and South Dakota) are immediately relevant, and that additional insight into certain special aspects can be gained by extending comparisons even further afield, particularly into the Illinois-southern Wisconsin region. The positions of sites or other cultural units included in the comparative study are indicated on Map 2.

THE CENTRAL PLAINS

The first area to be discussed is that of the Central Plains, or more exactly, Nebraska. Here a large group of excavations and several summaries offer a convenient starting point. Cultural groupings which are especially pertinent in the placing of the Arzberger site are the Upper Republican Aspect (or Culture), the Nebraska Aspect (or Culture), and the Lower Loup Focus (Wedel, 1940, Fig. 22). The relative chronological position of these units has been the subject of study for a number of years, and there can be little doubt of the general accuracy of the conclusions reached by Strong (1935: 271–82) and supported by more recent work (Champe, 1946; Wedel, 1949: 336–37 and Fig. 83).

The Upper Republican Aspect. Convenient generalized descriptions of the Upper Republican Aspect as it is found in Nebraska, especially the Lost Creek and Medicine Creek foci in the drainages of the Republican and Loup rivers, are presented by Strong (1935: 245–50) and Wedel (1940: 310–12). More detailed references include Champe (1936), Wedel (1935*a* and 1935*b*), and Strong (1935: 69–123).

The settlement pattern of the Upper Republican peoples was characterized by small, loosely arranged villages of earth lodges which were invariably unfortified and were most frequently situated on terraces along the tributary creeks. Wedel (1940: 310) inferred that each house sheltered two or three families and doubted that many villages contained more than 50 to 100 inhabitants. More recently, extensive work in the Medicine Creek Reservoir (Kivett, 1949: 279) provided additional and very informative data. Here almost every suitable terrace produced some evidence of settlement, and the village boundaries were often very poorly defined. Characteristic units of occupation were small, more or less isolated clusters of two to four houses. The over-all impression is one of a rather intensive occupation over a considerable period by a people to whom military considerations in village planning were a matter of indifference. The very small nuclei and generally sprawling nature of the settlements suggest that convenience for gardening and perhaps hunting for local game were the primary concern.

This casual attitude toward village layout offers a sharp contrast to that of the Arzberger inhabitants. Although the Arzberger site can hardly be described as compact with its average of about one observed house per acre, the village is a definite, clearly circumscribed unit, and the presence of the fortification is good evidence of the motive for such an arrangement. It is not inconceivable that other factors may have influenced the settlement pattern, but there does not appear to be any very convincing reason to invoke them. Physical environment and methods of food production seem to have been of the general type found in the Upper Republican Aspect, which leaves military necessity as the paramount motive for the Arzberger arrangement. Thus the contrast is inferred to be entirely the result of differing relationships to other social groups rather than an expression of fundamental distinctiveness in the environmental-cultural interaction.

In the more detailed field of architectural features both contrasts and similarities can be observed. The Upper Republican sites lack completely anything comparable to the Arzberger stockade and ditch, as was noted above. At Medicine Creek (Kivett, 1949: 279–80) the houses are described as rectanguloid with a central fireplace (in one case, two fireplaces), four or rarely six center posts, and a single set of smaller wall posts defining the boundaries of the floor. Floors were excavated from 6 to 20 inches or in some cases were on, or only slightly below, the old ground surface. They were not puddled or burned, in contrast to a common practice in historic village sites. Entrance passages some 8 to 10 feet in length extended out from approximately the middle of one wall. Cache pits were found both outside the houses and beneath the floors; they expanded toward the bottom and did not exceed 4 to 5 feet in depth. There is no direct evidence of the manner in which the outer walls were enclosed, but it is inferred that the roof covering was constructed of brush, grass, and sod. Refuse deposits were usually situated near the entrance of the house. Wedel (1949: 329) commented, "It is noteworthy that house construction on the Medicine seems often to have been haphazard, unlike the carefully laid out structures of the protohistoric and historic periods farther east. One wonders whether these village-dwellers were so preoccupied with making a livelihood that they had scant time for more careful work, or alternatively, were experimenting with a house complex that was still new, unfamiliar, and unformalized." A rectangular shape, usually with rounded corners, appears to be characteristic elsewhere, although nearly circular houses are also reported (for example, Wedel, 1935*a*: 150; Champe, 1936: 258 and Fig. 3).

A basic resemblance between the Upper Republican structures and those of the Arzberger site seems plain. The limited number of houses excavated at Arzberger precludes sweeping generalizations, but the available examples share with the Upper Republican houses the fundamental features of a four-center-post foundation, central fireplace, long entrance projecting from one side, an external row of vertical wall posts, external and internal cache pits, and presumably similar types of rafter arrangements and roof coverings. In both instances no very deep cache pits of the type occasionally reported from sites of the protohistoric and historic periods were found. The two well-defined outer wall patterns found at Arzberger appear to be within the reported range of Upper Republican structures, although the Arzberger House II is definitely more circular than most of the Upper Republican examples. The obscure pattern of House IV also suggests a circular outline. The numerous extra posts inside the outer walls of Houses II and III are not reported for the Upper Republican sites, but whether they represent a genuine structural difference or simply more substantial furniture is not clear. A second difference is the larger size of the Arzberger houses, the minimum dimensions of which usually exceed by several feet those reported for various Upper Republican sites (cf. Wedel, 1935*a*; Champe, 1936). It must be remembered, however, that the Arzberger excavations were conducted in the more prominent depressions and hence may represent selection of the larger houses. Insofar as a conclusion can emerge from the restricted Arzberger sample, it would appear that the houses are in general very similar to those of the Nebraska Upper Republican Aspect, but that a possibility of significant differences exists in the direction of larger structures, a more complex post mold pattern, and a greater tendency toward a circular periphery at the Arzberger site.

Stone artifacts show both similarities and differences. An outstanding difference is the presence of catlinite at the Arzberger site. Moreover, the pipe forms and grooved tablets for which the catlinite served as raw material are absent in the Upper Republican sites. The neatly made small pipes of the Arzberger site, and especially the painstakingly carved projecting stem fragment, contrast sharply with the stone, or rarely pottery, elbow pipes characteristic of Upper Republican. Another trait which is present at the Arzberger site and totally lacking in Upper Republican is the grooved maul. In the category of chipped stone the large specimen from Arzberger thought to be a hoe seems to have no exact counterpart in the Upper Republican sites, and conversely nothing closely comparable to the Upper Republican chipped celt is present at Arzberger. The distinctive vein chalcedony specimens of the Arzberger site are probably of little comparative value, their form being largely the result of the peculiar nature of the raw material. Projectile points, end scrapers, other types of scrapers, four-bladed knives, elliptical knives, and other forms appear to be substantially alike at Arzberger and Upper Republican sites, although the fairly numerous ribbon flakes may be an Arzberger specialty and T-shaped flint drills an Upper Republican specialty. The general conclusion is that the chipped stone tools and some other stone forms, for example, sandstone abraders, indicate a rather close relationship, but that the presence of catlinite, certain forms of smoking pipes, catlinite tablets, and grooved mauls at the Arzberger site represents a genuine difference. It is probable that a more detailed comparison with the specimens in hand would reveal other similarities and contrasts.

Bone, antler, and shell artifacts again show impressive similarities combined with minor but almost certainly significant differences. An obvious difference is the occurrence of scored hump spine and rib artifacts at Arzberger and their total absence at the Upper Republican sites; the inferred relationship of these artifacts to pottery stamping has been discussed above. On the other hand, the Upper Republican sites have produced deer metapodial beamers, antler shaft straighteners, and antler flakers or handles, all types which appear to be absent at Arzberger. The blunt, awl-like artifacts described as flint flakers at the Arzberger site do not seem to occur at the Upper Republican sites, nor do the polished ribs thought to be beamers, although Kivett (1949: 280) reported bison spine beamers from Medicine Creek. If future investigations indicate that these distinctions are genuine, they presumably reflect differences in flint and skin working techniques. Similarities will not be listed in detail; they are numerous and certainly indicative of participation in a common tradition. Most of the bone, antler, and shell artifact types appear in both Upper Republican and Arzberger, sometimes with differences in detail. Thus, notching of scapula hoes is quite frequent at Upper Republican sites but absent at Arzberger, and the Arzberger fishhook blank differs in principle from the loop-shaped, two-hook blank illustrated by Strong (1935, Pl. 9, Fig. 2*a*), although the finished products are very much alike.

A comparison of the pottery of the Arzberger site and that of the classic Upper Republican components gives an even clearer view of the situation because of the larger numbers of specimens available. Nearly all of the physical attributes characteristic of the pottery of Upper Republican sites are found at Arzberger, frequently in the same combinations, so that the resulting vessels resemble each other quite closely, but Arzberger has in addition a considerable number of attributes which are not at all characteristic of Upper Republican. Outstanding ceramic differences between Arzberger and the Upper Republican sites of the Republican River drainage are the presence at Arzberger and absence in Upper Republican of grooved paddle-stamped and check-stamped surfaces; handles, lugs, and other rim modifications in quantity; shoulder incising; and rather small vessels with low, usually everted, simple rims and elliptical orifices.

To turn to a more detailed comparison, it is at once apparent that the vessels of the Arzberger Group resemble strikingly the collared specimens from the Republican River drainage. Paste is very much alike in all of the pottery of the two groups, and the rim forms figured by Wedel (1935*a,* Fig. 5*a–i*) can be fitted into those of the Arzberger Group without undue strain (cf. Pl. VI, rim forms 72–79). The Republican River forms, however, seem to be on the average somewhat more outslanting than the Arzberger specimens, and the true S form (Arzberger rim form 74) is not illustrated by Wedel. Another point of difference is the apparent absence in the Arzberger Group of the high shoulder and flat shoulder area often seen on Upper Republican specimens (Wedel, 1935*a,* Fig. 4*a*), although the evidence for shoulder form at Arzberger is admittedly unsatisfactory. Differences in surface finish have already been mentioned; briefly, most of the Upper Republican collared specimens show evidence of primary surface finish, although some smoothing is reported, and the primary surface finish where identifiable is invariably cord-wrapped paddle stamping. In the Arzberger Group, however, primary surface finish could not be identified because of smoothing on most of the rim fragments (244 out of 297 rims), but 22 rims have traces of cord-wrapped paddle stamping, 26 of grooved-paddle stamping, and 1 of checked-paddle stamping. Decorative attributes associated with the collared vessels of both groups show a decided overlap. Incised designs on the band provided by the surface of the collar are characteristic, as are plain collars in small numbers. Moreover, the three important Arzberger Group motifs—horizontal lines, opposed diagonals, and coarse cross-hatching—are prominent in the Upper Republican sites, although it is probable that each group has a small number of distinctive designs. Notching, incising, or punctating on the lip of collared vessels was comparatively rare in the Upper Republican area, but at Arzberger most of the collared vessels had lips decorated by these techniques, chiefly by means of short, diagonally incised strokes. Strong (1935 : 248) reported that rim base pinching is a characteristic mode of decoration on the collared rims of the Upper Republican Aspect, but it seems to be rare on the specimens discussed by Wedel, who figured one example (Wedel, 1935*a,* Pl. VI, 1*j*). Rim base pinching, modeling, or incising is very common at Arzberger. Despite these differences in relative popularity and perhaps in the presence or absence of minor attributes, there can be no doubt that a close relationship exists between the two groups. Individual pairs of specimens are in many instances virtually identical, for example, the horizontally incised sherds with incised base figured by Strong (1935, Pl. 21, 2*a* and *b*) and the rim of Plate VIII I. It is also significant that at Arzberger shoulder incising is not associated with collared rims, although it is relatively common on the other vessel forms; it does not occur on any vessel form in the Upper Republican sites. Finally, Wedel (1935*a*: 190) estimated that about 70 per cent of the rims from the Republican River sites are collared, the proportion rising in the more westerly sites. At the Arzberger site about a third of the rims are collared, perhaps a reflection of the addition of important new vessel types to the ceramic complex.

To extend the comparison of Arzberger with what might be called upper Republican River Upper Republican to the non-collared vessels, it is at once apparent that a greater number of attributes are found at Arzberger, but that a considerable number are common to both. Many of the Arzberger vessels resemble quite closely illustrated noncollared Upper Republican specimens; others differ especially in having elliptical mouths, low rims, strap handles, and decorated shoulders; still others show a mixture of the attributes of these two extremes. Clear evidence of a pronounced clustering of the non-Upper Republican attributes in vessels is lacking, however, and it would be an oversimplification to consider the Arzberger complex merely the result of addition of new vessel types to an Upper Republican base. Comparative evidence, as discussed below, suggests that this is the ultimate explanation, but so far as the Arzberger site itself is concerned, the situation appears to be primarily one of blending, even if it is possible to show that the various attributes were derived from discrete traditions.

Specific attributes linking the noncollared vessels of Arzberger and the Upper Republican sites include chiefly surface finish, lip incising, rim incising, and rim form. Upper Republican vessels were stamped with the cord-wrapped paddle and often subsequently smoothed, although seldom to such an extent as to obliterate the paddle impressions. Most of the Arzberger vessels are smoothed, but a few have traces or clear impressions of a cord-wrapped paddle. Additional types of surface finish found at Arzberger but unknown in the Upper Republican sites include grooved-paddle and checked-paddle stamping. Traces of a red film or stain were observed on five noncollared rims at Arzberger (and also on one collared specimen), and red staining was common on the Arzberger body sherds, where it usually occurred on the interior. Strong (1935: 247) reported in summarizing Upper Republican pottery that a bright red hematite stain on the inner surface of a small proportion of sherds occurred at nearly all of the sites known to him, and Kivett (1949: 280) found a "limited number of sherds, some of which are from rather deep bowls," with red stained inner surface. Paste, as was mentioned above, seems to be much alike in all of the pottery of both areas. Lip incising or punctating is reported for about 50 per cent of the noncollared rims from the sites described by Wedel (1935*a*: 188), and Strong (1935: 247) stated that incisions occur across or along the lip of many vessels. Rim incising in the form of multiple horizontal lines occurs on about a fifth of the Arzberger noncollared vessels. A few sherds have traces of other rectilinear patterns. Similar decorations are present on Upper Republican vessels (Strong, 1935: 248 and Pl. 5, Fig. 1*h*), but appear to be very rare. A comparison of rim forms as illustrated by Wedel (1935*a*: 187, Fig. 5*j–r*) with those of Plate VI indicates that all of the Upper Republican forms can be matched by Arzberger specimens; however, the high, straight, outslanting rims of Arzberger are not illustrated for the Upper Republican sites.

Attributes separating the noncollared pottery of the Arzberger and Upper Republican sites have in several instances been mentioned. The chief differences appear to be the presence at Arzberger alone of noncollared vessels having high, straight, outslanting rims; handles, lugs, and rim projections in some quantity; shoulders decorated by incising; angular shoulders; grooved and checked-paddle stamping; and elliptical orifices. The Upper Republican sites show some patterns of rim incising not surely known for Arzberger (Strong, 1935: 248) and perhaps other distinctive traits. Detailed analysis of the Upper Republican specimens would surely result in significant differences in relative frequencies of shared traits; for example, lip incising is certainly far more important at Arzberger, as is rim incising.

A slightly variant Upper Republican culture from south-central Nebraska is that exemplified by the Sweetwater site (Champe, 1936), which is situated in the Loup River drainage some 70 miles to the north of the approximate geographical center of the Republican River sites. In most respects the Sweetwater and Republican River sites are quite similar, the chief difference being the use of cord-impressed rather than incised decoration on some 61 per cent of the decorated rims at Sweetwater. At the Arzberger site cord-impressed decoration is confined to five rims which were interpreted as trade pieces because of their rarity, and at the Republican River sites the trait is equally rare (Champe, 1936: 278). On the other hand, there are a few traits which hint at a closer connection between Sweetwater and Arzberger than between Arzberger and the Republican drainage sites. One of these is the presence of some lip decoration on the collared vessels of Sweetwater, although lip decoration was not as abundant (32 out of 151 rims) as it was at Arzberger. Three examples of handles were noted at Sweetwater; one was definitely associated with a vessel having a noncollared rim and an incised lip. One vessel (Champe, 1936; Pl. VII F) has a combination of noncollared rim, probably elliptical mouth, incised lip, and a long, narrow lug onto which the lip incising was extended; this combination is frequently seen in the Arzberger specimens. In the nonceramic field, House I at Sweetwater (Champe, 1936, Fig. 3) appears to resemble in outline the "four cornered circle" of the Arzberger House II more than it does the comparatively rare nonrectangular structures of the Republican sites. These special resemblances, however, do not counterbalance the fundamental similarities in surface finish and other respects between Sweetwater and the Republican drainage sites as opposed to Arzberger. Discounting the unique emphasis on cord-impressed decoration at Sweetwater, the Republican sites and Sweetwater resemble each other more than either resembles Arzberger, but the rather small remaining differences at Sweetwater seem to point in the direction of Arzberger.

In summary, it would appear that Strong's suggestion (1940: 382) that the Arzberger site represents a basically Upper Republican culture is amply justified. The similarities are detailed and extend through many segments of material culture. The differences are no less real, but in many instances they constitute an addition to the Upper Republican complex rather than a replacement. An impressionistic view is that the Arzberger people participated more fully in the main currents of Plains cultural development with a richer, more varied culture as a result; in comparison, the Upper Republican sites seem to be drowsy provincial hamlets. That the wider social contacts of the Arzberger people were not invariably pleasant is attested by the site fortification, but they were stimulating. Discussion of this difference is postponed to a later section dealing with a more exact chronological placement, but it seems probable that both geographical position and time difference were involved. The Arzberger people were living in an area and period which exposed them to diverse cultural influences; the Upper Republican peoples were living in an area which was farther removed from active centers and probably in a period of relative stability as well.

The Nebraska Aspect. A second prehistoric cultural manifestation of the Nebraska area is that of the Nebraska Aspect (or Culture). Like the Upper Republican Aspect, the Nebraska Aspect represents the remains of an earth lodge-dwelling and horticultural group. Several lines of evidence indicate that the two aspects were in some measure contemporaneous. The distribution of the more characteristic sites is essentially along the bluff zone of the Missouri River in eastern Nebraska, southwestern Iowa, and northeastern Kansas (Wedel, 1940: 313). The basic similarity of the Nebraska Aspect to Upper Republican has been noted by Strong (1935: 266–67) and Wedel (1940: 312–13), and the convenient list of apparent differences presented by the latter (1940: 312–13) indicates that the Nebraska Aspect can be distinguished from the Upper Republican by its possession of more abundant shell work (spoons, hoes, zoomorphic figures), pottery with a greater frequency of handles, many plain-surfaced vessels, pottery tobacco pipes in bent tubular form, and pottery effigy human heads. A number of other items which seem to be confined to the Nebraska Aspect appear in minor quantities. In addition to the distinctive sites of the Missouri River area, several other sites to the westward are intermediate in both culture and geographical position between the Nebraska and Upper Republican aspects (Wedel, 1940: 314). One of the chief evidences of the intermediate cultural position of these sites is the presence of substantial numbers of collared rims, otherwise rare or completely missing in Nebraska Aspect sites. From the standpoint of a generalized comparison, however, the numerous similarities are more impressive than the detailed differences; Wedel (1940: 313) suggested that the similarities were the result of "a common ancestry at no very remote time, but there is nothing to indicate that either, as such, was derived from the other."

Of interest in the question of Arzberger-Central Plains relationships is the fact that several of the pottery attributes which are characteristic of the Nebraska Aspect rather than the Upper Republican are also found at Arzberger. These attributes include strap handles (e.g., Bell and Gilmore, 1936, Pl. II), incised shoulders (*ibid.*, Pl. III), a pinched lip band reminiscent of the Hughes Beveled pottery type, and rim lugs of various forms. Taken at face value, this situation suggests a direct connection between Arzberger and the Nebraska Aspect, but a more detailed analysis of the similarities fails to support this view. Thus the handles are often round in cross section (loop handles in the terminology employed here) and are usually undecorated (Bell and Gilmore, 1936; Hill and Cooper, 1937*a, b, c*, 1938; Strong, 1935: 253). Shoulder incising is not particularly abundant and is usually applied to simple round-mouthed jars with globular bodies and plain lips. Lugs are often heavy appendages with vertical perforations in contrast to the prevalent flat tabs of Arzberger.

A plausible explanation for these differences in detail is not difficult to find. It seems altogether probable that both Arzberger and the Nebraska Aspect received a constellation of traits from the same ultimate source, the Middle Mississippi ceramic tradition, but that the Nebraska Aspect was influenced directly by Middle Mississippi groups, whereas Arzberger was influenced by a modified derivative of Middle Mississippi, the Oneota culture. Discussion of Arzberger-Oneota relationship is presented below. The question of Middle Mississippi-Nebraska Aspect connections is summarized by Wedel (1943: 213–14); briefly, in addition to Middle Mississippi-like attributes on the native grit-tempered Nebraska Aspect paste, there are repeated examples of actual Middle Mississippi pottery on the Nebraska Aspect sites, a situation which leaves little doubt as to the direction in which the ceramic influences flowed. The excavation of the Steed-Kisker site, a Middle Mississippi village in the Kansas City area, completes the demonstration by providing a convenient source. It is interesting to note that diffusion was by no means a one-way process as is shown by the typical Nebraska Aspect house found at Steed-Kisker. Taking into consideration the fundamental relationship of Upper Republican and the Nebraska Aspect, a possible interpretation is that in post-Hopewell times an ancestral culture arose in the Central Plains characterized by the nonceramic features common to the Upper Republican and Nebraska aspects and having as a sort of highest common ceramic factor a grit-tempered, cord-wrapped paddle-stamped jar with simple rim and little, if any, decoration. It may be significant that such pottery is characteristic of the Antelope Creek Focus, far to the south in the Texas Panhandle (Krieger, 1946: 44), although here a peripheral position might well result in retention of an early pottery complex to a relatively late date. The subsequent bifurcation of the ancestral tradition involved the addition of Middle Mississippi influences to the more easterly sites, resulting in the Nebraska Aspect, and the addition of the collared rim with associated decorative techniques to the more westerly sites to form the Upper Republican Aspect. The source of the collared rim tradition presumably lies to the north and east, where the Late Woodland cultures from Minnesota to the Atlantic coast show basically similar vessels. In the Great Lakes area these collars were most frequently cord impressed rather than incised, as at Aztalan, Wisconsin (Barrett, 1933: 303–13), although the Mill Creek culture of northwestern Iowa and adjacent regions exhibits collared and noncollared rims with incised designs. Whatever the source of the Upper Republican incising may be, it is clear that the Arzberger people participated fully in the same tradition, and consequently that the site is a representative of the Upper Republican rather than the Nebraska Aspect variant of Central Plains culture.

The St. Helena Focus. The excavation by the University of

Nebraska of three closely related village sites in Cedar County, northeastern Nebraska, on the Missouri River and the publication of the results by Cooper (1936) provide a substantial body of data on still another geographical and cultural variant of prehistoric Central Plains culture. In many respects the St. Helena Focus resembles the Arzberger site more closely than it does either the Upper Republican or the Nebraska Aspect sites, but in certain other features there are clear differences. As a result, the exact nature of the relation of the Upper Republican and Nebraska aspects to the St. Helena Focus and the relationship of the latter in turn to Arzberger becomes a question of importance.

In its general features the St. Helena Focus offers no startling novelties. As in the Arzberger site, the assemblage of cultural traits is compounded of elements which are familiar within the general context of the late prehistoric period in the Central Plains. The three villages of the Focus were situated in elevated positions near the Missouri River, two of them actually on the bluff edges overlooking the river. It is perhaps chronologically significant that two of the villages were large by Upper Republican standards, one having probably more than 18 houses; the second, at least 31 houses. No fortifications were reported.

Artifacts other than pottery for the most part represent types already familiar in the Nebraska and Upper Republican aspects; consequently, no attempt will be made at a detailed comparative study. Pottery is grit tempered and cord-wrapped paddle-stamped with frequent subsequent smoothing, and vessels consist almost entirely of jars with simple straight or outcurving rims or collared rims, the latter usually decorated with incised rectilinear patterns and notched collar bases. A few handles were noted, mostly round or elliptical in cross section with some straplike forms. Handles were associated exclusively with the noncollared vessels, and only two were decorated. Lugs also occur in small quantity in several types, most often as a small projection from the lip, but one example of a vertically perforated lug reminiscent of the Nebraska Aspect was noted; a bowl (Cooper, 1936, Pl. IV, 6) had probably two strongly projecting perforated tabs, and a few sherds have rough appliqué rim nodes. So far as the evidence goes, all of the vessels had round mouths and more or less rounding shoulders. Lip or extreme upper rim decoration on noncollared vessels is decidedly the rule and usually takes the form of incising on the lip or scalloping or notching on the extreme upper rim (or outer lip in the terminology used for the Arzberger pottery). Incised shoulder decoration is present but exceedingly rare, and two of the five examples are shell-tempered specimens which were probably trade pieces from an Oneota culture group.

A comparison of Arzberger and St. Helena pottery immediately reveals certain differences. The most obvious of these from the standpoint of the St. Helena pottery are the complete absence of checked or grooved-paddle stamping; the higher proportion of collared rim sherds (about 60 per cent) ; the absence of elliptical orifices and angular shoulders; the comparatively rare occurrence of handles, lugs, and decorated shoulders; the prevalence of plain lips on collared vessels; and the complete absence of incised decoration on the rims of noncollared vessels. The high, straight, outslanting rims found in some quantity at Arzberger (rim form 17) seem to be absent in the St. Helena Focus, and the common St. Helena practice of beveling lips and decorating the bevel as if it were a proper collar is not at all characteristic of Arzberger. Less easily apparent differences can also be detected, chiefly in the field of incised rim decoration; there is a greater variety and complexity of incised patterns on the rims of the collared St. Helena vessels, the plain horizontal incising of Arzberger (and the Upper Republican sites) is said to be rare, and the crosshatched design at St. Helena seems to be characterized by more closely spaced lines and a consequently tighter lattice.

Most of these differences are also true of the Upper Republican-Arzberger relationship, and it is at least partly true to say that the reason St. Helena differs from Arzberger is because it is so close to true Upper Republican. A few ceramic features point in the opposite direction, however. Both St. Helena and Arzberger lack the high, rather flat shoulder often seen on Upper Republican pottery, and both have a higher proportion of lip ornamentation on noncollared vessels. Handles and lugs are very rare or absent at Upper Republican sites, in contrast to St. Helena and Arzberger. Finally, St. Helena and Arzberger are further linked by the common presence of a few trade sherds which are almost surely Oneota.

Oddly enough, there are a few ceramic details which unite Upper Republican and Arzberger as opposed to St. Helena; one is the greater importance of the simple, horizontal, incised line pattern, another is the use of interior red staining, a third is the apparent common absence of the St. Helena beveled lip treated like a collar, and a fourth is incising on noncollared rims, which is seen occasionally in Upper Republican. This equivocal situation suggests that Arzberger and St. Helena are slightly divergent derivatives from a common Upper Republican base. Some of their shared traits can be explained by influence from a fourth and alien culture, the Oneota Aspect, rather than by direct connection, but the intermediate geographical position of the St. Helena Focus and the general character of its ceramic differences still leave a suspicion that it is not far removed from a true intermediate between Upper Republican and Arzberger. It can also be argued that certain distinctive traits at St. Helena, notably the loop handles and perforated lugs, should be attributed to influence from the Nebraska Aspect which was lacking at Arzberger. Finally, there appears to be a trace of influence from the Mill Creek culture of eastern South Dakota and Iowa present in St. Helena and absent at Arzberger. Reference is made again to this problem.

Certain of the nonceramic artifacts shed further light on the question of Upper Republican-St. Helena-Arzberger relationships. Two catlinite pipes, both of projecting stem elbow form, and two pecked or ground stone mauls were found on the St. Helena sites; thus the St. Helena Focus is linked with Arzberger rather than with Upper Republican. Both St.

Helena and Upper Republican lack the Arzberger grooved ribs or spines thought to have been pottery paddles and seem to lack the blunt-pointed, awl-like bone tools called flint flakers in this study. Antler cylinders, polished celts, and notched scapula hoes are missing at Arzberger but occur in St. Helena and Upper Republican. A detailed comparative study with the specimens in hand might well expand or modify this list, but the situation in general seems to support the intermediate position of St. Helena, although interpretation is hampered by the inherent uncertainty of reasoning from absence of artifact types which in some cases were not particularly abundant at any site.

The Lower Loup Focus. The last cultural entity in the Central Plains to be compared with the Arzberger site is a compact group of sites in eastern Nebraska in the general region of the confluence of the Loup and Platte rivers. They are an especially important datum in Plains prehistory because finds of trade material from European sources clearly indicate a protohistoric date for the type of culture exhibited, and because in all probability they are the remains of the Pawnee towns of the protohistoric period (Strong, 1935 : 68; Wedel, 1938). Description of artifacts and architectural features is presented by Dunlevy (1936), and a summary in the form of an extended trait list is included in Wedel's publication (1938 : 6–9). A generalized comparison involving a few broad characteristics of Lower Loup culture will be sufficient to indicate the basic nature of Lower Loup-Arzberger relationships.

Settlements of the Lower Loup Focus are described by Wedel (1938 : 6) as generally "large (from 15 to 100 acres or more) and compactly arranged; not infrequently they seem to have been located on bluffs or hilltops with an eye to defensibility and in a few instances they were further protected by earth walls and ditches." Bastioned fortifications have not been reported, but with this exception the general pattern of occupation is very much like that exemplified by the Arzberger site. Four excavated houses (Dunlevy, 1936 : 157–71) are described as essentially round, having four central posts and in one case a definite circle of intermediate posts, the usual entrance passage, central fireplace, outer posts, and cache pits. Dimensions were large, the range in diameter being from 36 to 49 feet. House Number 2 at the Burkett site (Dunlevy, 1936, Fig. 5) is reminiscent of Houses II and III at Arzberger in its general complexity and seeming departure from a true circular outline, but this situation has been interpreted as the result of rebuilding rather than a departure from the standard circular pattern. Refuse mounds are characteristic, and some external caches had depths as great as 10 feet (Wedel, 1940: 331).

Lower Loup pottery (Dunlevy, 1936: 171–93) offers a number of perplexing problems from the comparative point of view. There are obvious similarities to Arzberger in many ceramic attributes, including the basic paste. Lower Loup pottery exhibits grooved-paddle (or perhaps tooled in some instances) surface finish, frequently with subsequent smoothing or polishing; collared rims with pinched lower collar borders and incised collar decoration; high frequency of lip incising or punctating in all vessel forms; elliptical orifices; rectilinear body decoration, often involving patterns of opposed triangles; a variety of straight or outcurving noncollared rim forms, including high, straight or nearly straight outslanting rims; and an abundance of strap handles, frequently decorated by incising. These attributes and others not listed constitute such an impressive list of resemblances that the existence of a fundamental relationship can hardly be questioned. On the other hand, the ceramic differences existing are equally important in a consideration of the nature of the Lower Loup-Arzberger relationship. Outstanding among these are the complete absence in the Lower Loup of cord-wrapped paddle and checked-paddle stamping; apparently nearly complete absence of rim incising on noncollared forms (Division I of Dunlevy); high frequency of lips decorated by punctation rather than by incising in the Lower Loup pottery and the prominence of herringbone patterns on lips; abundance of handles and characteristic attachment somewhat below the lip of noncollared vessels in contrast to the Arzberger practice of merging the upper end of the handle smoothly into the lip; association of handles at Lower Loup sites with collared rims, often multiple handles giving a cloistered effect; association of body decoration with collared rims; and absence or near absence of the Arzberger crosshatching and multiple horizontal lines incised on collars. It should also be noted that the effect of a very low collar was produced at the Lower Loup sites by lip modifications, in this tendency resembling the St. Helena and Sweetwater foci; at Arzberger such a practice was not evident, the rims being in almost every instance clearly collared or not collared. Finally, the incised patterns on vessel bodies and handles give a quite different appearance in spite of the presence of shared elements, such as opposed diagonals.

Although this comparison and contrasting of Lower Loup and Arzberger pottery is far from exhaustive, it is hoped that sufficient data have been presented to illustrate the general character of the differences and similarities. In a broad sense Arzberger pottery looks like an assemblage of familiar and more or less distinctive Plains ceramic traditions. Some blending of attributes presumably derived from separate traditions is present, particularly in paste and surface finish, but the Arzberger vessels have a marked tendency to resemble either Upper Republican collared or noncollared vessels on the one hand, and basically Upper Mississippian vessels on the other. Thus, handles and shoulder decoration are confined to noncollared vessels, and the collared vessels bear patterns of collar incising which are quite familiar to students of the Upper Republican tradition. In contrast, many Lower Loup vessels may be described as exuberantly original in spite of the familiarity of their component attributes; an example is a collared vessel with a cloistered rim, elaborate herringbone lip incising, and body and rim incising which forms what is essentially a single decorative unit. It is possible to exaggerate the importance of the contrast, since many of the simpler Lower Loup vessels resemble typical Arzberger specimens quite closely, but the difference is nevertheless real. One inference which might be drawn from this situation is that Arzberger and Lower Loup represent collateral products of the same or nearly the same combination of ceramic traditions, one exhibiting a rather timid retention of the originally discrete traditions, and the other boldly mixing the attributes into new and distinctive combinations. A second inference is possible: Arzberger might represent an ancestral stage in which the process of recombination of attributes and invention to form the unique Lower Loup pottery tradition had barely begun. The question of relative age is fundamental in assessing the probability of the two hypotheses.

Nonceramic artifacts provide further evidence on the nature of the Lower Loup-Arzberger relationship. Traits shared by Arzberger and Lower Loup which seem to be absent in the Upper Republican sites include catlinite pipes of elbow and projecting stem varieties, grooved bison ribs, and grooved stone mauls. The presence or absence of certain other traits is more difficult to establish because of scarcity and descriptive difficulties, but it appears that the blunt-headed awls of Arzberger have fairly close parallels in Lower Loup (Dunlevy, 1936, Pl. XIII B, C, D), as do some of the worked bison ribs and large elliptical scrapers. The comparative abundance of small, basically triangular, unnotched projectile points is another feature linking Arzberger and Lower Loup. On the other hand, absence of fishhooks and the presence of such features as cancellous bone paintbrushes and toothed bone fleshing tools sets Lower Loup apart from both Arzberger and Upper Republican. It is hardly necessary to emphasize that many traits occur in all three cultural units, and that the comparison reveals no more than variations of a basic cultural pattern. A general impression is that Arzberger shows some, but not all, of the traits, the presence of which distinguishes Lower Loup from Upper Republican, and it might be added that Arzberger shows some of the traits otherwise peculiar to Upper Republican. This situation is not inconsistent with the hypothesis that Arzberger is culturally and chronologically intermediate between the Upper Republican Aspect and the Lower Loup Focus.

The Central Plains: Summary. The preceding section has reviewed briefly the empirical similarities of the Arzberger site to certain of the late prehistoric and protohistoric cultural entities of Nebraska. One general conclusion emerges clearly: The number and character of the parallels between Arzberger and the Upper Republican Aspect, the St. Helena Focus, and the Lower Loup Focus strongly suggest that the Arzberger culture is no very remote offshoot of a tradition which includes these manifestations. In fact, it is tempting to construct a speculative chain of development in which Arzberger forms an integral part. The arbitrary starting point in such a developmental sequence would be represented by the Upper Republican Aspect as it is known on the Republican drainage in Nebraska. A second phase is that of the St. Helena Focus, which is fundamentally Upper Republican, but shows in minor quantities such features as grooved stone mauls, projecting stem catlinite pipes, body decoration, lugs and handles on pottery, and a decided increase in lip incising on pottery vessels. The third phase is represented by the Arzberger site; here the Upper Republican ancestry is evident, but the St. Helena innovations and other new features appear, sometimes in considerable quantity. Important among these are the large, fortified village layout; a probable tendency toward larger and more nearly circular houses; grooved stone mauls and catlinite pipes of projecting stem and other forms; catlinite tablets; grooved-paddle stamping of pottery (although not to the exclusion of cord-wrapped paddle stamping, the only type found in Upper Republican and St. Helena) ; a very extensive use of lip incising; and a number of other pottery attributes which suggest that the Arzberger people borrowed and retained in partly intact form a vessel type which was a low, elliptical-mouthed jar with paired strap handles (often decorated), with a plain or rarely incised rim, and frequently with rectilinear shoulder incising. The final developmental phase so far as this comparison is concerned is the Lower Loup Focus, where large and sometimes fortified towns were the rule, houses were round, and various ceramic attributes, such as handles, body decoration, and lugs, were freely recombined in a distinctive and original manner. Other traits appearing for the first time in St. Helena and Arzberger continue and still more were added, for example, cancellous bone paintbrushes and toothed bone fleshers. The subsequent transformation of Lower Loup into historic Pawnee lies outside the scope of this paper—the Arzberger culture has already been bracketed.

The hypothesis that Arzberger is simply a direct representative of one phase in the development of the Central Plains sequence which led ultimately to the historic Pawnee has the merit of economy, and the evidence certainly suggests an intermediate cultural position, as Strong pointed out earlier (1940: 382–83). Moreover, the particular phase which Arzberger represents is one which is missing in Nebraska so far as the available evidence goes (Wedel, 1941: 26, footnote 12). There are, however, three basic factors which suggest that the simple explanation, i.e., that the Arzberger people were the direct cultural and physical ancestors of the historic Pawnee, is not true, even though they may have played a significant part in an indirect manner.

Geographical position is the first of these factors. The Arzberger site lies in the middle of South Dakota some 260 airline miles to the northwest of the fork of the Loup and the Platte rivers. Although this distance does not preclude an ancestral status for the Arzberger people, it certainly serves to direct attention to the south and east to a less remote area for the Upper Republican-Lower Loup transition. Hints are not lacking that a search for truly intermediate sites may be successful (Meleen, 1948), but the problem is by no means solved or solvable with the evidence currently at hand.

The second basic factor is the presence at Arzberger of a number of traits which do not appear at the Lower Loup sites. An obvious example is the bastioned fortification, which has not been reported in Nebraska, although it is known that wall and ditch earthworks surrounded some of the Lower Loup sites. In the field of pottery attributes the horizontally incised, noncollared rim appears to be absent or nearly absent in Lower

Loup, as do carinate shoulders and checked paddle-stamped surface finish. It may well be true that any one or all of these traits could disappear in an Arzberger-Lower Loup transition, but their combined weight, plus the fact that they are absent or exceedingly rare at any time in Nebraska, again suggests an indirect rather than a direct relationship. In this connection it is also relevant to repeat that St. Helena and Lower Loup have vessels with very low collars produced by lip beveling, a technique which is hardly present at Arzberger.

The third factor is the possibility that certain of the broad resemblances between Lower Loup and Arzberger may have been the result of parallel development owing to exposure to the same basic cultural and perhaps environmental circumstances. Certainly, one of the dominant motifs in the culture history of the Central Plains from Upper Republican to protohistoric times is the increasing influence of the Middle Mississippi culture and its derivative, Upper Mississippi culture. This influence is barely detectable in some of the classic Upper Republican sites in the form of trivial amounts of shell tempering in pottery, notched clam shells, and probably a few other items; it is very evident in the Nebraska Aspect farther to the east, where the source is clearly the Middle Mississippi extension represented by the Steed-Kisker site; and finally in the protohistoric period it seems to extend even to settlement pattern, the large, often fortified town being a very widespread Mississippi feature. It is interesting to note in passing that this long-continued pressure from an active and expanding culture center never resulted in an overriding of the native Central Plains tradition; Middle and Upper Mississippi culture remained simply a source from which traits were borrowed and fitted into the Central Plains pattern without destruction of its continuity or essential distinctiveness. To return to the major point, this influence was presumably at hand in central South Dakota as it was in eastern Nebraska or southern South Dakota, and the cultural assemblage seen at Arzberger could be derived without any great strain by the operation of Mississippi and other influences more or less *in situ* on an Upper Republican culture much like that of the Republican drainage itself. The reverse of this statement is more cogent—Lower Loup culture could have been developed from an Upper Republican base in northeastern Nebraska or adjacent South Dakota without the specific intervention of the Arzberger culture, although it almost certainly passed through a stage which was generally similar. If the latter statement was true, as is here considered to be the more probable, Arzberger is in the position of an elderly collateral relative to Lower Loup. This basically avuncular role would not rule out Arzberger as the source from which certain traits, grooved-paddle stamping of pottery, for example, were introduced to the Central Plains traditions. Additional support for the collateral interpretation is offered by Wedel's suggestion (1940: 328–30, 346; 1941; 1947*b*: 14–18) that the abandonment of the western part of the Upper Republican range involved a general eastward shift of population owing to unfavorable ecological changes, pressure of hostile hunting groups, or both. Such a shift might well have been the prime factor in the extension of the Upper Republican culture to South Dakota, and it would have occurred at a period when Upper Republican was still characterized by small villages and pottery not greatly modified by Mississippi influences. It must be admitted, however, that a local ancestor of more or less classic Upper Republican type is not currently available for Arzberger.

Although sufficient evidence is not at hand for an appraisal of the exact nature of the relationship between Arzberger and the Upper Republican-Lower Loup sequence, it does seem clear that the resemblances are sufficiently close to allow one to assume that there was no great time discrepancy, and consequently that Arzberger existed at about the same time as the corresponding phase in the Central Plains. Since an exactly corresponding phase is lacking, the most that can be done is a bracketing based on cultural comparisons. The evidence cited above suggests that Arzberger is later than Upper Republican proper (specifically the Lost Creek and Medicine Creek foci) and the Nebraska Aspect; later than the St. Helena Focus, which is in turn later than classic Upper Republican; and earlier than the Lower Loup Focus. The firm anchoring of the latter in the protohistoric period permits a not entirely uncontrolled estimate in terms of absolute chronology; accepting Wedel's estimate (1947*a*: 155) that Lower Loup was in existence by *ca.* A.D. 1550 and making the further estimate that Arzberger did not long precede Lower Loup, a fifteenth century date seems reasonable.

IOWA—EASTERN SOUTH DAKOTA—MINNESOTA

The Oneota Aspect. In the foregoing discussion it has been asserted repeatedly that an important element in Arzberger culture, and one which distinguishes it from Upper Republican, was derived by diffusion from the Upper Mississippi Phase, and it was further suggested that this influence was exerted in approximately the area of the Arzberger site rather than in eastern Nebraska. The empirical evidence underlying this assertion is quite simply the specific, detailed, and unmistakable similarity of many Arzberger vessels to illustrated Oneota specimens. The original outline for the discussion of this point prescribed a detailed comparison of Arzberger with a group of Oneota and other Upper Mississippi foci, but a review of the pertinent literature indicates that such a procedure would be decidedly overweight for several reasons, among which are (1) the widespread distribution of the attributes which Arzberger exhibits, (2) the apparent failure of Arzberger to resemble any particular Oneota manifestation much more closely than it does other manifestations, and (3) the unevenness with which the cultural materials are described for the various Oneota foci. Further difficulty is introduced by the absence of a well-developed chronological sequence within the Oneota tradition, although sites can be separated on the basis of whether or not European trade materials are associated. In brief, the illustrations and descriptions of Oneota pottery presented by Hill and Wedel (1936), Mott (1938), Wilford (1941 and 1945), Griffin (1943), and McKern (1945) are held to be sufficient evidence to postulate a direct and intensive contact between Arzberger and an Oneota group, presumably one of the western groups such as the Blue Earth Focus of Minnesota or the Orr Focus of Wisconsin, Iowa, and Minnesota. No attempt will be made to compare attributes in detail. Instead, discussion will be restricted to inferences as to the general nature of the contact and comments on correspondences of the nonceramic artifacts and other features.

Perhaps the best entry into the comparative notes is a paraphrase of McKern's generalized description (1945: 145–47) of the pottery of the Orr Focus as it is known in Wisconsin. Orr Focus vessels are characterized by simplicity and standardization of form. Bodies are without exception ellipsoidal with rounded bases and shoulders and are rather squatty in appearance. Rims are usually straight and outslanting; there is some variation in rim height, but most rims may be described as medium. About half of the vessels observed have two oppositely placed handles connecting lip and upper shoulder. More commonly, strap handles (flat in transverse section) were used, but loop handles also occur. There is variation in the point of attachment of the upper end of the handle, some being attached immediately below the lip and others flush with the lip. Some handles rise upward from the point of attachment and then curve sharply down to the shoulder. Lip and shoulder area usually shows decoration, lips having "notched or scalloped" decoration, and shoulders incised rectilinear patterns sometimes embellished by marginal punctations. Solid areas are sometimes filled by punctations. Plain strap handles occur, but typically the handles bear three or four vertical incised lines; one handle has a design of opposed diagonals. Incising was sometimes done by a method leaving broad, smooth flutings with corresponding ridges on the interior, but more commonly designs were executed in narrow, rough lines. Although rims are typically undecorated, a few examples of multiple horizontal incised lines are figured, one on a vertical rim. Surfaces are smooth, and there are a few examples of the use of a pinkish slip. Shell tempering seems to be present in every instance.

The basic resemblance of much of the noncollared Arzberger pottery to the Orr Focus material is obvious and need not be emphasized. Certainly, most of the Arzberger attribute combinations can be matched quite closely by selected Orr Focus specimens. The reverse is not true, however; certain Orr Focus traits are either rare or absent at Arzberger. Examples are vertical fluted lines on the shoulder area, loop handles, handles with upper end attached slightly below the lip, and so on. Particularly with respect to decorative patterns, Arzberger resembles a simplified version of the Orr Focus concepts. More obvious differences include the almost universal use of grit tempering at Arzberger as opposed to Oneota shell tempering, and the occasional presence of traces of grooved, checked, or cord-wrapped paddle-stamped surface finish at Arzberger on vessels which are otherwise very much in the Oneota tradition. The angular shoulder seen at Arzberger appears to be completely absent from the Orr Focus, although it is reported from the Grand River Focus (McKern, 1945: 149). If the detailed comparison were extended to all of the Oneota and other Upper Mississippi manifestations, more specific similarities could be pointed out. For example, cord-wrapped paddle-stamped sherds have been found at other Oneota sites (Wilford, 1945: 35), and grooved paddle-stamped sherds occur in the sites of the Grand River Focus (McKern, 1945: 149) and other Upper Mississippi sites. Wilford (1945: 34–35) reported that the prehistoric Humphrey site, a component of the Blue Earth Focus in south-central Minnesota, differs from the Orr Focus in having vessels in which the handles are flush with the rim, the lips are more commonly incised or punctated (on the inner surface), and there is a small amount of cord-marked surface finish, an encouraging trend in the direction of Arzberger. Unfortunately, certain other pottery characteristics at the Humphrey site seem to point in the opposite direction; for example, no elliptical vessels were found. Another likely candidate on geographical grounds is the Oneota material from the vicinity of Correctionville in northwestern Iowa (Mott, 1938: 290, Table II, pp. 303–4). The Correctionville pottery differs from that of other Iowa sites in having relatively abundant outward curving, outward slanting rims, sometimes quite low; decoration of the lip surface and of the inner lip also; and shoulder decoration composed of hachured areas adjacent to each other. These features appear to lean in the direction of Arzberger.

Diffusion was not limited to ceramic ideas, as is shown by the catlinite pipes from Arzberger. The specimen illustrated as Plate V N is the projecting anterior end of what may well have been a disk or elbow pipe of Oneota type (McKern, 1945, Pls. 32, 33), and the other pipe fragments at least could have been from types within the Oneota range. It is hardly necessary to point out that the source of the catlinite was undoubtedly the famous quarry at Pipestone in southwestern Minnesota. The Arzberger catlinite tablets or sharpening stones (Pl. V Y) also have parallels at the Leary site (Hill and Wedel, Pl. VI, p. 48) and in the Iowa Oneota (Mott, 1938: 299), but the Oneota specimens bear purposeful designs rather than random scratchings. All of the Wisconsin Oneota foci produce ribbon flake knives (McKern, 1945: 134, Pl. 38) much like those of Arzberger; in view of the apparent scarcity of this type on the Plains and its long history farther east, it appears likely that the idea was borrowed from the Oneota people. In Iowa earthen enclosures are associated with some of the Oneota sites (Keyes, 1927: 223), but no bastioned fortifications have been reported. Over a much wider area, villages occur in high terrace situations suitable for defense. Abundant end scrapers and bison shoulder blade hoes in Iowa and Minnesota may indicate that Oneota was not invariably a cultural donor to the Plains villages.

If the evidence for a direct connection with Oneota culture is accepted, it follows that Arzberger could be as early as the first recognizable Oneota manifestation, and if the absence of trade goods is considered conclusive evidence of the prehistoric position of Arzberger, it must be earlier than the Oneota sites which produce materials of European origin. Unfortunately, there does not appear to be any independent dating of Oneota materials which is more reliable than the estimate already available for the Central Plains sequence. Wedel (1947) estimated that Oneota extends back to perhaps the mid-sixteenth century, with trans-Missouri sites probably in existence by A.D. 1650. Certainly, it seems probable that Oneota is as old as Lower Loup in view of the resemblances existing between the two. It is said that Upper Mississippi sherds appear in the middle level at the Kincaid site in southern Illinois and become more common in the late level, and it is further suggested that "the Late period at Kincaid may have been coeval with the developing Oneota aspect" (Cole, *et al.*, 1951: 230). Suggested occupation dates based on tree-ring analysis for Middle and Late Kincaid are A.D. 1525–1613 with the Middle Period ending about 1600 (Cole, *et al.*, 1951: 292). An exclusively seventeenth-century date for the development of Oneota seems too cramped, and the tree-ring dating can hardly be accepted as a lower terminus for Oneota when the considerable distance between Kincaid and the Oneota area is taken into consideration. If J. B. Griffin's hypothesis (1946: 90) that Oneota is essentially a development from the relatively early Aztalan type of Middle Mississippi is accepted, and it seems to be the most likely on the basis of present evidence, these chronological restrictions are removed. On this hypothesis Oneota would be developing from the Aztalan base in the Wisconsin-northern Illinois area at about the time when a similar type of early Middle Mississippi was influencing the Nebraska Aspect, and the development of a full Oneota in the northern area would be paralleled and perhaps influenced by the rise of the late Middle Mississippi Spoon River Focus farther to the south in Illinois. In support of this position, it can be said that sites in northern Illinois seem to show contemporaneity of late Middle Mississippi and Oneota in prehistoric times (H. G. Smith, 1951: 30 ff.; J. B. Griffin, 1946: 87; J. W. Griffin, 1948: 126; Bennett, 1945: 157–58). In summary, it appears that the best possible estimates of the age of both Arzberger and Oneota in the absence of definitive tree-ring or other absolute dates are essentially derived from Wedel's data on Lower Loup. The particular contribution of the Arzberger site is its exhibition of Oneota characteristics in association with material which suggests a cultural level corresponding to an early phase of Lower Loup. If the proposed fifteenth-century dating for Arzberger mentioned above is maintained, then it must also be argued that Oneota was in existence in the fifteenth century, a somewhat earlier date than that indicated by Wedel (1947*a*, Fig. 51). This dating has the merit of providing a comfortably early source for Upper Mississippi influence in Lower Loup and for the "occasional pot with Oneota-like decoration" (Wedel, 1947*a*: 153) of the Nebraska Aspect, not to speak of the Oneota vessels of the St. Helena Focus or the mixture of Upper Republican, Nebraska Aspect, and Oneota artifacts exhibited by the Lynch site (Wedel, 1940: 317) in northeastern Nebraska.

The Mill Creek-Mandan Tradition. A second major cultural tradition of the area which impinges on the Arzberger problem is that which is here called, though perhaps not too accurately, the Mill Creek-Mandan tradition. It is hardly necessary to undertake a full review of Mandan culture history for an adequate discussion of Arzberger, and the purpose of these comments is to sketch the probable cultural background of certain components found in the general vicinity of the site in order to discuss specific Arzberger features which are foreign to the Upper Republican-Lower Loup and the Oneota traditions, especially cord-impressed design, the frequent use of lugs and appliqué nodes, checked-paddle stamping, and the bastioned fortification.

The basic pattern as it appears to be emerging in the recent literature is one of development of a distinctive cultural tradition which is chronologically parallel to that of Oneota. This cultural tradition shares with Oneota the Aztalan-Cahokia Old Village type of early Middle Mississippi as an important basic ingredient, but, unlike Oneota, it has as a second important ingredient a definitely Woodland pottery tradition very much in evidence at Aztalan itself (Barrett, 1933: 303–22). Data presented by Wilford (1945) demonstrate that the Woodland element is itself a composite one involving the remarkably uniform Great Oasis vessel type (Wilford, 1945, Fig. 3*a*) and the Cambria Type B vessel with S-shaped cord-impressed or incised rim. At the Great Oasis site (in southwestern Minnesota) intensive Middle Mississippi influence does not appear, and the stratigraphic situation indicates that the Great Oasis pottery precedes that of both Cambria and Oneota. The Cambria site (in south-central Minnesota) has three presumably contemporaneous types of pottery, of which one (Cambria Type C in Wilford's terminology) might fairly be described as a grit-tempered version of Aztalan-Old Village angular shouldered, rolled rim jars; Cambria Type B vessels have S-shaped rims with incised or cord-impressed decorations and occasional incised or cord-impressed shoulder decorations; Cambria Type A, numerically very important, has a straight, outslanting rim and trailed or incised shoulder decoration and other features of Mississippi type, but shows crosshatched lips, interior cord impressing, and other features which can be attributed to Woodland influence. Surprisingly, in Type A there seems to be a foreshadowing of Oneota in the higher rim, chevron incising or trailing and other patterns on shoulders, and punctate markings associated with bands of parallel lines. A small amount of shell tempering appears at Cambria, but most vessels of all types are grit tempered. Cord-wrapped paddle stamping is found on all types, but is very rare on Type C, and all types are predominantly smoothed. It should be added that for economy's sake this brief and selective review does not do justice to either the importance of the material or Wilford's exposition of relationships.

From the Great Oasis and Cambria components outlined above as a base, two related but substantially distinct complexes seem to have emerged. The first is represented by the frequently mentioned but as yet undescribed Mill Creek sites of northwestern Iowa, primarily those on the Little Sioux River. The interpretation of Mill Creek (in the strict sense) adopted here, which is based on photographs and notes in the Ceramic Repository assembled by J. B. Griffin with the aid of Charles R.

Keyes, is that it is the result of expansion and refinement of the solitary pottery type of Great Oasis plus a rather heavy dose of Aztalan-Old Village Middle Mississippi. As was true at the Cambria site, the Middle Mississippi types were tempered with grit, but it does not seem possible to derive Mill Creek from Cambria by adding the Great Oasis type because of the absence of cord impressing as a decorative technique in Mill Creek, although a few S-shaped rims are present. Hence Cambria and Mill Creek are probably parallel developments, with Mill Creek perhaps slightly earlier.

The second complex related to Great Oasis and Cambria is that now called the Over Focus (Over and Meleen, 1941 : 41; Meleen, 1938; Hurt, 1951: 15 ff.) and as originally defined composed of three sites in South Dakota on the James and Big Sioux rivers. In these sites there are present both Great Oasis-Mill Creek types of vessels and the S-shaped, cord-impressed rim which appears at Cambria (Meleen, 1938; Over and Meleen, 1941). A possible explanation, and the one here considered most probable, is that the Over Focus is the result of a fusion of the Cambria and the Great Oasis-Mill Creek traditions. Strong Middle Mississippi influences continue in the Over Focus; indeed, a sherd from the surface of the Twelve Mile Creek site in the collections of the Ceramic Repository is an unqualified example of the Ramey Incised type which might well have been made at Cahokia or Aztalan. Since Cambria, Iowa Mill Creek, and the Over Focus all fall within a presumably restricted period when powerful Middle Mississippi influence was operative on the eastern margin of the Plains, it seems likely that no great time span separates the three units, and they may be in part overlapping. The absence of cord impressing in Iowa Mill Creek suggests, however, that the compact group of sites on the Little Sioux and their outliers on the Big Sioux were abandoned before the Over Focus was firmly established. It is possible, of course, that the Over Focus represents the immediate descendants of the Iowa Mill Creek population, but it is equally tempting (though undeniably speculative) to attribute the disappearance of the Mill Creek tradition in Iowa to the traditional westward movement of the Omaha and perhaps other Dhegihan-speaking Siouan groups (Champe, 1946:48; J. B. Griffin, 1946:89; Cooper, 1949:306) at a period slightly too early for them to be exposed to strong influence of the Cambria tradition. If the latter is true, it would be necessary to postulate an ancestor geographically and culturally intermediate in the Great Oasis-Mill Creek continuum for the Over Focus, which is a troublesome complication. A more detailed discussion of these relationships and a redefinition and expansion of the Over Focus is presented by Hurt (1952).

However these relationships may be interpreted ultimately, two major points stand out. The first is that the Over Focus is prehistoric and was probably in existence when Aztalan was a flourishing center; its general time period is presumably that of the Nebraska Aspect, where similar influences were reaching southeastern Nebraska by a quite different route. The second point is that the Over Focus seems to stand at the beginning of a cultural sequence which emerges in the historic period as the culture of the Mandan Indians and in view of the Mandan migration traditions (summarized in Hurt, 1952: 21) may very well be the actual sites of some of the ancestral Mandan. An obvious relationship of certain sites in the immediate vicinity of the Arzberger site to this tradition brings up the question of their chronological and cultural relationship to Arzberger.

THE UPPER MISSOURI

The Fort Pierre Branch. The task of assessing the relationship of the Arzberger site to its immediate neighbors has been very much lightened by the timely publication of Lehmer's study (1951, 1952) of what he has named the Fort Pierre Branch. To summarize Lehmer, extensive excavations at the Dodd site, a little less than 15 miles upstream from Arzberger and on the opposite bank, show the presence of three components which have been named in stratigraphic order the Monroe, Anderson, and Stanley foci, the Monroe Focus being the oldest. The Stanley Focus shows trade material of European origin, but the Monroe and Anderson foci are entirely prehistoric and generally similar. A still later protohistoric focus in the immediate neighborhood is that represented by the Phillips Ranch site and named the Snake Butte Focus; it is closely related to the Stanley Focus.

Broad characteristics of the Monroe and Anderson foci include a long rectangular house of a type utterly foreign to the Central Plains tradition and pottery with cord-wrapped paddle-stamped bodies and S-shaped, straight outslanting or, rarely, faintly collared rims. Although the Monroe and Anderson foci presumably represent a continuum, certain differences between them are apparent. The few collared rims are probably associated with the earlier Monroe Focus, and in general there is a shift from earlier horizontal incising to later horizontal cord impressing on the rims of otherwise quite similar vessels. Houses change in detail, although not in basic type; Monroe Focus houses had wall posts distributed evenly around the ends and sides of the rectangular pit, but most of the posts in the Anderson houses were on the longer side walls. Other distinctions are evident but need not be described here.

The cultural affiliations of the Monroe and Anderson foci seem clear, at least in a broad sense. Houses, pottery, and other traits are definitely in the Mandan tradition and have cognates both to the north on the Missouri and to the east and south in the Over Focus sites. Pottery is especially interesting and might with some degree of felicity be described as a sort of Cambria Aspect with most of the Middle Mississippi influence removed. Low curling rims, sharply angular shoulders, elaborate shoulder decoration, handles, and other Mississippi traits seem to be largely or completely missing, and only the straight, flaring, and S-shaped rimmed vessels with incised or cord-impressed decoration are left. Mill Creek influences can be seen in the crosshatched, beveled lips (Lehmer, 1951, Pl. *6c, f*) and the triangular patterns of rim incising (Lehmer, 1951, Pls. *6g; 7a, b, c*), but they are not strong. An interesting detail is the common occurrence in Great Oasis and Monroe of a distinctive hook-shaped scapula knife (Lehmer, 1951: 333, Fig. 102; Wilford, 1945: 34 and illustration in Wilford, 1951). What appears to be a similar implement was found at the Swanson site, an Over Focus component on the Missouri (Hurt, 1951, Fig. V, p. 24). This situation strongly indicates an early typological position in the Mandan sequence and presumably an early chronological position as well, even allowing for cultural retardation in this peripheral geographical position. The shift in house type from the Monroe to the Anderson Focus is exactly paralleled by a similar shift at the Mitchell and Brandon sites of the Over Focus in eastern South Dakota, as Hurt (1951: 16) has pointed out, and suggests contemporaneity. If this interpretation is correct, the early components at the Dodd site owe their ceramic simplicity, and particularly their lack of Middle Mississippi attributes, to a retention of an earlier type of Mandan culture than that exhibited by the Over Focus, and if the inhabitants of the Dodd site were actually the linguistic and physical ancestors of the later Mandan, they must have been the result of an early westward movement of a part of the group. Hurt's conclusion (1951: 21) that the Mandan migration legends have complicated implications for archaeology seems to be eminently sound.

The chronological relationship of Arzberger to the Monroe-Anderson sequence is easily assessed. The Arzberger site is later, and it is separated from the Anderson Focus by an unknown but substantial time interval. A more recent date for the Arzberger culture can be inferred from its possession of numerous traits which persist to the protohistoric or the historic period and which are completely absent in the Monroe and Anderson foci. Examples are grooved-paddle stamping of pottery, strap handles on pottery vessels, a circular or near circular house pattern, perforated bison ribs, and the use of catlinite. The same data provide evidence for the hiatus—it is extremely unlikely that the Anderson Focus would fail to show such common Arzberger traits as grooved-paddle stamping or tabular vein chalcedony knives if there was an appreciable amount of chronological overlap. By extension it can be argued that the Arzberger occupation was later than that of most or all of the sites of the Over Focus. A final observation concerns the St. Helena Focus, which was considered somewhat earlier than Arzberger in the discussion of the Nebraska sequences. Briefly, there seems to be a Great Oasis-Mill Creek element in the pottery of St. Helena, possibly as a result of early Omaha-Ponca contact, just as there is in Monroe and Anderson. It is shown particularly by thickened crosshatched lips (Cooper, 1936, Pl. V) and two motifs of rim incising (Cooper, 1936, Pls. VIII, 4, and IX, 1, 2), but here it is encountered in a recognizably Upper Republican context. St. Helena appears to be a variant of Upper Republican probably of the same general period as the older Dodd components, and the relationship of the latter to Arzberger confirms the earlier position of St. Helena inferred from Central Plains data.

The Middle Mandan. Elimination of the local sites of the early Mandan type and probably also of the Over Focus as a direct source of influence suggests that Arzberger was in contact with a somewhat later phase of the Mandan sequence. Attention is immediately drawn to the Huff site on the Missouri in North Dakota, a little more than 150 miles directly north of the Arzberger site. Limited information on the Huff site is presented by Will and Hecker (1944), and it has long been known among Plains archaeologists because of its rectangular, bastioned fortification. It also enjoys traditional importance among the Mandan as the town where the culture hero chief Good Furred Robe taught the Mandans agriculture and the technique of building a fortified town with houses laid out in rows like corn fields (Will, 1924: 338; Will and Hecker, 1944: 60). In addition to its rectangular ditch jutting out in bastions at regular intervals, the Huff site has houses of Anderson Focus type (Will and Hecker, 1944, Pls. 2, 6). The Huff pottery is predominantly smoothed or grooved paddle-stamped, but a checked-stamped surface finish appears on a little more than 1 per cent of the body sherds (Bowers, MS). Other pottery attributes of interest described by Will and Hecker (p. 67) include rectilinear and curvilinear cord-impressed rainbow designs, a few "lattice work" designs incised on rims, and a "low everted rim incised on outer lip with shoulder decoration opposed diagonal." If the low everted rim is the vessel illustrated as Plate 8, top, the opposed diagonal shoulder decoration is accompanied by punctations, and the rim is straight and nearly vertical rather than everted. Lugs, rim projections, and handles are not mentioned, but appliqué nodes at the top of the upward pointing chevrons are illustrated repeatedly (Pl. 9, bottom; Pl. 14) for the Middle Mandan period to which Will and Hecker assign the Huff site. It might be added that a collection of Middle Mandan sherds presented to the Ceramic Repository by the North Dakota Historical Society includes high straight rims, some of which could be included in the Hughes Beveled Type of Arzberger. A similar collection of early Mandan sherds contains numerous examples of rim projections.

If the Huff site is taken as representative of the Middle Mandan period, there appears to be a strong probability that most of the cultural elements at Arzberger which are rare or lacking in the Central Plains and Oneota traditions were derived from this source, and possibly from the Huff site itself. The few cord-impressed rim sherds found at Arzberger are probably the result of trade with this source; very high, straight rims with beveled lips are another feature in common; checked stamping and nodes associated with upward pointing chevrons are characteristic of the Middle and later Mandan sites and are almost surely the result of Middle Mandan influence; the same may be true of rim projections and horizontal lugs projecting from the lip, although lack of detailed information prevents any very definite conclusion on this point. Certainly these lugs are known earlier in the Mandan sequence, especially in the Over Focus (Meleen, 1938: 26; Over and Meleen, 1941: 25–26). Lugs appear to be the result of Middle Mississippi influence on the Over Focus; they are a prominent attribute in many Middle Mississippi assemblages. Rim projections are a well-known feature of Late Woodland pottery in the area west of Lake Michigan (at Aztalan, for example), and the strong Mandan connection with this area again suggests that Arzberger was the recipient of this attribute, not the donor. The prominence of S-shaped rims at Arzberger is another point of resemblance. The balance of evidence also seems to suggest that the bastioned fortification was borrowed by Arzberger people from the Middle Mandan. This type of fortification is definitely at home in Middle Mississippi, where it is found in the Tennessee-Cumberland area (Thomas, 1891, 1894), at the Angel site in southwestern Indiana (Black, 1944), and at Aztalan (Barrett, 1933). The Huff fortification is a miniature Aztalan, including the general rectangular plan and the stream forming one side. The Arzberger fortification is less regular and much larger, although this can be discounted in part because of the Arzberger topographic situation. Moreover, the intensive Middle Mississippi influence evident early in the Mandan sequence provides a plausible link with Aztalan. It certainly cannot be claimed, however, that anything like an unbroken chain of bastioned forts connects Huff and Aztalan. In fact, the only link is the tenuous connection provided by Keyes's statement (1927: 225) that two uncultivated Iowa Mill Creek sites are rectangular in form and surrounded by a broad, shallow ditch. The opposite explanation, that the Middle Mandan people acquired the idea of a bastioned fort from Arzberger, fails to account for the faithful adherence to the Aztalan layout at Huff and demands, presumably, some sort of link with Middle Mississippi through Oneota. Such a link is even less supported by evidence than is the case with Huff and Aztalan. In any event, the bastioned fortifications are a strong tie between Arzberger and Middle Mandan in view of their absence in other periods and areas in the Plains.

Traits suggestive of diffusion from Arzberger to Huff are not clearly present, at least with the information now available. One might speculate on the Oneota-like shoulder incising and a few other characteristics, but it is not possible to assert that Arzberger was the only source from which Oneota concepts might reach North Dakota, and the "lattice work" designs at Huff could have been derived from Mill Creek via early Mandan (for the Over Focus see Hurt, 1951, Fig. X, *xi;* for the Monroe or Anderson Focus, Lohmer 1951, Pl. 56).

Whatever the exact relationship between Arzberger and Middle Mandan may have been, the similarities seem distinctive and numerous enough to suggest approximate contemporaneity. Will (1946: 15–16) has dated 11 timbers from the Huff site by dendrochronological methods. Cutting dates range from A.D. 1485 to 1543, which agree reasonably well with the date suggested for Arzberger on the basis of its putative position in the Central Plains sequence.

Contemporaneity of Arzberger and Huff presents some interesting implications. The first is concerned with the problem of grooved paddle-stamped surface finish. At Huff this is the only type reported except for a minor amount of checked-paddle stamping, but at Arzberger cord-wrapped paddle stamping was found on about a third of the body sherds which showed traces of paddling, the remainder being grooved paddle-stamped except for a minor amount of checked-paddle stamping. This situation suggests that grooved-paddle stamping moved down the Missouri from the Mandan to the Arzberger people, and from the Arzberger people in turn to the Central Plains. A dogmatic assertion in this matter would be out of place owing to lack of absolute proof of Middle Mandan-Arzberger contemporaneity and owing to the sporadic occurrence of grooved-paddle stamping in many Upper Mississippi assemblages, but the southward diffusion does appear to be the most probable explanation. Had the transition from cord-wrapped to grooved-paddle stamping occurred in Nebraska, intermediate sites should have been discovered by this time.

A second important implication of contemporaneity is the matter of house types. Late prehistoric, protohistoric, and historic Mandan houses were large circular earth lodges definitely in the Central Plains tradition, but only the long rectangular house is reported in the Over Focus, the Monroe Focus, the Anderson Focus, and the Middle Mandan sites. Middle Mandan-Arzberger contact would provide the stimulus which initiated this basic modification of Mandan culture in the direction of the Central Plains tradition, although no trace of circular or subcircular houses of Arzberger type has yet been reported from the Huff or other Middle Mandan sites.

Other Mandan Sites. It has been argued above that the data presented by Lehmer (1952) on the Monroe and Anderson foci of the Dodd site clearly indicate that Arzberger postdates these early Mandan components, and their apparent contemporaneity with the Over Focus (on the evidence of house type) further implies that Arzberger is later than the Swanson component of the Over Focus, a site perhaps 40 miles downstream from Arzberger (Hurt, 1951). There is, however, some reason to suppose that the Swanson site is later than even the Anderson Focus, since it has such traits as worked catlinite, a toothed hide flesher (a decided anachronism), and grooved mauls; in addition, it hardly seems likely that the Dodd components would retain their simple and typologically early pottery if there was appreciable temporal overlap with the Swanson site. If this conclusion is correct, the Swanson site would fall chronologically between the Anderson Focus and Arzberger and would help to explain the apparently very close resemblance between some of the Foreman Incised rims (present at Swanson and the Anderson Focus) and some of the Arzberger Horizontal Incised rims. The connection, if it existed, must have been indirect, however, as the total absence of grooved paddle-stamped pottery at Swanson would certainly seem to establish its priority in the area.

Limited excavation at the Thomas Riggs site (Meleen, 1949), which is situated about 20 miles upstream from Arzberger, provides another assemblage with a typically Anderson-Huff house type. Lehmer (1952) has discussed the relationship of the Riggs site to the Anderson Focus and concluded it must be later, among other reasons because of the absence of cord-wrapped paddle-stamped surface finish on the pottery. High, straight, vertical or outsloping rims in quantity are another distinguishing feature. Many of the illustrated specimens (Meleen, 1949, Fig. 80) resemble Arzberger sherds strongly, but an obvious difference is the absence of cord-wrapped and checked-paddle stamping. Although the Riggs sample of rims is very small (only 85 rim sherds), there appears to be a high proportion of cord-impressed decoration; true collared rims are rare. Finally, the horizontally incised straight rim of Arzberger is completely absent. The Riggs site shows tabular vein chalcedony knives according to Lehmer (1952: 332). At first thought, the absence of cord-wrapped paddle stamping would suggest that the Riggs site is later than Arzberger, but the small sample, plus the fact that the supposedly contemporaneous Huff site also lacks cord-wrapped paddle stamping, indicates the need of caution in interpretation. Many pottery details and the chalcedony knives hint at contemporaneity and raise the question of the possibility of coexistence of two fundamentally discrete traditions within such a short distance. If this was the situation, the Riggs people were on friendly terms with those of the Arzberger site and also with the groups against whom the Arzberger people were fortifying themselves, to judge by the small and unprotected village. Coexistence would furnish a convenient source for the Arzberger cord-impressed sherds, rim projections, and so on, but it would hardly serve to explain checked-paddle stamping and the bastioned fortification. Will's tree-ring dates (Meleen, 1949: 321) for the Riggs site indicate that it was established about A.D. 1480, and the latest date is A.D. 1516, or precisely in the Huff date range, and by inference in the Arzberger date range too. It does not appear profitable to carry speculation further with the data in hand, but the analysis above is certainly far from a satisfactory solution of the problem.

The Arikara. If the outline of the cultural background of the Arzberger site given above is substantially correct, there should be contemporary and ancestral sites to the south and east, and the ancestral site would lack fortifications, grooved-paddle stamping, cord-impressed decoration, and other ceramic traits, all elements thought to be the result of Mandan influence on a northern outlier of the Central Plains tradition. That such sites are not lacking is indicated by Cooper's description (1949:

308) of sites 39 BR13 (p. 308) and the lower level of 39 CH5 (p. 308) and by Wedel's summary (1949: 332) of the Somers site.

To follow the same principles, sites in the same tradition but later than Arzberger would exhibit circular houses, exclusively grooved paddle-stamped pottery, and other traits which persist to the protohistoric horizon. Lehmer (1952) has pointed out that such sites do exist in the Meyer-La Roche horizon of the Pierre area. Disagreeably enough, Will's dendrochronological dates (Meleen, 1948: 31) for La Roche range from A.D. 1434 to 1457 plus 5 to 10 years, thus flatly contradicting the chronological equation of Arzberger and Huff. It is extraordinarily difficult to believe that Arzberger was an archaic survival of the Upper Republican tradition although sites so close and so obviously related had already progressed to better things (Wedel, 1949, Fig. 83). Alternatives would appear to be (1) to ignore one or the other set of dates, or (2) to find an earlier source for the Arzberger fortification and checked stamping. A second shock suffered during the course of this comparative study was provided by the Talking Crow site (C. S. Smith, 1951) less than 50 miles downstream from Arzberger; here, except for a small amount of protohistoric or historic Arikara ware, all of the pottery seems to fit reasonably well into the capacious Arzberger repertory. Smith divided the pottery into three sequent periods, however, and stated that all three show European trade goods, a distressing anomaly from any point of view, including Smith's (personal communication). By way of further complication, it is only necessary to point out that Arzberger exhibits pottery resembling both Category B and Category C types of Cooper, which are thought to show a tendency to segregate in the Fort Randall and Oahe reservoirs (Cooper, 1949). It is obvious that better control of these data in the form of intensive excavation, especially of short-duration sites, will be required before the exact position of Arzberger can be assessed. Meanwhile, a comparatively early dating for Arzberger on the basis of its cord marking and other Upper Republican characteristics seems undeniable; from the point of view adopted here the sites in the general area which are more Upper Republican-like are to be regarded as earlier, and the sites which are less Upper Republican-like, particularly in such matters as circular houses and grooved-paddle stamping, are thought to be later than Arzberger. The course of the Missouri River from the northern boundary of Nebraska to the southern boundary of North Dakota is a long one, and there is room for a considerable amount of local cultural variation. Moreover, the late prehistoric period is known to have been a lively one almost everywhere in the eastern United States. It is encouraging to be anticipated in this conclusion by Wedel (1949, Fig. 83).

The question of tribal affiliation of the people of the Arzberger site does not demand a lengthy discussion. Strong (1940: 359) summarized Arikara history as a northward movement up the Missouri from a starting point in the neighborhood of the Nebraska-South Dakota line. That a still earlier starting point can be found is indicated by linguistic and legendary evidence that the Arikara "were once in close relationship, if not identical, with the ancestral Pawnee." That the ancestral Pawnee in the prehistoric period in Nebraska had an Upper Republican culture seems generally regarded as highly probable, although absolute proof is yet lacking. The appearance of a community with strong Upper Republican cultural affinities on the Missouri in central South Dakota can hardly be interpreted as anything but an early movement of an Arikara group, quite possibly the first to advance so far north into what was to become the heart of the Arikara territory in the eighteenth century. The confused discussion immediately above will have made it clear that an unbroken chain of development from Arzberger or similar sites to the south to the historic Arikara Leavenworth site (Strong, 1940: 366–70) cannot be demonstrated from the data now available, but it seems probable that such a demonstration will be achieved in the future. Again, it should be pointed out that Wedel (1949, Fig. 83) has earlier advanced the same suggestion.

SUMMARY

THE physical characteristics of the Arzberger site and the uniformity of artifacts and features in the various excavation units are thought to indicate a homogeneous site. A comparison of the cultural assemblage with other material from the Plains area has led to the conclusion that the Arzberger culture was basically of Central Plains Upper Republican type, but that it had been subjected to strong Oneota influence and to less intensive but nevertheless important influence from Middle Mandan culture. As a result of these diverse influences, Arzberger culture was in many respects intermediate between the Upper Republican and Lower Loup cultures of Nebraska and may in fact have served as an intermediary in the transmission of grooved-paddle stamping of pottery to the Lower Loup culture. The basic affinity with the Central Plains cultural sequence further suggests that the Arzberger community was a representative of an early stage in the separation of the Arikara tribe from the parent Pawnee, and that this separation occurred prior to the Lower Loup phase of cultural development in Nebraska. Estimated dates for the Lower Loup culture and dendrochronological dates for a Middle Mandan site which may have been the source of the Mandan influence noted agree in assigning a date for Arzberger approximately on the boundary between the fifteenth and sixteenth centuries.

APPENDIX—CERAMIC ANALYSIS

INTRODUCTION

THE following detailed analysis of Arzberger pottery is based on a total of 5,124 sherds. The collections obtained in the 1939 excavations, with the exception of a pottery sample taken to Columbia University for study, were deposited in the Museum of the University of South Dakota. In 1940 the University of South Dakota donated a small sherd collection to the Ceramic Repository for the Eastern United States at the University of Michigan. The sherds discussed below were assembled for this study at the University of Michigan from the Columbia University, University of South Dakota, and Ceramic Repository collections. It is evident from a comparison of my tabulations with the field catalogue and with a preliminary analysis of the pottery made by Dorothy E. Fraser during the field season of 1939 that some of the sherds were not included in the group at hand. Most of the sherds not currently available are apparently body sherds from House I, the rim series for the entire site being virtually complete. In spite of various discrepancies in sherd totals, the result of Fraser's analysis of body sherds is in substantial agreement with mine in regard to the relative popularity of surface finish types by excavation units and for the site as a whole. The chief difference between the two studies appears to be a greater willingness on my part to place sherds in such categories as cord-wrapped paddle-stamped rather than smoothed on the evidence of a nearly obliterated trace of primary surface finish. This practice did not result in any great differences, however. The general agreement in classification, which extended to the rim sherds as well, indicates that the sherds studied are in every respect characteristic, and for this reason the results of the Fraser study have not been incorporated here. Absolute numbers and percentages of the sherds included in this analysis are presented by provenience within the site in Table I.

I am indebted to Glenn Kleinsasser for invaluable assistance in the analysis of the body sherds.

METHOD OF ANALYSIS

Rim sherds and a few special body sherds were classified by a method which differs in some respects from the commonly used technique of sorting into types by inspection, with subsequent use of the types thus established as descriptive units.

TABLE I

PROVENIENCE OF ALL RIM AND BODY SHERDS

Excavation Unit	Rim Sherds		Body Sherds		Total	
	Number	Per Cent	Number	Per Cent	Number	Per Cent
House I	606	53.9	1,675	41.9	2,281	44.6
House II	177	15.8	681	17.0	858	16.7
House III	168	14.9	704	17.6	872	17.0
House IV	154	13.7	835	20.9	989	19.3
Ditch	0	0.0	4	0.1	4	0.1
Unknown	19	1.7	101	2.5	120	2.3
Total	1,124	100.0	4,000	100.0	5,124	100.0

Here the pottery mode (in the sense used by Rouse, 1939: 11–12) was employed as the criterion of classification rather than considered as an attribute of a pottery type. This procedure, which is by no means novel, was thought to have special value in the case of the Arzberger site because of the occurrence there of certain unprecedented combinations of modes; in other words, a number of the Arzberger rim sherds could not be forced into the familiar categories of Plains pottery (e.g., vessels with decorated shoulders and checked paddle-stamped surface finish), a situation which has particular interest from the historical standpoint. The actual steps employed in the rim sherd analysis were (1) preliminary inspection of the entire rim series and listing of the attributes observed and considered to be significant, (2) coding and recording of the observed modes on punch cards suitable for mechanical sorting, (3) sorting and counting of the cards to provide data on the homogeneity of the site and the tendency of modes to cluster into types, and (4) use of the data thus obtained to compute four-cell coefficients (Kroeber, 1940) and to prepare tables and ratio diagrams to aid in the discovery and exposition of meaningful relationships. It should be emphasized that this procedure does not appear to have any marked advantage with regard to objectivity—its usefulness is plainly a function of the wisdom with which the modes to be recorded were chosen and the maintenance of consistent classification standards during recording. Its merit would seem to lie rather in the ease with which a tremendous number of questions can be investigated once the recording is completed. There is, perhaps, a slight gain in objectivity owing to the fact that the recorder completes his work without being fully aware of the ultimate significance of the data and consequently is less likely to be influenced by an anticipated conclusion. At any rate, the actual presence of modes on each rim is verified rather than assumed, a procedure which offers a higher degree of precision than do many conventional sortings.

Preliminary inspection of rim sherds to identify modes for coding resulted in 80 categories, of which 38 were various rim forms (Plate VI). The remaining 42 dealt with such items as lip form, treatment of rim base on collared vessels, placement and technique of lip and rim decoration, motif of rim decoration, motif of body decoration, techniques of surface finish, and paste characteristics. Selection of modes was, naturally, influenced by previous knowledge of ceramic trends in the Plains area; thus the various types of surface finish were known to have value as time markers and were included as a matter of course. On the other hand, the lip form categories—rounded, flattened, and narrowed and rounded—were listed in an experimental spirit, there being no advance knowledge as to their significance or lack of significance. It was anticipated that the listed modes would not provide sufficient variety, and accordingly a sort of safety valve category labeled "other" was provided in each series. For example, the paste characteristic series includes fine grit, medium grit, coarse grit, and other. The last category was exceedingly useful for the few shell-tempered sherds which turned up in the detailed examination.

The type of punch card used provides 73 positions marked by perforations regularly spaced around its margins. Coding of two types was necessary because the number of modes to be recorded exceeded the available positions. Recording of the 38 rim forms was accomplished by notching various combinations of three positions in a set of eight positions. The peculiar numerical designations of rim forms are a result of this practice. All other modes were simply assigned a single position, which was notched when that particular character was present. Additional positions were reserved for provenience data and certain information as to the condition and number of the sherd or sherds represented by a single card. The fundamental unit of association, represented by one card, was intended to be a single vessel. It is plain that intention and reality diverged somewhat, with the result that some vessels are represented by more than one card, although an attempt was made to repair all broken sherds and to group together nonmatching sherds which were clearly from a single vessel. The existence of 19 sherds of unknown provenience (Table I) is a measure of error in this determination; their lack of field catalogue numbers is presumably the result of breakage in shipping and subsequent failure in matching. A total of 893 cards, putatively representing as many vessels, was required for the 1,124 rim sherds. This total seems unduly large for the amount of excavation accomplished. It is possible to say in defense that a diligent attempt to group similar sherds was made. It is hoped that any personal error remained more or less constant so that relative frequencies are not seriously misrepresented.

Body sherd analysis was conducted in a different and somewhat more conventional fashion. The sherds were first sorted into two groups on the basis of the presence or absence of red filming or staining, and the resulting major groups were divided and subdivided by using such characters as surface finish (other than red staining) and decoration, which here means an incised shoulder area. After sorting was completed, the results were tabulated by provenience within the site to serve as a set of basic data which could be analyzed and recombined for various purposes. This process was fundamentally different from that used with the rim sherds in that the subject of classification was the sherd, not the vessel. This principle was maintained even in the case of sherds which were glued together. It is thought that such a practice provides the most generally useful data for comparative purposes. The information provided by the partly reconstructed body sections is not ignored as a result,

TABLE II

PROVENIENCE OF RIMS BY MAJOR SUBDIVISIONS

Excavation Unit	Collared		Noncollared		Unclassified		Total	
	Number	Per Cent	Number	Per Cent	Number	Per Cent	Number	Per Cent
House I	148	49.9	324	56.8	12	46.2	484	54.2
House II	52	17.5	90	15.8	7	26.9	149	16.7
House III	44	14.8	61	10.7	4	15.4	109	12.2
House IV	49	16.5	82	14.4	3	11.5	134	15.0
Unknown	4	1.3	13	2.3	0	0.0	17	1.9
Total	297	100.0	570	100.0	26	100.0	893	100.0

but is rather considered in connection with the pottery type descriptions. The 36 detached handles in the collection were included in Table III with some misgivings. It would probably have been more logical to segregate them in a separate category, but the resulting complications of presentation seemed to more than offset the minor distorting effect of 36 sherds in a total of 4,000.

SITE HOMOGENEITY

A question of fundamental importance in describing the artifacts and evaluating the significance of the Arzberger site is that of its homogeneity. In the absence of clear-cut stratigraphy or even nonstratified deep deposits, the only approach to this problem is a quantitative and qualitative comparison of the artifacts from the several excavation units and features within the excavation units. Since pottery is by far the most useful sort of material for this comparison because of its abundance, I have placed great reliance on the results of the ceramic analysis. It is difficult to answer with complete satisfaction the query as to whether or not four house excavations represent an adequate sampling of the site. In view of the fact that the excavations were widely scattered over the site and, to anticipate a conclusion, that the sherds from each were so similar, it appears highly probable that the sampling is adequate. A conclusion that none of the pottery data at hand hints at the presence of more than one component at the site appears to be justified.

Tables I, II, and III present absolute and relative frequencies of various classes of body sherds and rims. In the case of Table I, which deals with both rim and body sherds, relative frequencies are somewhat misrepresented in the "Body Sherds" and "Total" columns by the absence of a part of the House I body sherds. Tables II and III are confined, respectively, to rims and body sherds, thereby eliminating this source of distortion. The tables show in general that the frequency at a particular excavation unit of any pottery attribute which is reasonably common at the site tends strongly to be a function of the total body sherd or rim count at that excavation unit. As a result, it is possible to predict with a fair degree of accuracy, for example, the number of body sherds at House IV having a grooved paddle-stamped surface finish if the total number of body sherds at House IV and the ratio of grooved paddle-stamped body sherds to all body sherds at the site are known. A less cumbersome statement of the same idea is that one excavation unit is much like another so far as the proportions of the more popular pottery modes are concerned.

Figures 6 and 7 constitute an attempt at a trenchant presentation of the data of Tables I, II, and III and of some additional information. The logarithmic method of plotting used for these figures has not been employed heretofore in archaeological publications to my knowledge, and consequently an

TABLE III

Provenience of Body Sherds by Surface Finish

Excavation Unit	Smooth		Grooved Paddle		Cord-Wrapped Paddle		Checked Paddle		Brushed		Total	
	Number	Per Cent	Number	Per Cent	Number	Per Cent	Number	Per Cent	Number	Per Cent	Number	Per Cent
House I	916	37.1	396	43.9	267	56.0	84	65.7	12	54.6	1,675	41.9
House II	483	19.6	135	14.9	35	7.3	21	16.4	7	31.8	681	17.0
House III	443	17.9	172	19.1	70	14.7	17	13.3	2	9.1	704	17.6
House IV	557	22.5	178	19.7	96	20.1	3	2.3	1	4.5	835	20.9
Ditch	4	0.2	0	0.0	0	0.0	0	0.0	0	0.0	4	0.1
Unknown	67	2.7	22	2.4	9	1.9	3	2.3	0	0.0	101	2.5
Total	2,470	100.0	903	100.0	477	100.0	128	100.0	22	100.0	4,000	100.0

explanation is in order.[1] The particular advantage of logarithmic plotting is that it represents ratios in a fixed scale, so that 2 is separated from 4 by the same distance that 50 is separated from 100, 35 from 70, 25 from 50, or the components of any other pair in a 1 : 2 ratio. With the horizontal axis plotting of differences of logarithms, the true ratio of any two points can be determined by simply comparing the horizontal distance separating them with the logarithmic percentage scale at the

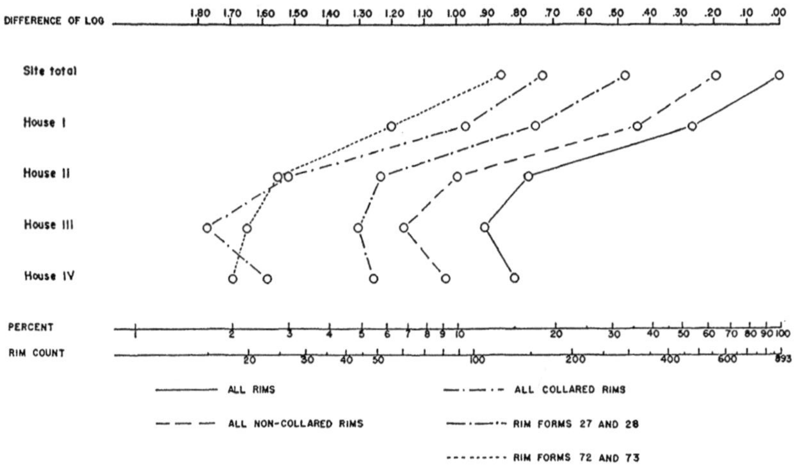

FIG. 6. Ratio diagram of various rim characteristics by excavation units.

bottom of the figure. A still more important effect from the standpoint of an investigation of homogeneity is that the curves produced by similar series will be identical and will be separated on the horizontal axis by a distance proportional (on a logarithmic scale) to the number of specimens in each series. Thus, in a perfectly homogeneous site plotting of mode frequencies by excavation units would result in a series of identical curves, of which that on the extreme left would represent the series having the smallest total and that on the right the series with the largest total.

[1] A discussion of this type of plotting, together with examples of its application to vertebrate paleontology, is available in Simpson (1941).

Five curves are shown in Figure 6, all of which deal with the rim series. The major feature of the diagram is the reasonably close adherence to a common pattern of the three curves on the right, which represent, respectively, all rims and the two mutually exclusive major form categories, noncollared rims and collared rims. House III appears to be slightly aberrant in its higher collared to noncollared rim ratio, but the discrep-

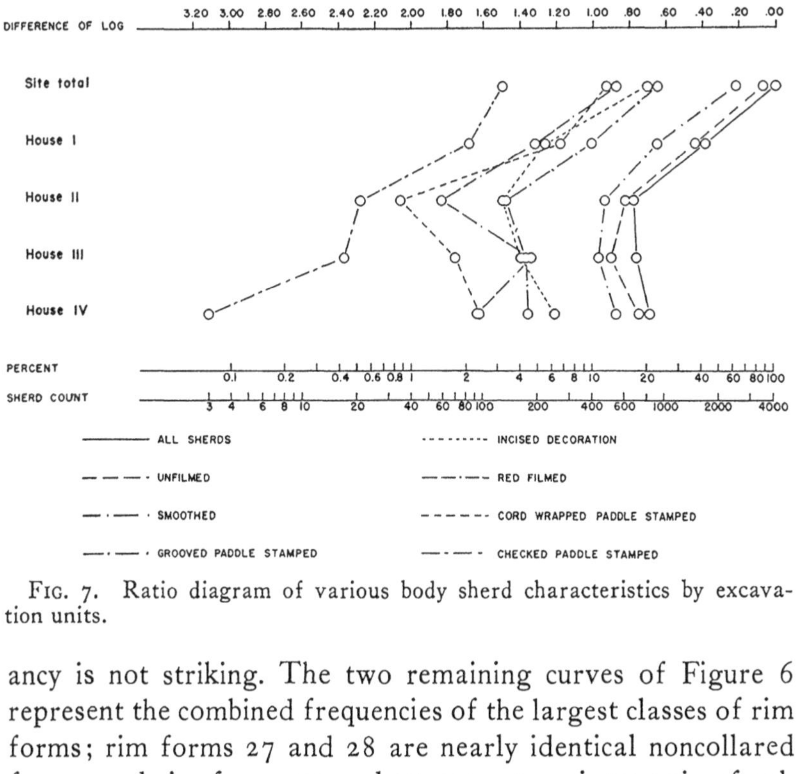

FIG. 7. Ratio diagram of various body sherd characteristics by excavation units.

ancy is not striking. The two remaining curves of Figure 6 represent the combined frequencies of the largest classes of rim forms; rim forms 27 and 28 are nearly identical noncollared forms, and rim forms 72 and 73 are a prominent pair of collared forms. Frequencies were combined in order to obtain larger series for plotting. The curve for rim forms 27 and 28 exhibits a fairly normal pattern in terms of the larger classes, although House III again is somewhat out of position because of a deficiency in these rim types. The final curve, representing the collared rim forms 72 and 73, is, on the other hand, distorted by a House IV deficiency. If these unusual positions are checked against the rim count scale at the bottom of the diagram, however, it will be seen that the distortions involve no more than a few sherds, and the erratic behavior of the plotted curve can be dismissed as an obvious result of the use of a small series.

Figure 7 presents eight curves derived from various body sherd statistics. Results here are more difficult to interpret than in Figure 6, but the approximate correspondence of the three curves to the right is surely significant. These curves are the plotted frequencies of the three large series: all body sherds, unfilmed sherds, and smoothed sherds. Curves for grooved paddle-stamped sherds and for decorated (incised) sherds are the next in numbers of sherds involved; these conform fairly closely to the pattern of the three curves on the right, but are somewhat irregular. The three remaining curves, those for red filming, cord-wrapped paddle stamping, and checked-paddle stamping, are still more irregular but at least bear some relationship to the major trends. Here again the series are comparatively small, although larger than those on the left in Figure 6. Interestingly enough, the mode frequencies of House III again seem to be an important disturbing factor, which suggests that the differences may not be due altogether to chance.

The general conclusion drawn from these curves is that the site is substantially homogeneous so far as the available ceramic data are concerned. Discrepancies are thought to be primarily the result of comparatively small series, although it is admitted that some possibility of culturally significant differences exists, particularly for House III. This confirms an impressionistic judgment formed during the original analysis, when sherd by sherd handling of the material left a distinct feeling of uniformity so far as the more striking types were concerned. It is possible, however, for this sort of analysis of large series to mask meaningful differences in the distribution of minor elements. In an attempt to avoid this, a number of modes were checked by provenience to detect possible absences and, more particularly, combinations of absences which might be interpreted as reflecting genuine differences in the ceramic tradition at a given house. The results of this investigation were negative in the sense that there were no conspicuous blanks on the master charts of the distribution of modes. For example, the distribution of rim projections on noncollared rims is: House I, 7; House II, 3; House III, 1; and House IV, 4. A final check, theoretically of considerable importance, involved a study of the pottery from the various cache pits, where a presumably limited period of filling might result in segregation of a chronologically restricted group of sherds. Again the results were negative, but tended to be inconclusive because of the small number of sherds used. The maximum number of rims was 15 from Feature 6, House I, and here, as well as for other pits with a fair number of rims, there appeared to be a random sprinkling of modes. In summation, no clear evidence of significant horizontal or vertical segregation of pottery characteristics was detected, and the pottery is considered to be the product of an essentially homogeneous group over a fairly short period of time. The observed differences between excavation units may prove to be meaningful in the light of future excavations, but this does not appear probable on the basis of the data at hand.

BODY SHERDS

Body sherds from the Arzberger site can be classified into two basic groups. The first of these includes practically all of the body sherds from the site; the second is a very small group of unusual sherds, mostly shell tempered, which will be described separately. Absolute and relative frequencies of certain body sherd modes thought to be useful for comparative purposes are presented on a total site basis in Table IV. Paste features are not included in this table because of the apparent uniformity in paste attributes of all the sherds from the larger group. One prominent characteristic of the body sherds, a fairly common red washing or filming, is the subject of Table V and is discussed as a separate feature.

Paste composition of the body sherds is quite uniform and appears to exhibit practically the entire range of texture noted on the rim sherds. In nearly every sherd angular fragments of quartz and orthoclase feldspar are visible, and occasional sherds show sparse or abundant flecks of mica. The fragments of grit are usually on the order of a millimeter in diameter, although larger and smaller fragments were noted frequently. The angular character and composition of the tempering particles suggest crushed granite as the standard source of aplastic

TABLE IV

Total Frequencies of Selected Body Sherd Modes *

Surface Finish	Undecorated		Decorated †		Total	
	Number	Per Cent	Number	Per Cent	Number	Per Cent
Smooth	1,668	42.0	763	19.3	2,431	61.3
Grooved paddle	894	22.5	9	0.2	903	22.7
Cord-wrapped paddle	458	11.6	19	0.5	477	12.1
Checked paddle	121	3.1	7	0.2	128	3.3
Brushed	22	0.6	0	0.0	22	0.6
Total	3,163	79.8	798	20.2	3,961	100.0

* Excluding detached handles and certain aberrant sherds.
† "Decorated" here refers to shoulder incising.

at the site. This was obtained, presumably, from the igneous glacial erratics of the region. No attempt has been made to measure carefully the relative proportions of clay and tempering material, but as a rule the sherds do not give an impression of abundant tempering particles, and the textures cannot be described as coarse. A few sherds (especially those belonging to the large vessel illustrated as rim form 24) have a high proportion of tempering material with a resulting friable paste. In general, the sherds are smooth to the touch rather than sandy or otherwise rough.

Hardness is relatively uniform at about 3.5 or a little more on the Mohs scale. A number of sherds show some tendency toward lamination, or more accurately, splitting, especially on the thicker rims. This is characteristically a spalling off of the outer surfaces, possibly as a result of incomplete firing so that the harder baked exteriors split away from the core. Fragments of tempering material can be seen on the outside surface of many sherds; these are usually flat mica particles, but occasionally are chunks of orthoclase or quartz. A quite smooth surface is characteristic, however, implying that some sort of floating technique was used habitually.

The exterior and interior color of the body sherds, as well as of the rim sherds, is typically tan or buff. Smoke clouding is common and sometimes covers large sections of a vessel. A few sherds are caked with soot, but there is no definite class of soot-caked cooking vessels. A number of sherds have creamy, light gray surfaces because of the action of weathering under the prevailing soil conditions, as is shown by those in which one of a matching pair has the normal tan or smoke-clouded black surface, whereas the other exhibits the light gray color. Quite often the lighter surface color does not penetrate deeply, with the result that a dark core is visible on broken edges.

Five categories of exterior surface finishing techniques (other than red filming) were recognized in the analysis of both body and rim sherds (sherd interiors were invariably smoothed, but sometimes show smoothing striations and a bumpy surface). The term "smooth" indicates that the surface was so thoroughly smoothed that no clear trace of any other surface finishing technique could be detected. Many of the sherds which were placed in one of the paddle-stamped categories were smoothed to a certain extent, and it is surmised that most, if not all, of the vessels at the site were subjected to paddle stamping at one stage in their manufacture. Moreover, the range of treatment subsumed by my "smoothed" division may include some examples of another classifier's "polished" category, as some of the Arzberger sherds exhibit at least a faint ability to reflect high lights. Unqualified polishing or burnishing, in the sense of a vessel surface compacted and polished by rubbing with a smooth object when the clay was at a leather-hard stage, was not observed. The significance of comparisons of the surface finish types is further weakened by lack of knowledge of finish on complete vessels; it is possible, for example, that basal sections are smoothed on most vessels.

The term "grooved paddle" is used here to describe what is thought to be the same technique elsewhere called thong-wrapped paddle-stamped or simple-stamped. Individual ridges (corresponding to grooves on the paddle) on the sherds finished with a grooved paddle are from 2.0 to 2.5 mm. wide, are spaced about 4 mm. apart, and are approximately rectangular in cross section. Grooves and ridges are usually vertical, but a number of sherds show application of the paddle at different angles with slightly overlapping strokes. One large sherd has what superficially appears to be an impression of a basketry fabric with splint warp, but a close examination also suggests paddle edge stamping with a carved or thong-wrapped paddle. Frequently the ridges were smoothed over, particularly in the case of sherds from the lower rim and shoulder area. Grooved paddle-stamped sherds are best illustrated in Plates VIII H; X C; XII G, H, L; and XVII J, K, L.

Cord-wrapped paddle-stamped sherds usually have the paddle applied so that the cord impressions are vertical insofar as this can be judged from body sherds, but overlapping strokes at various angles also occur. Individual impressions are clear except on those sherds which have the cord impressions partly obliterated by smoothing. The interval between the impressions runs from 2 to 4 mm., and the cords were hard twisted. Individual cord diameters are in the neighborhood of 1 to 2 mm. Examples of cord-wrapped paddle-stamped sherds are illustrated as Plates VII E; IX K; XI M; XIII H; XIV H, J, L, Q; and XVII F, G, H, I.

Checked-paddle stamping, although present on only 128 body sherds, is an interesting surface finishing technique from the comparative point of view. On the Arzberger specimens the checked markings are diamond-shaped rather than square, and the individual diamonds measure about 6 mm. or less on a side. A number of the sherds have quite delicate ridges, sometimes no more than a millimeter in width, indicating that the paddle grooves were narrow. The paddle was applied neatly in most instances, resulting in clear impressions with little overlapping. Most of the check-stamped sherds were well smoothed after paddling. In general, they give an impression of a more careful finish than that shown by other types of sherds, and there is also a tendency toward a thinner section; I would infer that check stamping is characteristically associated with small, well-made vessels. Some error in classification probably resulted from confusion with overlapping simple grooved-paddle ridges on a few small sherds. Check-stamped sherds are illustrated in Plate XVII M, N, and O.

Brushed body sherds (Pl. XVII D, E) are a very minor element in the surface finish classification and probably should be considered an insignificant variant of the smoothed category. The criterion for placing sherds in the brushed class was the presence of faint parallel striations which were presumably the result of smoothing with the aid of some tool or material having an uneven surface. The result is not a true roughened or brushed surface finish in the sense in which the term has been used in other areas.

An interesting feature of many body sherds and a few rim sherds is the occurrence of what is called here red filming. In its most obvious form the filming is a definite cherry red coating on the sherd interior which was probably produced by rubbing or soaking the vessel with a hematite batter. Frequently the coloring can be rubbed off on the fingers as a powder or even flaked from the interior surface. From this unmistakable coating there appears to be a complete gradation to a faint and irregular red coloring which cannot be distinguished from the unintentional product of an ordinary oxidizing firing atmosphere. As a result, there is a wide area of indecision in classifying sherds, and an independent check might well alter the counts as given here. Our analysis indicates that of the 540 body sherds thought to have some filming, 465 are colored on the interior only, 21 on the exterior, and 54 on both interior and exterior surfaces. Although exterior filming is rare and in many cases dubious, it definitely does occur. Six rims also were thought to have red staining; one of these was classified as a collared rim (rim form 76), four were from the small, low-rimmed vessels of rim form 48 type, and one represented the larger straight-rimmed vessel of rim form 27. This almost complete absence of red filming on rim sherds seems to indicate clearly that the coloring was essentially a body treatment; it also emphasizes the perverse tendency of rims to break from the vessel at the juncture with the shoulder. Data on the association of red filming with other modes are presented in Table V. There does not appear to be any pronounced inclina-

TABLE V

Association of Red Filmed Body Sherds with Other Modes

	Undecorated		Decorated		Total	
Surface Finish	Number	Per Cent	Number	Per Cent	Number	Per Cent
Smooth	184	34.0	98	18.1	282	52.1
Grooved paddle	131	24.3	5	0.9	136	25.2
Cord-wrapped paddle	110	20.4	1	0.2	111	20.6
Checked paddle	8	1.5	0	0.0	8	1.5
Brushed	3	0.6	0	0.0	3	0.6
Total	436	80.8	104	19.2	540	100.0

tion toward association with the various surface finishes, although the percentage of cord-wrapped paddle-stamped sherds is surprisingly high. With regard to body sherds decorated by incising, the percentages of undecorated and decorated red filmed sherds are virtually identical with those for all body sherds (compare Table IV). This lack of clear association with definite vessel types makes a functional interpretation of the red filming difficult. It is found on large and rather thick sherds, obviously from sizable vessels, and on sherds from small pots, which would argue for a simple decorative value rather than for a real or supposed utilitarian function connected with some special purpose for which a given vessel was intended.

No great variation in thickness of body sherds was observed. Most of the sherds fall within a 4 to 6 mm. range. Sherds from large vessels show thicknesses of 10 mm. or a little more in a few instances, and there are many sherds in the 3.5 to 4.5 mm.

class. Curvature and other details of the last class suggest vessels of moderate or small size of the general type illustrated by rim forms 44–49. It was mentioned above that check-stamped sherds seemed thinner on the whole; this is true of red filmed sherds also, although exceptions to this generalization are by no means rare.

A total of 798 body sherds, approximately 20 per cent of all body sherds, was classified as decorated (Table IV). The only form of decoration observed consists of incised and punctate rectilinear patterns on the shoulder area, since red filming has rather arbitrarily been considered a form of surface finish. Execution of the incising is ordinarily neat. Closely spaced shallow lines about 2 mm. in width are characteristic, but cruder examples were observed on which the lines are narrower and V-shaped in section and have a careless, scratchy appearance; there seems to be some tendency for this sort of incising to be associated with small vessels (Pls. XI B, XII D). A few sherds have broad, shallow lines approaching what is sometimes described as trailing. Occasionally, the incised lines are so deep that they produce corresponding ridges on the vessel interior. The pattern is essentially a band which extends from the plane of the maximum diameter of the vessel to the base of the rim. The typical element of the design is a group of parallel straight lines. These are frequently arranged to form simple series of alternately erect and inverted triangles (Pls. XI A; XII A, E, F, I; XIII C, L). One example shows a still simpler pattern of widely spaced elements consisting of diagonally oriented rectangular units encircling the shoulder area (Pl. XII K). On other specimens a rather complicated arrangement of sets of lines truncating each other at various angles produces irregular triangles and four-sided figures (Pl. XVI B, C, E, H). Occasionally, unincised areas are left in designs of this type, and the borders of the blank space are characteristically embellished with punctates or incised dashes (Pls. XV F; XVI A, C, E, I, L). Another motif consists of a large triangle, probably upward pointing, within which are incised punctate-bordered, downward pointing chevrons (Pl. XVI D). Examples of a herringbone pattern are also present (Pls. XV C, XVI K), and large units are sometimes bordered by zigzag lines which, in turn, may be ornamented by incised hatching (Pl. XVI E, M). There are other minor design features which are thought to be adequately described by illustration. Practically all of the decorated body sherds have a carefully smoothed surface finish (Table IV), but all of the important types of surface finish are represented to some extent in the decorated body sherd category. In addition, a number of rim sherds having parts of decorated bodies attached show evidence of paddle stamping, leading to the conclusion that the decorated vessels were ordinarily finished by paddle stamping with subsequent smoothing. There is no special association of red filming and incised decoration (compare Tables IV and V). Thickness and curvature of the incised body sherds suggest that small and medium-sized vessels were most frequently decorated, an inference which is supported by the data from rim sherds. On a number of specimens the lower border of the decoration is sharply delineated by an angular break in the curvature of the wall of the vessel—a true carination or angular shoulder (Pls. XV E; XVI F, G). Very exceptionally, the decorated areas may extend a short distance below the angular shoulder. It should be noted that the angular shoulder is not confined to decorated specimens, although it is characteristically associated with them. Usually, however, the shoulder of the decorated vessels is rounded rather than angular, although there is a tendency for a sharper curvature and thinner cross section to occur in this area so that the shoulder can be defined by something more than the plane of maximum horizontal diameter.

Information on vessel size and shape provided by the body sherds is unfortunately limited because of their comparatively small size. Nearly all of the sherds are smoothly curved (except the carinate specimens discussed above), indicating that an essentially globular body was the rule at the site. Although statistical verification has not been attempted, it seems likely on an impressionistic basis that the body sherds fall into two overlapping series, one of relatively thick sherds and the other of those which are thinner in cross section. The thicker sherds would presumably belong to collared vessel types and the thinner primarily to the straight or everted rim types with which incised shoulder areas are also associated. One cord-wrapped paddle-stamped sherd shows part of a flattened area, possibly a base, but this is unique.

The aberrant body sherds mentioned at the beginning of this section consist of 19 shell-tempered sherds found in House III, 1 shell-tempered sherd from House II, and 1 smoothed and ostensibly painted sherd from House IV. The House III specimens range in thickness from 3 to 6 mm., most of the sherds being very thin. Tempering is rather sparse, with small particles of shell, and the paste is compact. These sherds have a pronounced tendency toward lamination; more than half are split so that only one surface is present. Exteriors are well smoothed, and two sherds have traces of red filming. One sherd has a pink interior surface. The only hint at decoration on the House III specimens is on a sherd from which the outer surface has spalled; the rough surface thus produced still shows a series of regular grooves suggesting a design of opposed diagonals. The House II specimen is generally similar to those from House III; it is about 4 mm. thick and has a smooth exterior and a red filmed interior. The final specimen to be given a special description, the supposedly painted sherd, was found in the fill of House IV (Pls. XV I; XVII C). It is a small body fragment slightly less than 6 mm. in thickness with well-smoothed, almost polished, exterior and interior surfaces. A uniform, thin, rather glossy black coating covers the interior of the sherd, but the outer surface is an unmodified gray. On the outer surface are two converging black stripes about 4 mm. wide which look superficially like painted bands. An almost obliterated trace of a third stripe cuts across the first two. If this is a painted sherd, it is unique at the site. I have observed other black striped sherds on collections from the Plains areas, and in some of these the stripes appear to be accidental features caused by running of some black pigment. It is possible to interpret the Arzberger sherd in the same way; the stripes may be accidental by-products of special interior treatment which produced the glossy black coating observed there. A similar treatment, however, occurs in some quantity at the Rygh site (Strong, 1940: 378) and is known elsewhere. In many instances it is undoubtedly a genuine trait.

RIM SHERDS

Rim sherds, like the body sherds, are here treated as a unit because of the absence of clear evidence of horizontal segregation discussed earlier. Gross data on rim sherds by provenience and in relation to all sherds are shown in Table I. Additional information is provided in Table II, which presents rim counts (thought to represent individual vessels) rather than sherd counts; here the classic central Plains ceramic subdivisions, collared and noncollared rims, are distinguished. The range of such paste characteristics as hardness, color, and tempering material does not appear to be significantly different from that discussed in the section on body sherds. Description of the various minor attributes of rims and their tendency to cluster into types will be included in the pottery type descriptions. A few rim sherds which differ sharply from the usual Arzberger rim in that they have cord-impressed decoration will be described individually.

POTTERY TYPES

The classifications of the Arzberger ceramic material into pottery types is intended to be a classification of vessels, not of potsherds. This is not a universal practice among archaeologists working in eastern United States, but it does have a number of virtues. Among these is a probably greater tendency for the classification to coincide with the mental categories of the makers of the vessels, a feature which is at least not without a certain humanistic value; a second advantage is the larger number of associated modes for statistical manipulation when the unit of classification is the vessel; finally, the dilemma of the vessel composed of two pottery types, a situation disturbing to all but the most hardened sherd classifier, is avoided. An obvious disadvantage is the fact that it is necessary to have a moderately clear idea of the appearance of the vessels if the classification is to be meaningful, from which it follows that in many instances a sherd classification is the only practicable procedure. Moreover, the sherd classification has amply demonstrated its utility as a tool for the investigation of chronological change and diffusion. It would appear that the two sorts of pottery classification are not in fundamental opposition, but rather are supplementary and represent different levels of empirical analysis. Unfortunately, the same sorts of names are applied to both, and the basis of classification is not always explicit, or perhaps not always recognized, which may reduce the value of the classification for comparative purposes (this subject is discussed more thoroughly in Krieger, 1949: 75–77). For this reason no names have been assigned to various categories of body sherds; their characteristics and frequencies have been described under each generalized category, such as smoothed or checked-paddled, with conscious avoidance of such rubrics as Arzberger Simple Stamped to denote the presence of a few modes on a body sherd. The type descriptions which follow are accordingly based on a rim analysis supplemented by the body sherd data which can reasonably be associated with the various types of rims. No amount of theoretical purity, however, can compensate for the dearth of information on the body characteristics resulting from the pronounced tendency for breakage at the rim base, and the descriptions suffer in consequence. This situation is deplorable, but it is inherent in the material.

Two basic criteria, validity and utility, were recognized in describing pottery types. Validity is here taken to mean a demonstrable tendency for a specific group of modes to be associated on a vessel within the general context of the Arzberger pottery. An attempt was made to investigate clustering tendencies through the use of four-cell coefficients (the Z coefficient of Kroeber, 1940), but the process was not carried through to its logical conclusion of a mathematical expression of the validity of pottery types. The primary difficulty encountered was a misleading effect caused by a very low count in one or two of the four cells. As a result, each coefficient seemed to require special interpretation, a circumstance which vitiates the particular advantages of statistical presentation. It is possible that a more persistent or a more artful use of the method would have resulted in a satisfactory presentation, but the effort was not wasted in any case because the process of statistical analysis and interpretation itself constituted a most valuable check on naive impressions. This sort of analysis was supplemented by a number of ratio diagrams like those constructed to investigate site homogeneity. In those instances where a definite clustering of modes seemed to be present, it was assumed that a valid pottery type had been established. Overlapping of modes with other types and the actual character of the modes used in the definition of the type were not considered relevant to the problem of whether or not a type was to be described, although such considerations are, of course, vital in the interpretation of the historical significance of types. Types more or less bound together by a considerable overlapping of modes have been given a group name to emphasize this fact.

The concept of utility operated primarily at the level of selection of modes for recording and tabulation, i.e., the recording code was devised largely to investigate modes which were known or thought to have historical meaning within the context of previous Plains archaeological studies. It was assumed that any clustering of the modes so chosen constituted not only a valid but also a historically significant pottery type worthy of a formal name and description. This assumption conflicts with the recommendation of Krieger (1949: 71–74) that the named type should be restricted to classes of empirically similar artifacts whose comparative value and range of variation have been demonstrated through extensive distributional studies. My feeling is, rather, that the artifact type established on the basis of central tendency and range of variation within the context of the culture of a prehistoric community over a reasonably restricted period of time is a datum of the first order of importance for historical and cultural studies, and that it is entitled to the dignity of a formal name if any typological category is so entitled. One classificatory difficulty with which Krieger is concerned is the verbal separation of closely related types through formal names which give no hint of wider relationships. A workable solution, always assuming that archaeologists are careful to check tentative types against existing published descriptions, would seem to lie in the direction of naming groups of types when a need for unification becomes apparent.

With regard to the question of allowable variability within a named type, it appears impossible to set up any universal standards. The common-sense definition, which is based on a general impression of previous archaeological research, requires no more than an avoidance of the two extremes of types so rigidly defined as to include only a few virtually identical specimens or so broadly defined as to include a wide range of specimens with a few basic characteristics in common. The practice followed in this study was an investigation of each proposed type to discover whether or not it differed from similar types in at least two empirical modes. Differences in frequencies were considered significant. This practice is well illustrated by the typing of the collared sherds. It was not at all obvious from inspection whether or not sherds should be lumped into one type, but the presence of undecorated rims and three distinctive design patterns on rims suggested that subdivision might have some value. The process of investigation consisted of preparing ratio diagrams to discover whether or not other modes showed any tendency toward special association with the distinctive rim designs. There appeared to be a significant difference in the frequencies of certain rim forms in the trial types, and accordingly it was decided to describe them as four separate types rather than as variants of one type. It is entirely possible that another investigator would have come to the opposite conclusion on the ground that the sample was inadequate, or through a different conception of the underlying typology of the component modes, or from a conviction that frequency differences of this order are not sufficient warrant for adding a new name.

No attempt was made to respect conventions with regard to the importance of certain attributes which have developed in pottery typing in the eastern United States. Surface finish and presence or absence of incised shoulder decoration, for example, have been treated in the same manner as any other distinguishable attributes in arriving at the delineated types. The behavior of such modes with relation to other characteristics was considered a problem to be investigated, and consequently there was no automatic typological boundary established between, say, cord-wrapped paddle-stamped and grooved paddle-stamped vessels.

Data on the distribution of the pottery types and inferences as to their chronological range have been relegated to the section of the report dealing with the cultural affiliations and temporal position of the site and will not be repeated in the type descriptions.

The Arzberger Group

The Arzberger Group consists of the 297 vessels with thickened or collared rims of the rim form 72–79 group (Pl. VI). It is here divided into the four pottery types: Arzberger Plain, Arzberger Horizontal Incised, Arzberger Crosshatched, and Arzberger Diagonal Incised. Although this division is based on pattern of rim decoration or its absence, there is a tendency for other attributes to be more or less strongly associated with these primary criteria. In no instance, however, is this association exclusive, and the four types must be regarded as closely related variants of a unifying structural concept.

Paste characteristics of the series do not appear to differ from those of the grit-tempered body sherds described above, nor is there any significant variation associated with the component types. Briefly, the paste is tempered with angular particles of quartz and orthoclase feldspar with occasional fragments of mica, suggesting a crushed granite aplastic. Sherds exhibit characteristically a tan or buff hue on the surface with some darker smoke clouding. Paste cores are often darker than the surfaces. Hardness is about 3.5 on the Mohs scale with little variation.

Surface finish is difficult to describe satisfactorily owing to the very marked tendency for these vessels to break at the rim base and also to the prevailing practice of smoothing the neck and rim area, whatever the basic surface treatment may have been. The relatively few sherds which include both rim and a sizable part of the shoulder show paddle marking, and it is assumed that all vessels of the Arzberger Group were originally finished by paddle stamping of some sort. Of the 297 collared sherds, 244 were listed as smoothed only; on some sherds included in this group traces of paddle stamping were visible but were too obscure to permit definite assignment to one of the stamped categories. Rim surfaces are as a rule well smoothed, but the neck area beneath the overhanging collar often shows horizontal marks as a result of imperfect smoothing with some sort of narrow tool. Recognizable grooved-paddle stamping was observed on 26 rims, cord-wrapped paddle stamping on 22, and checked-paddle stamping on one. One cord-wrapped paddle-stamped rim showed an exterior red wash. Interior surfaces are invariably smoothed, although sometimes so carelessly that a striated or bumpy effect is produced.

The 72–79 rim profile group illustrates quite completely the form range and variation in height of collar of the Arzberger Group. Extremes in the basic rim shapes of the collared vessels are represented by profiles 78 and 79, in which the collar is produced by thickening at the base of an essentially straight rim, and by profile 72, in which the collar is formed by bending the rim rather than by thickening. Other forms shown appear to be intermediate between those extremes. Profiles 73 and 74 are perhaps a special case because of their inward curving upper rims; they approach a true S form and may be the result of specific influence from other ceramic traditions instead of inconsequential variations of the Arzberger collared form. Recorded collar heights vary from about 25 mm. to as much as 60 mm., but a majority would fall within a 30–40 mm. range.

Both size and form were considered in setting up the rim form categories, so that designation of the rim form implies that there is not too radical a departure from the dimensions indicated by the specimens of Plate VI.

Comparatively little information is available on shoulder and lower body form. The vessel shown in profile 72 is the most nearly intact of the entire group. All the rims which have some part of the shoulder remaining suggest that the smoothly rounding 72 shoulder profile is characteristic. By inference from the body sherds, the lower body was also essentially globular. All of the larger rim fragments suggest an orifice and body which were round in the horizontal plane. Estimated diameter at the lip ranges from 14 to 30 cm., with an average of probably a little more than 20 cm. The maximum body diameter would be a few centimeters more. Total vessel height is difficult to estimate, but projecting the shoulder curve downward on a few of the larger fragments indicates that this dimension is probably about the same as the lip diameter, or a little more.

Decoration and modeled appendages are discussed in detail in connection with the type descriptions. Major features for the group as a whole are prevalence of lip and rim incising, frequent decoration of the rim base by modeled knobs or short incised strokes, complete absence of handles and shoulder decoration, and the very rare occurrence of lugs, rim projections, and other modeled protuberances.

Table VI presents the absolute number and percentage frequency of the various Arzberger Group types with relation to the series and to the rims of the site as a whole. The classification "Unknown Incised" includes four small sherds with traces of incising which might belong to any of the well-known patterns. Seven sherds are listed as "Unclassified Incised"; these have parts of patterns not otherwise recognized, although possibly all represent variants of the three major designs. Two of these (Pl. X D, E) show what may be an uninterrupted band of diagonal incising on the rim. One (Pl. X H) has two sets of parallel diagonal lines interrupted by an oppositely slanted line. The remaining four have interrupted horizontal or slightly sloping lines which in two cases are associated with a vertical line. All of the latter sherds are too small to give any clear idea of the design element represented. The 22 rims not otherwise classified are those which are plain but are too small to indicate whether or not they should be placed in the Arzberger Plain type.

TABLE VI

COMPOSITION OF ARZBERGER GROUP RIMS BY POTTERY TYPES

Pottery Type	Number of Rims	Per Cent of Arzberger Group Rims	Per Cent of All Rims
Arzberger Plain	35	11.8	3.9
Arzberger Horizontal Incised	79	26.6	8.8
Arzberger Crosshatched	78	26.3	8.7
Arzberger Diagonal Incised	72	24.2	8.1
Unknown Incised	4	1.3	0.5
Unclassified Incised	7	2.4	0.8
Unclassified	22	7.4	2.5
Total	297	100.0	33.3

POTTERY TYPES OF THE ARZBERGER GROUP

Arzberger Plain (Pl. VII)

Paste: See introductory section on Arzberger Group and discussion of body sherds.

Surface Finish: Of the 35 Arzberger Plain sherds, 22 are smoothed (Pl. VII A, C, D, H, I, K, L), 7 are cord-wrapped paddle-stamped (Pl. VII E), and 6 are grooved-paddle stamped (Pl. VII B, F, G, J). Paddle-stamped sherds usually have some smoothing over the stamping.

Vessel Form and Size: All the forms illustrated in the 72–79 series (Pl. VI) were observed, but nearly half (15) were recorded as 75 or 72. The remainder are quite evenly distributed among the other categories. Estimated lip diameters of the larger rim fragments are noted in the description of Plate VII. They tend to cluster at 18 cm. A general impression of the Arzberger Plain rims is that collars tend to be lower and vessels smaller than in the other Arzberger types. The 27 rims having a part of the lip preserved were divided as follows: round lip (Pl. VI, 72), 4; flattened lip (Pl. VI, 75, 76), 19; narrowed and rounded lip (Pl. VI, 29), 4. The term "flattened" as used in this study means only that some sort of flattened area occurs at the top of the lip; it does not necessarily imply a neat bevel. On many lips the closely spaced incising made determination of the basic lip form difficult.

Decoration: Three of the 27 lips (all were narrowed and rounded in form) have no decoration. The remaining 24 were decorated on the top by short, diagonally incised strokes or, in one instance, by longitudinally placed punctate marks. Diagonal strokes slanting from upper left to lower right and from lower left to upper right occur in about equal frequency in all of the types of the Arzberger Group.

All of the rims proper are, of course, undecorated, since this is the primary criterion for definition of the type within the general context of the Arzberger Group.

A majority of the rim bases were decorated, in most cases by modeled knobs or finger notching (Pl. VII C, H, J, K, L) or by simple pinching (Pl. VII A, F). The distinction between knob modeling and pinching is difficult to make in intermediate examples and is of doubtful utility. Twenty-one rims were placed in the pinched or modeled category. Three rim bases were notched with a tool in a manner very similar to that employed in lip decoration. The other rims with base present (10) have a simple, undecorated ledge as a base (Pl. VII B, D, E, I).

Appendages: No examples of lugs, rim projections, or other appendages were observed.

Frequency at Site: The 35 Arzberger Plain rims constitute 11.8 per cent of the Arzberger Group rims and 3.9 per cent of all rims at the site (Table VI). The listed total is probably somewhat low because only in the case of a fairly large sherd is it possible to be certain that no incising is present. On the other hand, even a trace of incising is sufficient to place a sherd in one of the incised categories.

Arzberger Horizontal Incised (Pl. VIII)

Paste: See introductory section on Arzberger Group and discussion of body sherds.

Surface Finish: On 69 of the total of 79 Arzberger Horizontal Incised rims a smoothed surface finish is present, 5 rims are cord-wrapped paddle-stamped (Pl. VIII E), and 5 rims are grooved-paddle stamped (Pl. VIII H). One of the cord-wrapped paddle-stamped sherds also has an exterior red wash (Pl. VIII E).

Vessel Form and Size: With the exception of rim form 78 all of the illustrated 72–79 rim forms were recorded for the 62 horizontally incised sherds whose forms could be classified. However, rim forms 73 and 72 were recorded for 41 of the sherds, and the 22 horizontally incised sherds of rim form 73 comprise nearly half of the 50 examples of this profile. It would appear that rim form 73 was specially associated with the horizontally incised rim, although the available sample is rather small for definite conclusions. Other forms are more or less evenly present in proportion to their over-all frequencies. Data on vessel size are scanty; in addition to the two large rim sections illustrated on Plate VIII (A, H), whose lip diameters were about 17 and 15 cm., one vessel with outslanting rim had an estimated lip diameter of 33 cm. Of the 52 rims having lips well enough preserved for observation, 15 had rounded lips, 27 flattened lips, and 10 narrowed and rounded lips.

Decoration: Nearly all (45) of the lips were decorated with short, incised strokes or, in one case, punctations. Most of the lips (32) were decorated on the top, but 11 specimens have an outer lip decoration which seems especially characteristic of this pottery type (Pl. VIII F, H). Two examples of inner lip decoration were noted, and 6 lips are undecorated. Outer lip decoration is definitely associated with the narrowed and rounded lip form. Most of the lip decoration consists of short diagonal strokes, but on 7 rims the orientation is transverse or vertical to the lip.

Rim decoration consists of a band of horizontal lines encircling the rim in the area between rim base and lip. The number of lines varies from 2 (Pl. VIII E) to 8 (Pl. VIII C), with three- and four-line patterns in the majority. The patterns having seven or eight lines appear to be associated with high, relatively straight rims of the general type of rim form 73. Three sherds (Pl. VIII C, G) show association of a band of horizontal lines with a panel of upward pointing chevrons composed in one case of four elements and in the second of six. The sherd figured as Plate VIII C has at the apex of the chevrons a depression which suggests that originally an appendage, presumably in the form of a clay knob, had been attached. A fourth sherd (Pls. XIII I and XV R) shows a more complete example of this pattern. All of the specimens are too fragmentary to offer any information as to the number of such chevron panels on a rim. A vertical node culminating in a rim projection (Pl. VIII A) occurs on one specimen of this pottery type and is the only intact example from the entire Arzberger rim group, although an apparently similar feature occurs on a noncollared sherd (Pl.

XI J). The four unclassified incised rims mentioned above which show fragments of horizontal lines may also be essentially members of the Arzberger Horizontal Incised type, and accordingly it is suggested that the possibility of other design variants should be recognized. In technique the incising ranges from the very deep lines of Plate VIII K to narrow, shallow scratching. More typical are shallow lines from 2 to 4 mm. broad. Two sherds which are not otherwise remarkable have bands of horizontal lines executed in a linear punctate technique (Pl. VIII B).

Rim bases, like all in the Arzberger Group, were simple ledges (Pl. VIII C, G) or were decorated by short incised strokes (Pl. VIII B, D, E, I, J) or finger pinching or modeling (Pl. VIII A). The tabulation shows 25 plain bases, 13 modeled or pinched bases, and 20 incised bases. Bases are missing on 21 rims. A high proportion of incised bases is characteristic of the type; this seems to be linked with a high proportion of rims with comparatively slight basal ledges which are better adapted to incising than to bolder, modeling techniques.

Appendages: The vertical node of the rim illustrated as Plate VIII A, and the inferred presence of some sort of node on the chevron-decorated specimen (Pl. VIII C) have been discussed above. One other sherd has an interrupted band of horizontal lines and traces of what was probably some sort of appliqué node.

Frequency at Site: As is indicated in Table VI, the 79 rims of the Arzberger Horizontal Incised type comprise 26.6 per cent of the Arzberger Group rims and 8.8 per cent of all rims at the site.

Arzberger Crosshatched (Pl. IX)

Paste: See introductory section on Arzberger Group and discussion of body sherds.

Surface Finish: Nearly all of the 78 Arzberger Crosshatched rims were smoothed. Five rims show stamping with a cord-wrapped paddle (Pl. IX K), 2 are grooved-paddle stamped (Pl. IX B, E), and 1 has faint traces of what appears to be checked-paddle stamping.

Vessel Form and Size: Of the 57 rims which were complete enough to be classified as to form, 33 were recorded as rim form 72 and 13 as rim form 75. The remaining 11 rims included 6 of rim form 73, 2 of rim form 79, 1 of rim form 77, and 2 of rim form 76. This heavy emphasis on the straight-collared rim forms is one of the major features other than the distinctive design which led to characterization as a separate type. Representative data on lip diameter are furnished in the description of Plate IX. The absence of large sherds or restorable vessels again makes an adequate description of vessel form impossible; the largest sherd, that illustrated as rim form 77 and shown in Plate IX M, has a slanting shoulder. No evidence was found of the existence of any unusual vessel forms. With regard to lip form, 51 rims were classified as flattened, 6 as rounded, and 2 as narrowed and rounded. Missing lips made classification impossible on 21 rims.

Decoration: Of the 57 lips present on the 78 Arzberger Crosshatched rims, 55 were decorated by short incised strokes. In nearly all examples lip decoration (53 rims) occurs on the top of the lip, the exceptions being two rims with decoration on the outer lip. One of the latter shows vertical decorating strokes instead of the typical diagonal incising. Two lips, both rounded, are undecorated.

The basic rim design for the type, as the name indicates, is an incised coarse crosshatching which is so arranged as to give the effect of a band of single lozenges with contiguous apexes (Pl. IX A, B, C,

E, L). Typically, the design was formed so that the lower point of a lozenge was placed on or over one of the modeled knobs at the rim base. The basic procedure is well shown on the rims illustrated as Plate IX B and E; here the design was constructed by starting at a point vertically over a knob near the lip and incising a line downward and to the right to terminate at the knob next to the right of the one marking the starting point. This procedure was continued until the entire rim was covered with diagonal lines slanting from upper left to lower right. The design was completed by incising the upper right to lower left lines in the same manner, giving the characteristic band of single lozenges. This order of construction (with upper right to lower left lines incised last) is evident on most of the rims and appears to be a genuine cultural trait. Occasionally examples occur in which the second set of elements is incised upward (from lower left to upper right). In one case (Pl. IX I) this single rank design is enhanced by vertical incised lines filling the open triangular areas between the lozenges and the lip. Some rims have patterns which do not conform closely to the basal knobs because of careless execution (Pl. IX K) or because of widely spaced lines on a rim with closely spaced pinched knobs (Pl. IX L). Lattice-like multiple rank designs occur on 15 sherds, of which 14 are of the two-lozenge type (Pl. IX D, F, G). The rim illustrated as Plate IX M has a confused and niggling design which appears to be basically a two-lozenge type plus some extraneous lines added in an unsuccessful attempt to capture the proper relationship. On the other hand, Plate IX H shows a smooth-based rim on which an essentially correct four-lozenge pattern is incised. A fundamental feature of the crosshatched design as used at the Arzberger site is the primary character of the upper left to lower right elements and the tendency for the slant of these elements to conform to the interval set by the basal knobs. As a result, the cutting across of two or more lines necessary to produce the multiple rank designs causes a more gentle slope in the secondary upper right to lower left elements, the lozenges become rhomboidal, and the whole lattice leans to the right. A few examples of nearly symmetrical lattices occur (Pl. IX G), but they are exceptional, and I infer that the Arzberger potters had little knowledge of, or interest in, the relations of slope to horizontal interval necessary to produce symmetrical lattices of varying complexity. The character of the decorative incising is adequately shown in Plate IX. In general, shallow lines 2 to 4 mm. wide are characteristic.

Tabulation of rim base decoration indicates that 54 bases were decorated by modeling or pinching (Pl. IX illustrates the range of treatment fairly well), 1 base was decorated by tool notching (Pl. IX G), and 3 bases were undecorated (Pl. IX H, M). On 20 rims no classification could be made because of missing bases. The very high proportion of finger modeled or pinched bases is a distinguishing feature of the type, and this association is not altogether fortuitous, as was noted above in the discussion of rim design. It would appear that the Indians often regarded the rhythm of horizontal interval set by the spacing of modeled knobs as a first step in the construction of a crosshatched design. The absence of rim base decoration on the atypical and complicated four-rank design of Plate IX H is probably not accidental—it would have been difficult to make such a design conform to the wide spacing of the ordinary knobs because of the extreme slant which would be imparted to the second set of elements. Similarly, the abortive design of Plate IX M occurs on a plain-based rim; the confusion, presumably, is the result of the absence of a defined unit of horizontal spacing.

Appendages: No appendages of any type were observed.

Frequency at Site: Arzberger Crosshatched rims constitute 26.3 per cent of the rims of the Arzberger Group and 8.7 per cent of all rims from the site.

Arzberger Diagonal Incised (Pl. X)

Paste: The paste characteristics of this pottery type do not differ significantly from those of the other components of the Arzberger Group or from the ordinary body sherds.

Surface Finish: Of the total of 72 rims assigned to the Arzberger Diagonal Incised type, 61 show no surface finish other than smoothing, 7 bear traces of grooved-paddle stamping (Pl. X C, K), and 4 had been stamped with a cord-wrapped paddle (Pl. X B).

Vessel Form and Size: Only 43 rims were considered complete enough to allow rim form classification. Of these, 17 were assigned to rim forms 74 and 73 (7 and 10 rims, respectively), another 17 were counted as rim forms 72 and 75 (11 and 6 rims), and the remaining 9 were scattered in the 76–79 rim forms. This situation recalls the distribution of rim forms 72 and 73 for the Arzberger Horizontal Incised type but differs from Arzberger Crosshatched with its heavy emphasis on the straight-rimmed 72 and 75 forms. The description of Plate X gives representative estimated lip diameters. The rim figured as Plate X K is notably large; the diameter of its 30 cm. orifice is the result of a rim form 73 which is outslanting instead of vertical or slightly inslanting. Tabulation of lip form observations resulted in a distribution much like that of Arzberger Crosshatched; 33 lips were more or less flattened, 5 were rounded, 8 were narrowed and rounded, and 26 rims were not classified because of missing lips. As is true of the other collared sherds, lip form is associated with decoration—plain lips tend to be rounded, lips decorated on the top are usually somewhat flattened, and the narrowed and rounded lips are often decorated on either the inner or outer surface. To a certain extent the two classifications are interdependent, in that closely spaced diagonal incising on the top of the lip actually produces a flattened effect, and inner or outer decoration a narrowed and rounded effect. It may be surmised that lips were characteristically somewhat rounded before decoration.

Decoration: Of the 46 rims still having a section of lip attached, all but one are decorated. Most of the lips (35) are decorated on the top by short diagonal strokes. In two examples the decorative markings are more nearly punctations. Five rims have lips decorated on the inner surface, in one case with vertical rather than diagonal strokes, and another five are decorated on the outer lip surface (or extreme upper rim). One of the outer lip decorations is formed by vertical instead of diagonal lines.

The characteristic incised rim designs of the type are often described as opposed diagonals. There are two major forms of opposed diagonals on the Arzberger material. The first gives the effect of a band of alternately erect and inverted triangles formed by sets of parallel lines (Pl. X A, B, F, K, L); the over-all effect of the second can be described as a series of rhomboids formed by sets of parallel lines (Pl. X C, J). Statistics on the relative frequency of the two patterns are inadequate because of the impossibility of distinguishing between the two on small sherds. It seems clear, however, that the triangular type was considerably more popular. Details of the construction process are not entirely clear because the lines were not intentionally overlapped. Enough accidental overlaps are present to suggest that the construction proceeded from left to right and that the bounding lines of the design element (triangle or rhomboid) were incised before the filling lines were added to the pattern. Many of the strokes were made in an upward direction. Both possibilities in the filling of erect and inverted triangles were utilized without marked preference, i.e., the incising on the inverted triangles may be directed from upper right to lower left (Pl. X L) or the reverse (Pl. X K). Filling lines on the erect triangles are, of course, in the opposite direction. In the case of the band of rhomboids, the rhomboidal elements may lean in either direction. Other, less regular designs which seem closely related to the opposed diagonal type also occur. Plate X D and E are rims which may have a continuous band of parallel diagonals. Plate X H and I illustrates two odd designs which are probably derivatives of the opposed diagonal concept. Not illustrated are two examples of what looks like a band of triangles with no filling in the upright elements and with opposing slope of filling lines on the inverted triangles; both specimens are small sherds of similar, but not identical, vessels from House IV. The Arzberger Diagonal Incised type shares with the crosshatched type an incising technique which is characterized in construction by diagonal straight lines, not zigzags, as primary elements, and these lines were frequently made from the rim base upward toward the lip in both types. The pattern comprising a band of triangles is also prominent in shoulder decoration of noncollared vessels. Execution of the diagonal patterns is sometimes good, but it is more often indifferent or even sloppy. Narrow, ploughed lines like those shown in Plate X L are frequent, and failure to achieve parallelism of lines, as well as other evidence of careless workmanship, is common. It would not be accurate, however, to state that the type gives an impression of marked inferiority to the other collared types.

The only form of rim base decoration observed was modeling, including modeled knobs and pinching, which occurs on 37 rims. If the rim of uncertain design shown by Plate X E is considered an example of the type, an incised rim base should also be listed. Seven bases are undecorated; they occur in comparatively weakly developed collars. On 28 rims classification was impossible because of the absence of the base.

Appendages: Four examples of lugs projecting laterally from the lip were noted. All of the sherds involved are small, and their assignment to the type and even to the Arzberger Group must be regarded as no more than probable. All of the lugs are broken, but two are complete enough to show that the incised strokes of the lip decoration were lengthened to extend to the edge of the lug. The small section remaining on the other two suggests that in one the lip decoration was carried through the lug sector on the lip only, leaving the top of the lug undecorated; the fourth example is too battered for determination of this point. Two lugs are estimated to project about 4 or 5 mm. beyond the outer wall of the rim, and one probably extended about 10 mm. No estimate was made on the fourth example because of its fragmentary condition.

Frequency at Site: Arzberger Diagonal Incised vessels have about the same frequency as the other decorated collared types. They constitute 24.2 per cent of the Arzberger Group and 8.1 per cent of all rims from the site.

Noncollared Vessels

The remaining vessels from the Arzberger site include 596 examples (Tables II and VII), of which 570 were placed in the noncollared category. The 26 unclassified rims include 19 whose basic form could not be determined because of their fragmentary condition, 5 cord-impressed rims, and 2 miniature vessels reserved for description as special units. Groups within the 570 noncollared rims which are accorded special description include 16 rims classified as the pottery type Hughes Beveled. This leaves for collective description 554 rims with more or less adequately defined forms.

TABLE VII

Pottery Types and Descriptive Groups of Noncollared and Unclassified Rims

Type or Descriptive Group	Number of Rims	Per Cent of Noncollared Rims	Per Cent of All Rims
Hughes Beveled	16	2.7	1.8
Horizontally incised rim	121	20.3	13.5
Other incised rim	9	1.5	1.0
Plain rim	445	74.7	49.8
Cord-impressed rim	5	0.8	0.6
Total	596	100.0	66.7

Obvious characteristics of the residual group are variations in form, presence or absence of rim decoration, and presence or absence of shoulder area decoration. With the exception of rim form 24, which practically defines the Hughes Beveled type, the relation of other characters to rim form did not prove to be a particularly fruitful channel into typological distinctions. Similarly, the presence or absence of rim decoration showed no striking complementary distribution with shoulder area decoration or the various forms of lip decoration. This absence of easily recognized clusters of modes results in a typological problem. The possible solutions appear to be (1) a multiplicity of named types defined by such characters as presence of rim and shoulder decoration, plain rim and decorated shoulder; (2) lumping of the entire group into one very loosely defined named type; or (3) subdivision into obvious groups for descriptive purposes only. The last solution has been adopted, although not without some misgivings because of the fact that certain of the differences between the major descriptive groups (plain and incised rims) seem to be of the same order as those between the members of the Arzberger Group. The reluctance to assign type names stems from the heterogeneity of the types which would result and which cannot be rationalized on the basis of any mathematical or other rigid concept of typology. A corollary of this failure to isolate and describe types is recognition of the many features which are shared by all the rims of the groups and which thus give it a certain unity. Those features include paste traits (also shared with the Arzberger Group), frequent occurrence of strap handles, incised lips (often the inner lip), decorated shoulder areas, elliptical orifices, and other attributes. On the whole, it would appear justifiable to consider the noncollared rims (other than the special groups mentioned above) a group of the same general order as the Arzberger Group, and they will be referred to below as the Hughes Group. The 16 rims of the Hughes Beveled type will be considered the only named type within the Hughes Group.

The Hughes Group

Paste characteristics seem to be quite uniform throughout the group and do not differ significantly from those of the Arzberger Group or the grit-tempered body sherds. Accordingly, no special description of the paste will be given. Surface finish is also much like that of the Arzberger Group, with most of the rims too completely smoothed for primary finishing technique to be determined. Grooved-paddle stamping, or traces of it, occurs on 94 rims, cord-wrapped paddle stamping on 43 rims, and checked-paddle stamping on 8 rims. Traces of red wash were observed on 5 rims. Data on vessel shape and size are by no means all that might be desired. The general range of rim profiles is illustrated in Plate VI, rim forms 17–49. These forms show a considerable variety, the extremes being the very small, low-rimmed vessels of forms 47–49 and the large vessels with the high, straight, outslanting rims of rim form 17. The most important forms numerically (Table VIII) are the nearly straight, slightly inward or outward slanting profiles of rim forms 29, 28, and 27. Most of the other forms are present in some quantity; the most poorly represented group is the curving, inward slanting type of forms 25 and 26, which totals only 28 specimens. Several relatively complete rim sections show that elliptical orifices were common, if not the rule, with vessels of this group. Information on body shape is limited, and the larger sherds figured in Plate VI present graphically almost all the evidence available. As was suggested in the discussion of body sherds, the thinner body sherds were probably derived from the smaller noncollared vessels. In particular, the angular shoulders appear to be associated with the small vessels of rim forms 46–49. Other vessels were probably subglobular or globular with a tendency toward total depth somewhat less than the maximum horizontal diameter. Data on orifice diameter are provided in Plates XI, XII, and XIII. Estimates of the major and minor axes of the elliptical vessels were difficult to make and cannot be considered to have any great reliability. A further complication is uncertainty as to whether or not a rim fragment represents an elliptical or a round orifice unless an unusually large segment can be observed. Extremes in size are furnished by a number of small vessels of rim forms 46–97 with mouth dimensions about 8 by 10 cm. and the large vessels of rim form 17 with estimated mouth diameters up to about 30 cm. The intermediate vessels having mouths about 18 by 20 cm. are more common than either of the extremes. Decoration and appendages are discussed in detail in connection with the descriptive subgroups.

TABLE VIII

RIM FORM FREQUENCIES OF HUGHES GROUP RIMS, EXCLUDING HUGHES BEVELED RIMS

Rim Form	Decorated Rims: Horizontal Incised		Decorated Rims: Other Incised		Decorated Rims: Total Incised		Plain Rims		Total Rims	
	Number	Per Cent	Number	Per Cent	Number	Per Cent	Number	Per Cent	Number	Per Cent
17	18	16.7	1	16.7	19	16.6	20	4.5	39	7.0
23	9	8.3	2	33.3	11	9.5	26	5.9	37	6.7
25	1	0.9	0	0.0	1	0.9	16	3.6	17	3.1
26	5	4.6	0	0.0	5	4.4	6	1.4	11	2.0
27	37	34.2	2	33.3	39	34.2	65	14.7	104	18.7
28	6	5.6	0	0.0	6	5.3	55	12.4	61	11.0
29	4	3.7	1	16.7	5	4.4	28	6.4	33	6.0
42	10	9.3	0	0.0	10	8.8	47	10.7	57	10.2
43	9	8.3	0	0.0	9	7.9	39	8.9	48	8.7
44	2	1.9	0	0.0	2	1.8	50	11.4	52	9.3
45	0	0.0	0	0.0	0	0.0	35	8.0	35	6.3
46	1	0.9	0	0.0	1	0.9	22	5.0	23	4.2
47	0	0.0	0	0.0	0	0.0	2	0.5	2	0.4
48	6	5.6	0	0.0	6	5.3	26	5.9	32	5.8
49	0	0.0	0	0.0	0	0.0	2	0.5	2	0.4
2–?	0	0.0	0	0.0	0	0.0	1	0.2	1	0.2
Total	108	100.0	6	100.0	114	100.0	440	100.0	554	100.0

Vessels with Incised Rims

This section of the Hughes Group is represented by 114 rims of classified form, of which 108 are decorated with horizontal lines and 6 with other patterns (Pls. XI, XII). Thirteen rims which could not be classified as to form have horizontal incised lines and may belong either to this group or to the Arzberger Horizontal Incised type. Three rims of unknown form carried other incised patterns. Of the latter group, two bear traces of crosshatched and diagonal designs which indicate that they probably should be considered a part of the Arzberger Group, but the third has parts of two parallel vertical lines which do not suggest any common pattern. Within the group of vessels known or reasonably inferred to be noncollared, the ratio of horizontally incised rims to plain rims is 108 : 440, or almost exactly 1 : 4.

Only 9 sherds have recognizable traces of primary surface finish. Three of these were cord-wrapped paddle-stamped and 6 were grooved-paddle stamped. Two vessels have traces of interior and exterior red filming.

The 6 rims with incised patterns other than horizontal lines include 2 of rim form 23, 2 of rim form 27, and 1 each of rim forms 29 and 17 (Table VIII). All are small sherds which do not permit an accurate conception of the designs involved. One specimen of rim form 23 shows three parallel diagonal lines in one direction and one opposed line; it could perhaps be considered some sort of variant of the opposed diagonal designs of the Arzberger Group and the body sherds. The second sherd of rim form 23 has at one side the ends of three horizontal lines, the rest of the fragment being smoothed. Interruption of horizontal lines is characteristic under handles, but in this instance no evidence of a handle was seen. A unique pattern is present on one of the sherds of rim form 27; it has a shallow horizontal line near the lip and another at the rim base with a zigzag line in the band thus defined. The triangles resulting are filled with oval punctations in a manner reminiscent of shoulder decoration at the site. The second sherd of rim form 27 has traces of two opposed diagonal lines nearly meeting at the base of the sherd. A small fragment, thought to be of rim form 29, has traces of parallel vertical lines at the rim base. It is possible that this is actually the lower part of a handle decoration rather than a new rim pattern. The final sherd, of rim form 17, has the ends of four parallel, upward slanting diagonal lines terminating under a broken lug or handle.

Range of pattern on the horizontally incised rims is illustrated by Plates XI and XII J. Extremes are the few and carelessly scratched lines of the small, low rimmed vessel of Plate XI B and the numerous and comparatively neat lines of Plate XI A and L. The rim form 17 sherds of Plate XI C, E, and I are a special case characterized by well-executed, widely spaced lines on the upper rim only. Future comparative studies may result in the segregation of this group as a named type. On the other sherds the general tendency appears to be a covering of the entire rim with more closely spaced lines. The number of lines observed varies from 2 to 12. The general similarity of the incising on these rims to that on the Arzberger Horizontal Incised type is obvious, although no examples of the chevron panels were seen on the Hughes Group specimens except for the very dubious sherd mentioned in the preceding paragraph. On those rims having handles the lines were invariably interrupted underneath the handle (Pl. XI G). The character of the incising itself is well within the range of that found on the Arzberger Group rims and on the decorated body sherds.

Lip ornamentation is decidedly the rule for the horizontally incised vessels—94 rims show lip decoration and only 1 lip is plain (lips were not present on the remaining rims). The technique of lip decoration is very similar to that found on the Arzberger Group sherds; it is usually a series of closely spaced, diagonally incised lines on the top, inner, or outer surface of the lip. In most instances a neat and regular appearance is attained. Lines may slant in either direction, i.e., from the upper left to lower right or the opposite, but the direction is constant on a given vessel. In 15 instances the incising strokes are transverse to the lip rather than diagonally oriented, and on 2 vessels the strokes were placed so that their long axes lie along the lip instead of across it. Two rims have roughly triangular impressions on the top of the lip in place of the very short incised lines. With regard to placement of the lip decoration, 16 vessels are decorated on the inner lip (or upper rim interior) only, 5 on both the inner lip and the top, 1 on inner lip, top, and outer lip, 8 on the outer lip only, and 64 on the top of the lip only. The placement of lip decoration appears to be related to rim form, which is discussed below. Briefly, the top placement is associated with, but not confined to, the straighter, more vertical rims of the general type of rim form 27. Inner lip decoration is similarly linked with outcurving, outslanting rims (rim form 42, for example). Outer lip decoration is uncommon in the Hughes Group, but seems to be primarily associated with rim form 17.

Shoulder decoration occurs on 21 of the 114 vessels with incised rims, a ratio very close to that of the vessels with plain rims of the Hughes Group. Plate XI A illustrates the only vessel on which a large part of the pattern is preserved. One instance of combined punctation and incising was recorded. All of the others consisted of incised lines only, but, typically, the area available for observation was so small that little more than the presence of shoulder decoration could be inferred. The relation of decorated shoulders to rim forms is discussed in connection with the plain-rimmed Hughes Group vessels.

Appendages observed on the decorated rims consist of 14 handles (Pl. XI F, G, H), 4 lugs (Pl. XI J), and 3 features which were probably rim projections. Unfortunately, fragmentary specimens may be broken in such a way as to make it impossible to determine which of the three classes of appendages are represented, and the counts given above represent an opinion rather than a fact. The illustrated specimens show the general character of the strap handles, which do not differ appreciably from those of the plain-rimmed Hughes Group vessels. They extend from the lip to the upper shoulder, where they are most commonly attached by riveting. Riveting appears to be considerably more frequent than welding at the lower attachment, although often satisfactory determination of this point is not possible. The lip attachment is skillfully done, and the handle appears to curve out as an extension of the lip. As a rule, handles are broader at the lip and taper toward the lower end, but there is an example with essentially parallel sides (Pl. XI G). Two of the handles are undecorated, 2 have vertical incised lines (Pl. XI F, H), and 1 has three horizontal rows of short diagonal strokes like those used for lip decoration. The remaining handles are too fragmentary for description of decoration. They consist of very small parts of the handle at the lip. Incising on the top of the lip is usually lengthened to cover the top of the handle, even if it is otherwise plain. The small vessel illustrated as Plate XI B is a special case because the rough, round area just below the lip and a small rough perforation directly below it on the upper shoulder suggest a loop (i.e., round in section) handle riveted at the lower attachment. The interruption of rim incising beneath the handles presumably indicates that handles were placed on the vessel prior to decoration. An unusual appendage which might be called both a lug and a rim projection occurs on the rim of the vessel illustrated as Plate XI J. Although most of it is now broken away, it was apparently a vertical lug or knob which rose above the level of the lip in a pointed projection. A very similar feature occurs on the Arzberger Horizontal Incised vessel shown as Plate VIII A. Two other rims have small, tabular lugs which extend out about 10 mm. from the lip. Both are decorated on the top with incised strokes. The remaining lug is a very small horizontal projection. Aside from the combined lug and rim projection described above, only three rims were listed as having rim projections. Two are broken, but suggest vertical points of the type shown in Plate XIII D. The third is complete and shows a heavy incised decorative stroke at the top like the lip decoration on the same vessel.

Absolute and relative frequency of the rim forms recorded for the 108 horizontally incised rims of determinable form is presented in Table VIII. The main impression given by this distribution is a tendency for association of the rim decoration with the higher, more or less vertical rims represented by rim forms 23 and 25–29. Rim form 17 is also strongly represented. Most of the other rim forms, however, are present; the absence of rim forms 47 and 49 is of little consequence since these are undoubtedly overly refined distinctions within the very low-rimmed group which are represented by only four specimens in the entire Hughes Group. The most significant deficiency is the virtual absence of rim forms 44 and 45, which are common profiles for undecorated rims. Rim forms 17, 23, 26, and 27 are relatively more popular in the decorated rim group than they are in the plain rim group. Rim forms 42, 43, and 48 are about equally common in both groups, and the remaining non-collared rim forms are relatively more numerous in the plain rim group. The general conclusion would appear to be that the Arzberger potters considered most of the noncollared forms suitable for rim decoration but favored especially the higher, less everted rim forms, possibly because the pattern is displayed to better advantage on such forms. It should be emphasized that every form found in the decorated rim group can be duplicated in the plain rims, and that on the basis of presence or absence of a mode the differentiation of the two groups is almost entirely a matter of the rim ornamentation.

Vessels with Plain Rims

Hughes Group vessels with undecorated rims total 440 specimens with the 16 Hughes Beveled rims excluded (Pls. XII, XIII, and XIV). There are in addition 5 plain rims of unclassified form, including 2 miniature vessels which may actually belong to this group but which are discussed as a special category. The discussion of the incised rim sherds of the Hughes Group has already emphasized the close relationship of the two descriptive groups, and their similarities and differences are given further consideration here.

Observations on surface finish indicate that 40 specimens were originally cord-wrapped paddle-stamped, 88 were grooved-paddle stamped, 8 were check-stamped, and 300 showed only smoothing. The rim surfaces of 2 were dimpled (Pl. XIII F) as if they had been stamped with the end of a rodlike tool, 1 sherd was finished with what appeared to be some sort of tooling slightly resembling cord-wrapped paddle stamping, and 1 rim had a roughened surface of unknown origin. Three rims, 2 of which belonged to the small rim form 47 class, had traces of red filming. The relationship of individual paddling techniques to the various rim forms did not give an impression of any marked association. All of the rim forms except the insignificant form 47 (total of two vessels) show some examples of paddle malleation, and the relatively small number of specimens in each rim category makes any but the crudest statistical analysis unprofitable. If the 31 per cent paddle-stamped vessels are used as a basis of comparison, rim forms 26 and 29 show the highest proportion of paddle-stamped vessels (67 and 68 per cent); rim forms 17 and 28 are also high with 50 and 47 per cent; rim forms 25, 44, 23, and 42 are about average (31, 28, 27, and 26 per cent); rim forms 45 and 46 are low with 20 and 18 per cent; and rim form 48 is very low with 4 per cent. These percentages probably represent no more than a rough measure of care in finishing, since most of the sherds are also smoothed to some degree. Checked-paddle stamping is numerically insignificant, but it is perhaps meaningful that the eight examples occur in six different rim form classes (rim forms 43, 29, 28, 27, 23, and probably 17). Both cord-wrapped and grooved-paddle stamped vessels are well distributed through the rim forms with the exception of rim form 48, in which only one is paddle-malleated in spite of its total of 32 plain and decorated rim vessels. This may mean either that the small vessels of this rim form were carefully smoothed or that the paddle was not ordinarily used at any stage in their manufacture. Paddle-stamped vessels of all types are far more common in the plain-rimmed group than they are in the incised rim group; only 9 out of 114 sherds show stamping in the latter group as opposed to 136 out of 440 in the former.

The data of Table VIII have already been discussed in connection with decorated rims. Major points are the comparatively even distribution of vessels through the various rim forms, particularly if similar forms are pooled to avoid excessively subtle distinctions; the very strong tendency of rim forms 44 and 45 to be undecorated; and the less strongly marked but nevertheless evident tendency for rim forms 17 and 27 to bear decoration. In terms of broad form groups, the high, nearly straight and vertical rim forms 27, 28, and 29 are most important (148 vessels) in the plain-rimmed group, and the thin everted rims of forms 44 and 45 and the thicker everted or outslanted rims of forms 42 and 43 are next in numerical importance with 85 and 86 vessels, respectively.

Lip form has not been discussed in connection with the incised rims, and the following summary is intended to cover the entire Hughes Group. The actual counts are: rounded lip, 170; flattened lip, 227; and narrowed and rounded lip, 128. No particularly striking associations for these lip forms have been noted, and it must be admitted that in many cases the classification was unsatisfactory owing to vague typology. Furthermore, the lip profile is in part produced by the lip decorating technique and hence is not a completely independent variable. In the most general terms, about 50 per cent of the vessels decorated on the inner lip only had narrowed and rounded lips and in the remaining half about 30 per cent had rounded and 20 per cent flattened lips. About 60 per cent of the vessels decorated on the top of the lip only had flattened lips, 35 per cent had rounded lips, and 5 per cent had narrowed and rounded lips. The comparatively few vessels decorated on the outer lip only show a scattering of lip form modes. A hypothesis suggested by those percentages is that the basic lip form was more or less rounded, and that subsequent modification, largely connected with decoration, was responsible for the narrowed and rounded and flattened extremes.

Lip decoration is very common on the plain rims, as it is on all Arzberger pottery; out of the 430 rims with lip sections preserved, only 27 had plain lips. Techniques of lip decoration noted are apparently identical with those previously described —most consist of short incised strokes on the top or inner lip, or, more rarely, on the outer lip. On 5 vessels the decorative markings seem to be punctations rather than incised strokes. All of the punctations occur on the lip proper, or what is called here the top of the lip. On 231 rims the lips were decorated on the top only, on 150 on the inner lip only, and on 10 on the outer lip only. Combinations of inner-top decoration occur on 8 vessels, of inner-outer decoration on 3 vessels, and of inner-top-outer decoration on 1 vessel (Pl. XIII K). There appears to be a definite relationship between rim form and the placement of lip decoration. Two-thirds of the 150 rims with inner lip decoration were classified as rim forms 42, 44, 45, and 46, and in each of these classes examples of inner decoration decidedly outnumber top decoration in spite of the considerably higher total of vessels in the latter category. An obvious explanation of this association is the fact that these profiles represent most of the strongly outcurving, outslanting rims on which the inner lip is the most accessible and easily visible area. Rim forms 23, 28, and 29 show inner and top decoration in something approaching the proportion of the totals, but top decoration in the remaining forms (excluding the numerically insignificant 47 and 49) is overwhelmingly preponderant, the totals being 16 rims with inner decoration and 128 rims with top decoration. All four of the vessels with rim forms 47 and 49 were decorated on the inner lip. The general conclusion seems to be that the preponderance of top lip decoration is the result of the greater number of vessels having a rim form suitable to this placement, and the relatively greater popularity of inner lip decoration in the plain as opposed to the incised rims can be explained on the same ground as a function of the preference for the straighter rimmed forms noted in the incised rim category. This relationship of form and placement of lip decoration is, however, a tendency and not an absolute association—inner lip decoration occurs in every rim form except 25, and top lip decoration is missing only in the rare rim forms 47 and 49. Six of the ten vessels which were decorated on the outer lip only are fairly evenly scattered through the 23–29 series of forms, one doubtful example was placed in rim form 42, and three vessels were placed in rim form 17. The special association of rim form 17 and outer lip decoration has been mentioned above. Plain lips, on the other hand, are scattered quite evenly through the entire series. Rim forms 27, 48, and 44 have a higher proportion of plain lips, but even here the numbers involved are comparatively small with seven, six, and five examples, respectively. Combinations in placement of lip decoration do not seem common enough to warrant any special analysis other than the observation that they appear in practically all rim forms except 17. Minor variations in lip decoration include 34 examples of transverse or vertical strokes instead of the more usual diagonals and a few instances in which top decoration was achieved by short strokes along the lip rather than diagonally or transversely across it. One short lip section had opposed diagonal strokes, the only example of this sort of thing in all the Arzberger rims. It may have been an accidental feature confined to a small section of rim.

Decorated shoulder areas occurred on 76 of the 440 plain rim vessels and hence have nearly the same relative frequency as do the vessels with incised rims. Most of the larger rim fragments with decorated shoulders are illustrated in Plates XII and XIII. In the great majority of fragments the only pattern observed was a trace at the juncture of the rim and shoulder, and the only course is to assume that the general description of incised shoulder patterns on body sherds applies equally to the plain and decorated rim groups of the Hughes Group. Tabulation by percentages of the rim forms of the vessels with decorated shoulders gives a series which resembles fairly closely a similar tabulation of all the plain rim vessels. In 9 rim forms the difference between the corresponding percentages did not exceed 2.9, and in 5 rim forms was less than 2. The sum of the percentage differences was 45.8, which was taken to be an indication of substantial agreement. Rim forms 48 and 44 showed a sizable excess of decorated vessels (the respective percentages are 5.9 and 14.5, and 11.4 and 17.1), and rim forms 28 and 23 had fewer decorated vessels than would be expected from the over-all 76 : 440 ratio (the percentages are for rim form 23, 5.9 per cent, and for shoulder decorated rim form 23, 2.6 per cent; the corresponding percentage figures for rim form 28 are 12.5 and 6.6). No shoulder decorated vessels were classified as rim forms 17 and 25 despite the totals of 20 and 17 rims in these categories. So far as the plain rim vessels are concerned, it seems reasonable to conclude that vessels of nearly all rim forms were regarded as suitable for shoulder incising, but that there was a certain tendency to favor vessels of rim forms 48 and 44 and to avoid those of rim forms 23 and 28. Vessels of rim forms 17 and 25 were not decorated at all.

A comparison of a similar pair of percentage tables (i.e., rim forms of all decorated rim vessels and rim forms of decorated rim vessels with decorated shoulders) for the decorated rim vessels of the Hughes Group leads to the conclusion that the presence or absence of rim decoration has little relationship to the presence or absence of shoulder decoration. It has already been remarked that the ratios of decorated shoulders to plain shoulders are about the same (1 : 5.4 for all decorated rims, 1 : 5.8 for all plain rims), and this similarity of ratio extends to the individual rim form percentages as well. The resemblance is particularly striking when the small number (20 vessels) of shoulder decorated vessels in the decorated rim group is taken into consideration. The most important exception is the presence of two vessels having incised shoulders in the rim form 17 category of the decorated rims.

Appendages, or traces of them, were observed on 83 plain rim vessels. The types recorded consist of handles, 39 vessels; lugs, 24 vessels; rim projections, 12 vessels; and unclassifiable traces of modeled appendages or other features, 8 vessels.

Handles are figured in Plates XII G and I, and XIII A, B, C, and E. In addition, the handles on decorated rims shown in Plate XIV can be regarded as typical. As was true with the decorated rims, fragmentary specimens make classification uncertain. The general description of handles on the decorated rim sherds applies equally well to those on the plain rim vessels. Unfortunately, no rim was complete enough to permit determination of the number of handles on a vessel, with the exception of the small vessel illustrated as Plate XIII E, and one other, a larger vessel; both had two handles placed at the ends of the major axis of an elliptical orifice. In 24 cases no more than a trace of handle was preserved, and it was not possible to observe decorative treatment. Of the more complete specimens, three handles were definitely undecorated (Pls. XIII B and XII G); four were decorated with vertical or nearly vertical incised lines (Pls. XIII A and XI F); the remaining eight specimens show horizontal rows of punctates or short dashes, horizontal incised lines, diagonal lines, opposed diagonals, and combinations of diagonal and vertical lines (Pls. XIII C, E and XII I). The Fraser manuscript figures and describes one loop handle on a small, plain rim vessel having a carelessly incised shoulder area. Handles are associated with most of the rim forms of the Hughes Group, but appear to be particularly characteristic of rim forms 43 and 44 (eight and ten examples, respectively). On the other hand, vessels with rim form 28 had no handles, and those of rim form 27 showed only three examples in spite of the 65 plain rim vessels of this form.

The 24 lugs reported are thought to be more or less tabular, horizontal projections of the lip (Pls. XII J; XIII K, M; XIV F, G; and XV J, K, L). As was pointed out above, it is not certain whether a small fragment should be considered a lug, a part of a handle, or even a rim projection, and the counts given are to be regarded as no more than a rough estimate of relative popularity. Lugs vary in size from very small projections extending no more than 5 or 6 mm. out from the lip (Pl. XIII K) to bold appendages projecting out 10 to 12 mm. Most of the vessels having lugs are decorated on the top of the lip, and ordinarily the decoration is extended to cover the flat upper surface of the lug. On one vessel having a plain lip the lug is also undecorated. Another example (Pl. XV L) with inner lip decoration has a special chevron design. No complete data are available as to the total number of lugs on a vessel, but certain large rim sections suggest that sometimes only two lugs were present. The comparatively few lugs are distributed in the various rim forms in what appears to be a random manner.

Rim projections (sometimes called castellations) differ from lugs chiefly in being directed upward rather than outward. An example is figured as Plate XIII D. Complete examples are very rare, but, again, extension of lip decoration onto the rim projection seems to be characteristic. Data on the number and placement of these features on the vessel are lacking.

Two minor features which have not been discussed are two small vessels (Pls. XII D and XVI B) with traces of small perforations on the rim base or extreme upper shoulder. In both the perforation was made from the outside while the clay was plastic.

Detached Handles

Detached handles are considered a part of the Hughes Group material, since all available evidence indicates that handles are confined to vessels of this group. Plates XV H, P, and Q and XVII A and B illustrate the range of designs noted. Most of the handles (24) are decorated with a panel of parallel vertical lines beginning at or close to the point where the top of the handle leaves the lip and terminating a short distance above the point of attachment to the upper shoulder. Two specimens have a panel of diagonal rather than vertical lines. Two special designs are shown in Plate XV H and P; in one the vertical line pattern is embellished with punctates, and in the second the surface of the handle is divided into four areas by an X, and these areas are further decorated by parallel incised lines. Five handles are plain, one shows traces of vertical and diagonal units of parallel incised lines, and the remaining two specimens are small fragments with no visible design. The forms of the detached handles fall within the range of those still attached to their rims. The characteristic form is a broad strap handle whose size is probably quite closely related to that of the vessel to which it was attached. Very often the handles are broadest at the lip and taper to the point of juncture with the shoulder. When viewed from the side, the handle usually forms a fairly smooth curve from lip to shoulder, but occasional specimens are rather sharply bent to meet the vessel shoulder, thus forming a sort of carination on the lower part of the handle.

Hughes Beveled

Paste: In most instances the paste of these vessels is indistinguishable from that of the other Hughes Group and the Arzberger Group vessels. Two large vessels, however, have a notable coarse paste with numerous tempering particles and a crumbly texture. One of these (from House I) is figured as Plate XIV P. The other is almost identical in general appearance but was found in the widely separated House IV excavation.

Surface Finish: In half of the vessels classified in this type (8), evidence of cord-wrapped paddle-stamping was observed. In a few vessels very little smoothing was evident; in others the paddle marks were nearly obliterated. No evidence of other types of paddle stamping was seen, and it is possible that all the vessels of this type were constructed with the aid of a cord-wrapped paddle. The large vessel mentioned above (Pl. XIV P) is smoothed but also shows horizontal striations which were presumably produced in the smoothing process. The remaining vessels are smoothed or have spalled surfaces.

Vessel Form and Size: Rim and lip form are the most distinctive features of this pottery type. The combination of a slightly everted, rather high rim with an outwardly beveled or filleted lip illustrated by the rim form 24 specimens of Plate VI is characteristic of the type. The distinctive lip form seems to have been achieved usually by a beveling technique, resulting in what might be considered from the structural standpoint an extremely low collar. A few rims, however, show what appears to be an added rim strip, but in view of the prevailing technique it may well be that even here the effect was produced by modeling rather than by the use of a true fillet. The scanty information available suggests that the orifices were circular in shape. Data on orifice diameter are given in the description of Plate XIV (J–N, P, and probably Q), the range being 16 to 25 cm. The vessels were quite large, although most of the sherds are not particularly thick (see rim profiles). The coarsely tempered vessels mentioned above were very thick, however (11 mm. near the rim base). The somewhat angular rim profiles of the last three examples of rim form 24 on Plate VI are thought to be especially characteristic. One rim (Pl. XIV I) included in the type has a true S-shaped profile, but otherwise seems to fall into the group. Another rim (Pl. XIV Q) has a rim profile classified as rim form 29, and the lip has a barely detectable bevel, but it has been included in the Hughes Beveled count. Practically no information is available on shoulder or lower body form. The profiles suggest a moderately or steeply sloping shoulder.

Decoration: The characteristic form of decoration observed consists of incising on the lip bevel or pinching on the fillet. One vessel (Pl. XIV K) also had incising on the inner lip. Lip incising is ordinarily oriented diagonally, like other lip incising at the site, but the interior lip incising mentioned immediately above was vertical. The sherd illustrated as Plate XIV M has a heavy zigzag line constructed by a technique like that used on the Arzberger Crosshatched type; it also has impressions at the base of the rim bevel in the style of the modeled rim base of the collared sherds. It might perhaps be considered an example of the Arzberger Group. One sherd has transverse rather than diagonal lip bevel notching. Plate XIV N illustrates a vessel with vertical ovoid punctations; here the base of the beveled lip has been treated as if it were a collar. True pinching is associated on two vessels with the fillet-like lip modification shown in Plate XIV P and also occurs on the curved rim shown as Plate XIV I. Shoulder incising or other types of decoration seem to be entirely absent.

Appendages: No examples of handles, lugs, or other appendages were observed.

Frequency at Site: Only 16 rims were classified in the Hughes Beveled type, and, as indicated in the discussion above, the inclusion of a few of these is of questionable propriety. In consequence, the legitimacy of the type is open to question until the significance of this association of attributes is demonstrated by new material. The rims constitute 2.7 per cent of the noncollared rims and 1.8 per cent of all rims (Table VII).

Miniature Vessels

Two examples of miniature vessels were collected. One of these, illustrated as Plate XIII J, is a small jar with a mouth diameter of about 3.5 cm. It is crudely smoothed, undecorated, and has very little tempering. Its bumpy exterior surface suggests that it was modeled without the aid of a paddle. The second miniature vessel appears to be a fragment of a very small bowl. Although its general orientation is uncertain, the available evidence suggests that the orifice was restricted. Curvature of the shoulder is pronounced, but there is not an angular break. Tempering seems normal, but the paste on a fresh break has a laminated appearance and a dark color. Both surfaces are bumpy but smoothed, and the exterior surface has traces of what looks like vertical grooved-paddle stamping. The total depth of the vessel is probably about 5 cm.

Cord-Impressed Rims

The five rim sherds, representing as many vessels, decorated by cord impressing are illustrated as Plate XIV A–E. With the exception of the first sherd illustrated, all have parts of the lip intact. No traces of surface finish other than smoothing were detected, and the paste is within the ordinary range of the Arzberger pottery, although perhaps a little finer in texture than the average. Two sherds (Pl. XIV D, E) are heavily soot-encrusted on the interior as if they had been used in cooking. In form all are slightly convex and were probably faintly S-curved rims on the general order of rim form 74. The lips are neatly finished and are rounded, but verge on a flattened form. Thickness about 1 cm. below the lip ranges from 5 to 7 mm., but two sherds are slightly thicker toward the base than they are at the lip. Orifice diameter was not estimated owing to the small size of the sherds. The range of decoration is illustrated in Plates XIV and XV M, N, and O. Three of the sherds are decorated with horizontal impressions formed by hard twisted cords about 2 mm. in diameter. The impressions are spaced at an interval of about 5 or 6 mm. Two sherds (Pl. XIV C, E) show five impressions and may have had more. The absence of rim bases makes accurate determination of this point possible. One sherd (Pls. XIV A and XV N) has part of a panel of three upward pointing nested chevrons; on this sherd the rim base is present, and it can be seen that the design extends to the bottom of the rim. The final cord-impressed sherd (Pls. XIV B and XV O) has at least six horizontal impressions, of which the top two bend down beneath a small lug. The top surface of the lug is crossed by a transverse groove, giving a spoutlike effect.

LITERATURE CITED

BARRETT, S. A.

1933 Ancient Aztalan. Bull. Pub. Mus. City of Milwaukee, Vol. 13.

BELL, EARL H., and G. H. GILMORE

1936 The Nehawka and Table Rock Foci of the Nebraska Aspect. *In* Chapters in Nebraska Archaeology. Lincoln: Univ. Nebraska Press. Vol. I, No. 4.

BENNETT, JOHN W.

1945 Archaeological Explorations in Jo Daviess County, Illinois. Chicago: Univ. Chicago Press.

BLACK, GLENN A.

1944 Angel Site, Vanderburgh County, Indiana. Indiana Hist. Soc., Prehist. Res. Ser., Vol. 2, No. 5.

BOWERS, ALFRED W.

1948 A History of the Mandan and Hidatsa. A Dissertation Submitted to the Faculty of the Division of the Social Sciences in Candidacy for the Degree of Doctor of Philosophy. Dept. Anthropol. Univ. Chicago. Microfilm.

CHAMPE, JOHN L.

1936 The Sweetwater Culture Complex. *In* Chapters in Nebraska Archaeology. Lincoln: Univ. Nebraska Press. Vol. I, No. 3.

1946 Ash Hollow Cave. University of Nebraska Studies, N.S., No. 1.

COLE, FAY-COOPER, *et al.*

1951 Kincaid: A Prehistoric Illinois Metropolis. Chicago: Univ. Chicago Press.

COOPER, PAUL L.

1936 Archaeology of Certain Sites in Cedar County, Nebraska. *In* Chapters in Nebraska Archaeology. Lincoln: Univ. Nebraska Press. Vol. I, No. 1.

1949 Recent Investigations in Fort Randall and Oahe Reservoirs, South Dakota. Amer. Antiq., 14, No. 4, Pt. 1: 300–310.

DELAND, CHARLES E.

1906 Aborigines of South Dakota, Pt. I. S. Dak. Hist. Coll., 3: 271–586.

DUNLEVY, MARION LUCILE

1936 A Comparison of the Cultural Manifestations of the Burkett and Gray-Wolfe Sites. *In* Chapters in Nebraska Archaeology, Lincoln: Univ. Nebraska Press. Vol. I, No. 2.

GRIFFIN, JAMES B.

1943 The Fort Ancient Aspect: Its Cultural and Chronological Position in Mississippi Valley Archaeology. Ann Arbor: Univ. Michigan Press.

1946 Cultural Change and Continuity in Eastern United States Archaeology. *In* Man in Northeastern North America, ed. by Frederick Johnson. Papers Robert S. Peabody Found. for Archaeol., 3: 37–95.

GRIFFIN, JOHN W.

1948 Upper Mississippi at the Fisher Site. Amer. Antiq., 14, No. 2: 124–26.

HILL, A. T., and PAUL COOPER

1937*a* The Schrader Site. Nebr. Hist. Mag., 17, No. 4 (October–December, 1936): 223–52.

1937*b* The Champe Site. *Ibid.,* pp. 253–70.

1937*c* Fremont 1. *Ibid.,* pp. 271–92.

1938 The Archeological Campaign of 1937. *Ibid.,* 18, No. 4 (October–December, 1937): 243–353.

HILL, A. T., and WALDO R. WEDEL

1936 Excavations at the Leary Indian Village and Burial Site, Richardson County, Nebraska. Nebr. Hist. Mag., 17, No. 1: 3–73.

HURT, WESLEY R., JR.

1951 Report of the Investigation of the Swanson Site 39Br16, Brule County, South Dakota. Archaeol. Studies Cir., No. 3, Pierre: State Archaeological Commission.

1952 House Types of the Over Focus, South Dakota. Plains Archeol. Conf. News Letter, 4, No. 4: 51–52.

KEYES, CHARLES REUBEN

1927 Prehistoric Cultures. The Palimpsest. Iowa City, Ia. 8, No. 6: 215–29.

KIVETT, MARVIN F.

1949 Archaeological Investigations in Medicine Creek Reservoir, Nebraska, Amer. Antiq., 14, No. 4, Pt. 1: 278–84.

KRIEGER, ALEX D.

1946 Culture Complexes and Chronology in Northern Texas with

Extension of Puebloan Datings to the Mississippi Valley. Univ. Texas Publ., No. 4640.

1949 The Southern Limits of Central Plains Cultural Complexes. Proceedings of the Fifth Plains Conference for Archeology, Note Book No. 1, Lab. Anthropol. Univ. Nebr., pp. 98–99.

KROEBER, A. L.

1940 Statistical Classification. Amer. Antiq., 6, No. 1: 29–44.

LEHMER, DONALD J.

1951 Pottery Types from the Dodd Site, Oahe Reservoir, South Dakota. Plains Archeol. Conf. News Letter, 4, No. 2: 3–15.

1952 The Fort Pierre Branch, Central South Dakota. Amer. Antiq., 17, No. 4: 329–36.

MCKERN, W. C.

1945 Preliminary Report on the Upper Mississippi Phase in Wisconsin. Bull. Pub. Mus. City of Milwaukee, Vol. 16, No. 3.

MELEEN, ELMER E.

1938 A Preliminary Report of the Mitchell Indian Village Site and Burial Mounds. Univ. S. Dak. Mus. Archaeol. Studies, Cir. 2, Pt. 1.

1948 A Report on an Investigation of the La Roche Site, Stanley County, South Dakota. *Ibid.,* Cir. 5.

1949 A Preliminary Report on the Thomas Riggs Village Site. Amer. Antiq., 14, No. 4, Pt. 1: 310–21.

MOTT, MILDRED

1938 The Relation of Historic Indian Tribes to Archaeological Manifestations in Iowa. Iowa Journ. Hist. and Polit., 36, No. 3: 227–304.

OVER, W. H., and ELMER E. MELEEN

1941 A Report on the Investigation of the Brandon Village Site and the Split Rock Creek Mounds. Univ. S. Dak. Archaeol. Studies, Cir. 3.

ROUSE, IRVING

1939 Prehistory in Haiti: A Study in Method. Yale Univ. Publ. Anthropol., No. 21.

SIMPSON, GEORGE GAYLORD

1941 Large Pleistocene Felines of North America. Amer. Mus. Novitates, No. 1136.

SMITH, CARLYLE S.
1951 Pottery Types from the Talking Crow Site, Fort Randall Reservoir, South Dakota. Plains Archeol. Conf. News Letter, 4, No. 3: 32–41.

SMITH, HALE G.
1951 The Crable Site, Fulton County, Illinois. Anthropol. Papers Mus. Anthropol. Univ. of Mich., No. 7.

STRONG, WILLIAM DUNCAN
1935 An Introduction to Nebraska Archeology. Smithsonian Misc. Coll., Vol. 93, No. 10.
1940 From History to Prehistory in the Northern Great Plains. *In* Essays in Historical Anthropology of North America, Published in Honor of John R. Swanton in Celebration of His Fortieth Year with the Smithsonian Institution. *Ibid.,* 100: 353–94.

THOMAS, CYRUS
1891 Catalogue of Prehistoric Works East of the Rocky Mountains. Bur. Amer. Ethnol., Bull. No. 12.
1894 Report on the Mound Explorations of the Bureau of Ethnology. Bur. Amer. Ethnol., 12th Ann. Rep., pp. 3–730.

WEDEL, WALDO R.
1935*a* Contributions to the Archaeology of the Upper Republican Valley, Nebraska. Nebr. Hist. Mag., 15, No. 3 (July-September, 1934): 133–209.
1935*b* Appendix: Preliminary Classification for Nebraska and Kansas Cultures. *Ibid.,* pp. 251–55.
1938 The Direct-Historical Approach in Pawnee Archeology. Smithsonian Misc. Coll., Vol. 97, No. 7.
1940 Culture Sequences in the Central Great Plains. *In* Essays in Historical Anthropology of North America, Published in Honor of John R. Swanton in Celebration of His Fortieth Year with the Smithsonian Institution. *Ibid.,* 100: 291–352.
1941 Environment and Native Subsistence Economies in the Central Great Plains. *Ibid.,* 101, No. 3.
1943 Archeological Investigations in Platte and Clay Counties Missouri. U. S. Nat. Mus., Bull. 183.
1947*a* Culture Chronology in the Central Great Plains. Amer. Antiq., 12, No. 3, Pt. 1: 148–56.

1947*b* Prehistory and Environment in the Central Great Plains. Trans. Kans. Acad. Sci., 50, No. 1: 1–18.
1949 Some Provisional Correlations in Missouri Basin Archaeology. Amer. Antiq., 14, No. 4, Pt. 1: 328–39.

WEDEL, W. R., and A. T. HILL
1942 Scored Bone Artifacts of the Central Great Plains. Proc. U. S. Nat. Mus., 92: 91–100.

WILFORD, LLOYD A.
1941 A Tentative Classification of the Prehistoric Cultures of Minnesota. Amer. Antiq., 6, No. 3: 231–49.
1945 Three Villages of the Mississippi Pattern in Minnesota. *Ibid.,* 11, No. 1: 32–40.
1951 Three Villages of the Mississippi Pattern in Minnesota. Minn. Archaeologist, 17, No. 4.

WILL, GEORGE F.
1924 Archaeology of the Missouri Valley. Amer. Mus. Nat. Hist., Anthropol. Papers, Vol. XXII, Pt. 6.
1946 Tree Ring Studies in North Dakota. Agricultural Experiment Station, N. Dak. Agricultural College, Bull. 338.

WILL, GEORGE F., and THAD. C. HECKER
1944 The Upper Missouri River Valley Aboriginal Culture in North Dakota. N. Dak. Hist. Quart., 11, Nos. 1–2: 5–126.

PLATE I

Fig. A. General view of site from Missouri River flood plain, looking north. Columbia University negative No. 312.

Fig. B. Pitted boulder at east side of site. Columbia University negative No. 311.

PLATE I

Fig. A

Fig. B

PLATE II

Fig. A

Fig. B

PLATE II

Fig. A. House II, looking south. House I excavation in background. Columbia University negative No. 301.

Fig. B. House IV, looking north. Columbia University negative No. 319.

PLATE III

Fig. A. House III, looking east. Columbia University negative No. 305.

Fig. B. Vertical section of Feature 4, House III. Columbia University negative No. 302.

PLATE III

Fig. A

Fig. B

PLATE IV

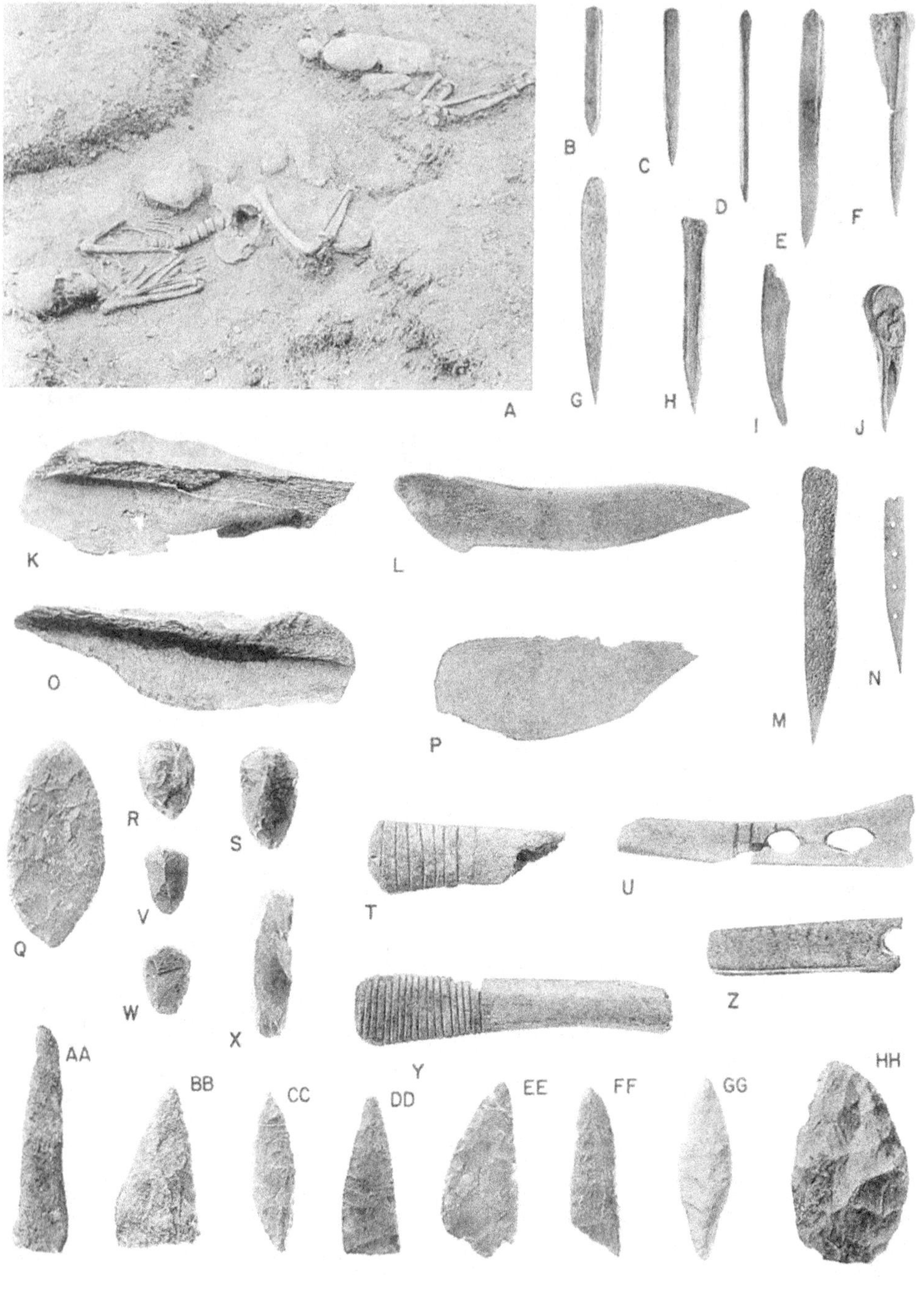

PLATE IV

Burials and bone, antler, and flaked stone artifacts.

A. Burial 3 (foreground) and Burial 4, looking southwest.

B, C, D, and E. Flakers or pins from split shafts of long bones. Lengths 6.6, 8.0, 9.7, 12.0 cm. House I, Feature 6; House II, fill; House I, fill; House I, Feature 6.

F, G, and H. Awls from unidentified bone, bison rib, and deer(?) metapodial. Lengths 10.5, 11.5, 10.0 cm. House I, Feature 9; House I, Feature 8; House I, Feature 8.

I. Polished deer antler tine. Length 8.1 cm. Provenience unknown.

J. Awl from split pronghorn metapodial. Length 7.3 cm. House I, fill.

K. Bison scapula tool. Length 28.0 cm. House II, Feature 5.

L. Scapula knife (probably bison). Length 19.0 cm. House I, fill.

M. Awl from bison rib. Length 14.1 cm. House I, fill.

N. Awl, broken and reused, probably from bison rib. Length 9.0 cm. House I, Feature 9.

O. Bison scapula tool. Length 28.4 cm. House III, Feature 3.

P. Scapula knife (cutting edge at top). Length 14.0 cm. House I, fill.

Q and R. Flint knives. Lengths 9.8, 4.1 cm. House II, Feature 6; House II, fill.

S. Flint end scraper. Length 4.8 cm. House III, fill.

T. Scored paddle from dorsal spine of bison hump vertebra. Length 16.7 cm. House I, fill.

U. Shaft wrench(?) from bison rib. Length 15.7 cm. House IV, fill.

V, W, and X. Flint, quartzite, and flint end scrapers. Lengths 3.6, 3.6, 7.5 cm. House I, fill; House I, fill; House I, Feature 2.

Y. Scored paddle from dorsal spine of bison hump vertebra. Length 26.2 cm. House IV, fill.

Z. Shaft wrench(?) from bison rib. Length 10.4 cm. House IV, fill.

AA. Knife fragment, tabular chalcedony. Length 11.3 cm. House I, fill.

BB. Knife fragment, Bijou Hills quartzite. Length 7.7 cm. House II, Feature 5.

CC. Flint knife. Length 7.6 cm. House II, Feature 4.

DD. Quartzite knife fragment. Length 8.2 cm. House II, fill.

EE. Tanged flint knife. Length 8.2 cm. House II, fill.

FF. Knife, Bijou Hills quartzite. Length 8.8 cm. House III, Feature 3.

GG and HH. Quartzite knives. Lengths 8.5, 10.4 cm. House I, Feature 9; House IV, fill.

PLATE V

Flaked and ground stone, bone, and shell artifacts.

A, B, C, and D. Flint projectile point fragments. Lengths 1.9, 2.1, 2.7, 2.5 cm. House I, Feature 9; House I, fill; House II, fill; House II, fill.

E. Quartzite projectile point fragment. Length 1.7 cm. House I, fill.

F. Sandstone shaft smoother. Length 9.1 cm. House I, fill.

G, H, and I. Flint projectile point fragments. Lengths 1.7, 1.0, 1.7 cm. House I, fill; House II, fill; House I, fill.

J. Quartzite projectile point fragment. Length 1.7 cm. House I, fill.

K. Flint projectile point fragment. Length 2.0 cm. House I, Feature 9.

L. Flint projectile point. Length 1.5 cm. House II, Feature 7.

M. Sandstone shaft smoother. Length 9.0 cm. House I, Feature 3.

N. Catlinite pipe fragment, top view. Length 5.9 cm. House I, fill.

O. Catlinite tube fragment. Length 3.1 cm. House II, fill.

P. Specimen "N," side view.

Q. Catlinite pipe fragment. Length 2.9 cm. House II, fill.

R. Notched mussel shell. Length 9.2 cm. House I, Feature 10.

S and T. Worked mussel shells. Lengths 8.2, 7.2 cm. House I, Feature 6; House II, fill.

U and V. Bone fishhooks. Lengths 4.0, 5.0 cm. House I, fill; House I, Feature 6.

W and X. Heavy flint scrapers. Lengths 7.3, 10.4 cm. House I, Feature 9; House III, Feature 4.

Y. Grooved catlinite fragment. Length 7.2 cm. House III, fill.

PLATE V

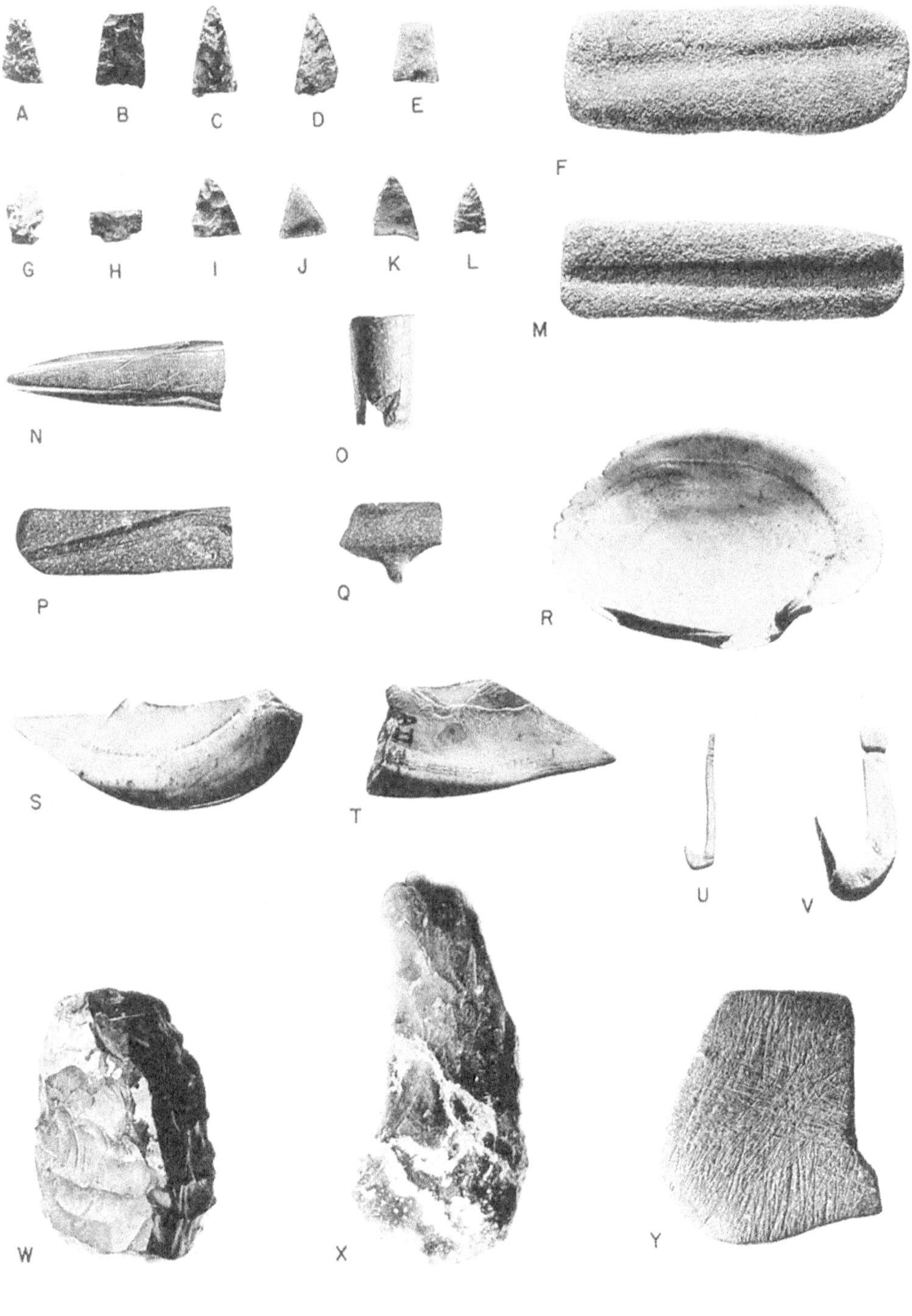

PLATE VI

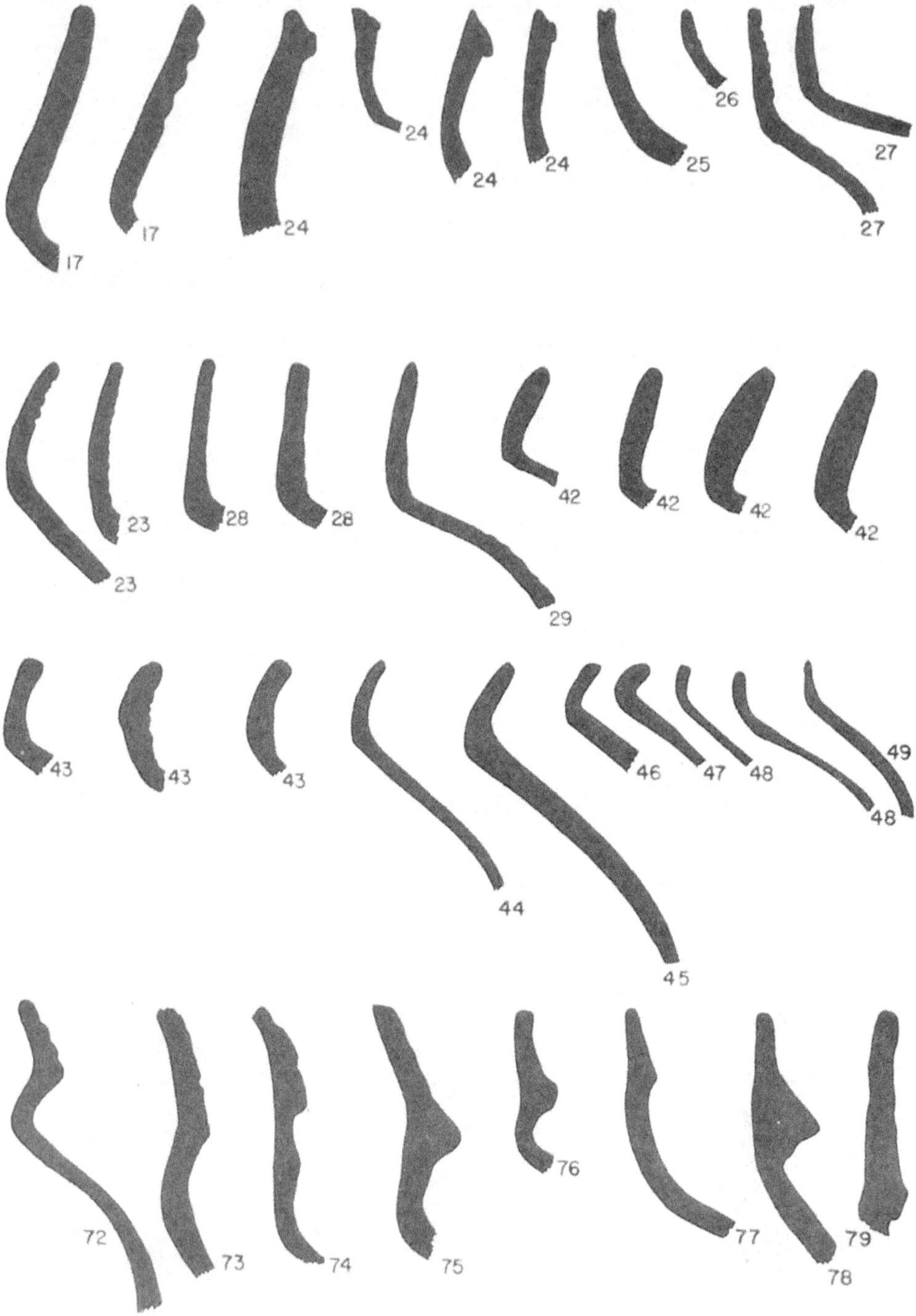
17
17
17
24
24
24
24
25
26
27
27
23
23
28
28
29
42
42
42
42
43
43
43
44
45
46
47
48
48
49
72
73
74
75
76
77
78
79

PLATE VI

Rim profiles of pottery vessels. Exteriors are toward the right. $\times\frac{1}{2}$

PLATE VII

Arzberger Plain rims.
(Reduced approx. ½.)

	Field Cat. No.	Provenience (H = House)	Est. Lip Diameter (in cm.)	Rim Form	Basic Surface Finish	Remarks
A	AI 71	H I, fill	18	76		
B	AI 18	H I, fill	15	74	Grooved-paddle stamped (?)	
C	AI 121	H I, fill		72		
D	AII 86	H II, fill	14 (?)	72		
E	AIII 50	H III, post mold		78	Cord-wrapped paddle-stamped	
F	AI 12 UMMA 7750	H I, fill	18	76	Grooved-paddle stamped	
G	AI 71	H I, fill	18	7–	Grooved-paddle stamped	Like 76 but far more outslanting than any other collared sherd
H	AI 174	H I, Feature 7		72		
I	AII 67	H II, Feature 3		74		
J	AI 71	H I, fill	23	72	Grooved-paddle stamped (?)	
K	AI 123	H I, fill		76		
L	AII 8	H II, fill		78		

PLATE VII

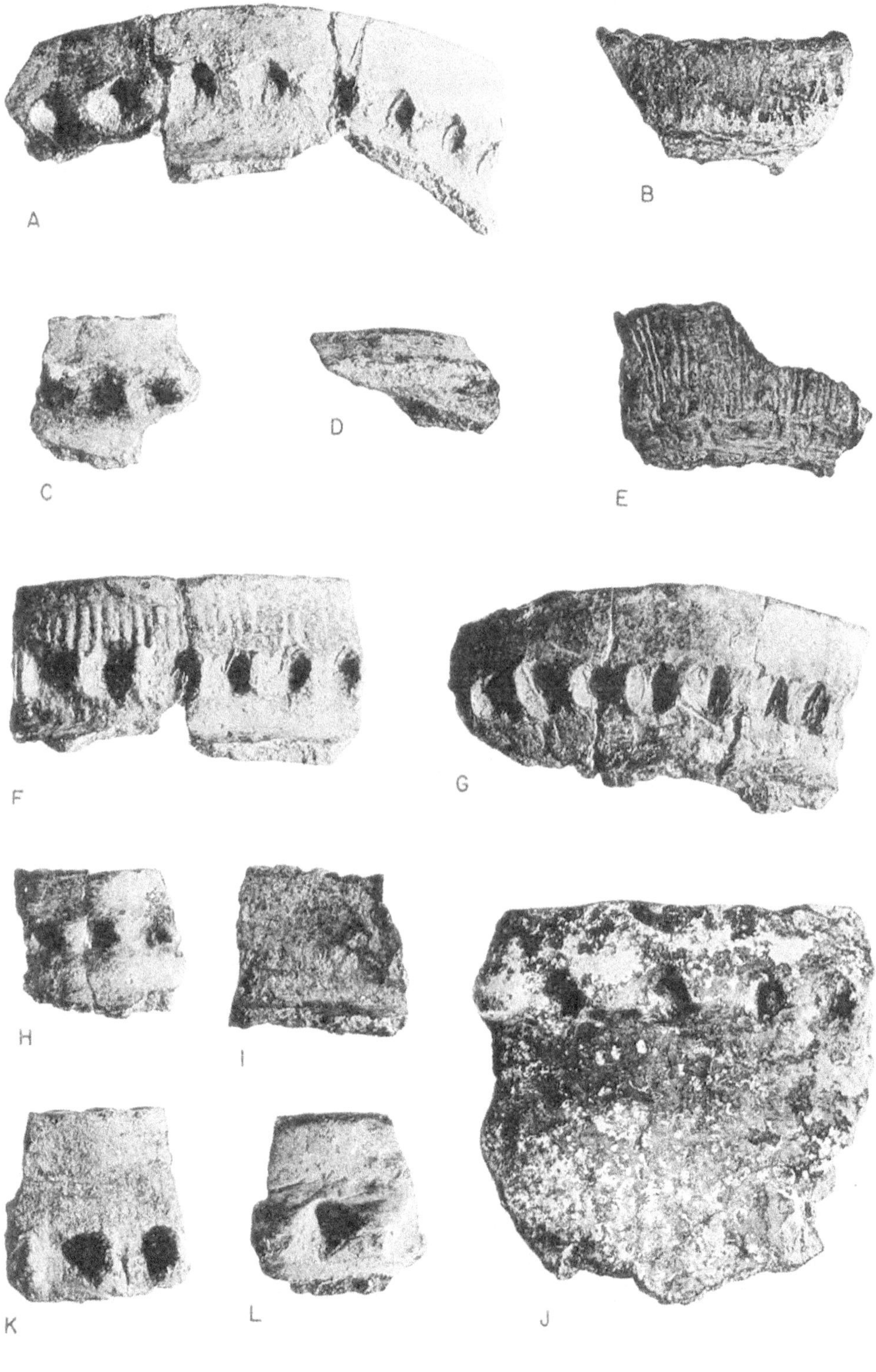

PLATE VIII

PLATE VIII

Arzberger Horizontal Incised rims.
(Reduced approx. ½.)

	Field Cat. No.	Provenience (H = House)	Est. Lip Diameter (in cm.)	Rim Form	Basic Surface Finish
A	AI 123 UMMA 7750	H I, fill	17 (not quite circular)	73	Unknown
B	AIV 7	H IV, fill		75	Unknown
C	AIV 48	H IV, Feature I		73	Grooved-paddle stamped
D	AIII 50	H III, post mold		72	Unknown
E	AIII 55	H III, Feature 3		76	Cord-wrapped paddle-stamped. Red wash
F	AIII 62	H III, fill		72	Unknown
G	AI 57	H I, fill		73	Unknown
H	AIII 55 UMMA 7755	H III, Feature 3	15	72	Grooved-paddle stamped
I	AIII 30	H III, fill		79	Unknown
J	AIV 6	H IV, fill		72	Unknown
K	AIV 6	H IV, fill		76(?)	Unknown

PLATE IX

Arzberger Crosshatched rims.
(Reduced approx. ½.)

	Field Cat. No.	Provenience (H = House)	Est. Lip Diameter (in cm.)	Rim Form	Basic Surface Finish
A	AI 243	H I, fill	16	75	
B	AI 11	H I, fill		72	Probably grooved-paddle stamped
C	AI 78	H I, fill	20	75	
D	AI 10	H I, fill	22	72	
E	AII 23	H II, fill	22	72	Grooved-paddle stamped (?)
F	AI 71	H I, fill	15	75	
G	AII 35	H II, fill		72	
H	AII 30	H II, fill		72	
I	AII 8	H II, fill	19	75	
	UMMA 7753				
J	AI(?)	H I	14	72	
K	AIII 24	H III, fill	20	73	Cord-wrapped paddle-stamped
L	AIV 6	H IV	24	79	
M	AIV 7	H IV, fill	19	77	

PLATE IX

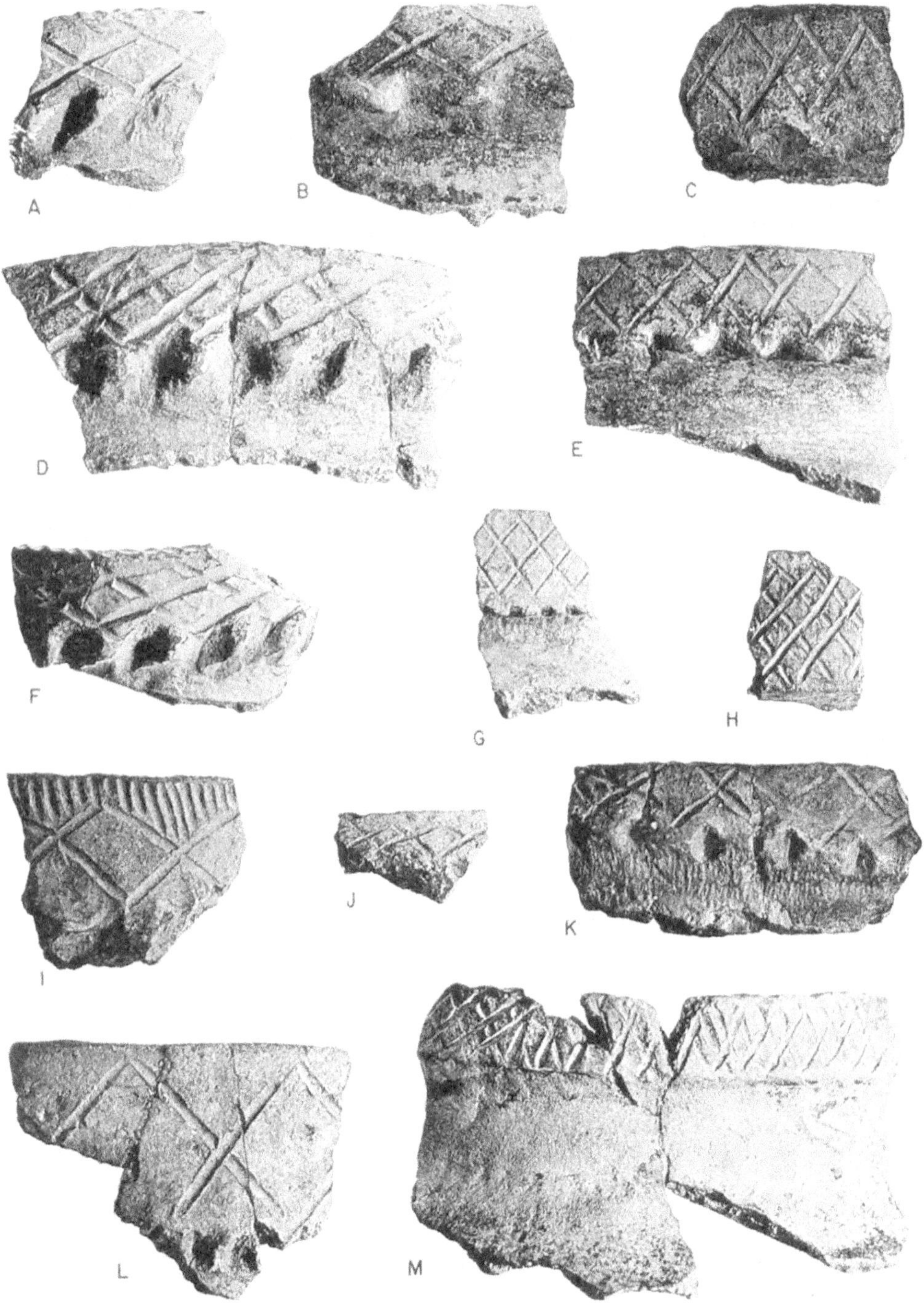

PLATE X

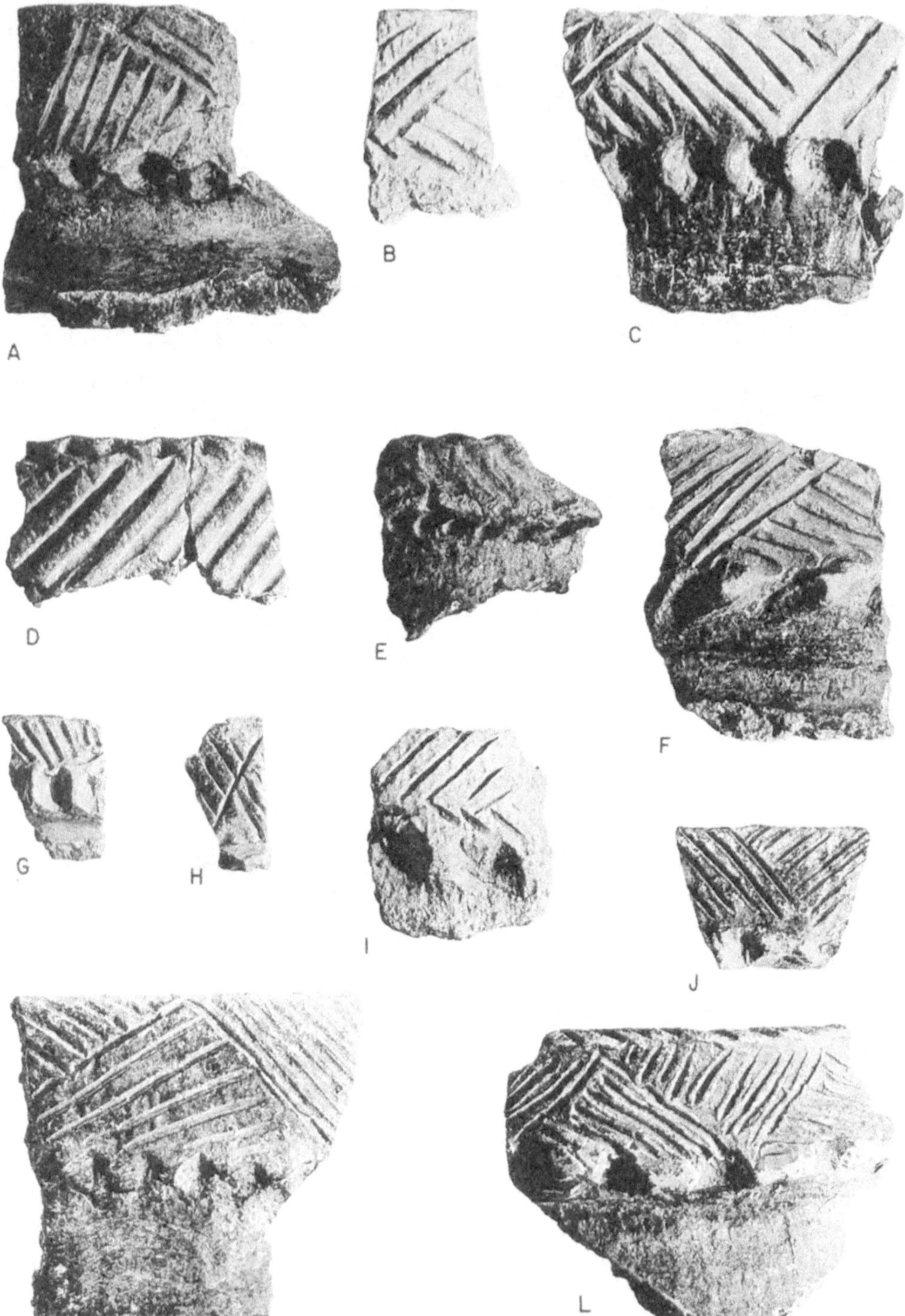

PLATE X

Arzberger Opposed Diagonal rims.
(Reduced approx. ½.)

	Field Cat. No.	Provenience (H = House)	Est. Lip Diameter (in cm.)	Rim Form	Basic Surface Finish
A	AII 51	H II, fill	20	75	
B	AIV 3 UMMA 7755	H IV, fill		75	Cord-wrapped paddle-stamped
C	AIV 17	H IV, fill	22	74	Grooved-paddle stamped
D	AIII 3	H III, fill	20	74(?)	
E	AIV 11	H IV, fill	15	72	Grooved-paddle stamped
F	AIII 1	H II, fill	25(?)	75	
G	AII 7	H II, fill		72	
H	AIII 62	H III, fill		73	
I	AI 91	H I, fill		75	Grooved-paddle stamped (?)
J	AIV 48	H IV, Feature 1		73(?)	
K	AI 12	H I, fill	30	73	Grooved-paddle stamped
L	AII 30	H II, fill	25	78	Grooved-paddle stamped (?)

PLATE XI

Horizontally incised noncollared sherds (Hughes Group).
(Reduced approx. ½.)

	Field Cat. No.	Provenience (H = House)	Est. Lip Diameter (in cm.)	Rim Form	Basic Surface Finish	Remarks
A	AI 20	H I, fill	10	27		
B	AI 63	H I, fill	8	26		Interior and exterior red filming
C	AIII 55	H III, Feature 3		17	Grooved-paddle stamped	
D	AI 1	H I, fill		23	Grooved-paddle stamped	
E	AIII 55 UMMA 7755	H III, Feature 3	30(?)	17	Grooved-paddle stamped	
F	AII 67	H II, Feature 3		45		
G	AI 198	H I, Feature 9	14(?)	44		
H	AIII 24	H III, fill		45	Cord-wrapped paddle-stamped	
I	AIII 24	H III, fill	28	17	Grooved-paddle stamped(?)	
J	AI 1	H I, fill	20 x 22(?)	29		
K	AI 10	H I, fill	16 x 18(?)	43		
L	AII 51	H II, fill		23	Grooved-paddle stamped(?)	
M	AI 243 UMMA 7750	H I, fill	21	23	Cord-wrapped paddle-stamped	

PLATE XI

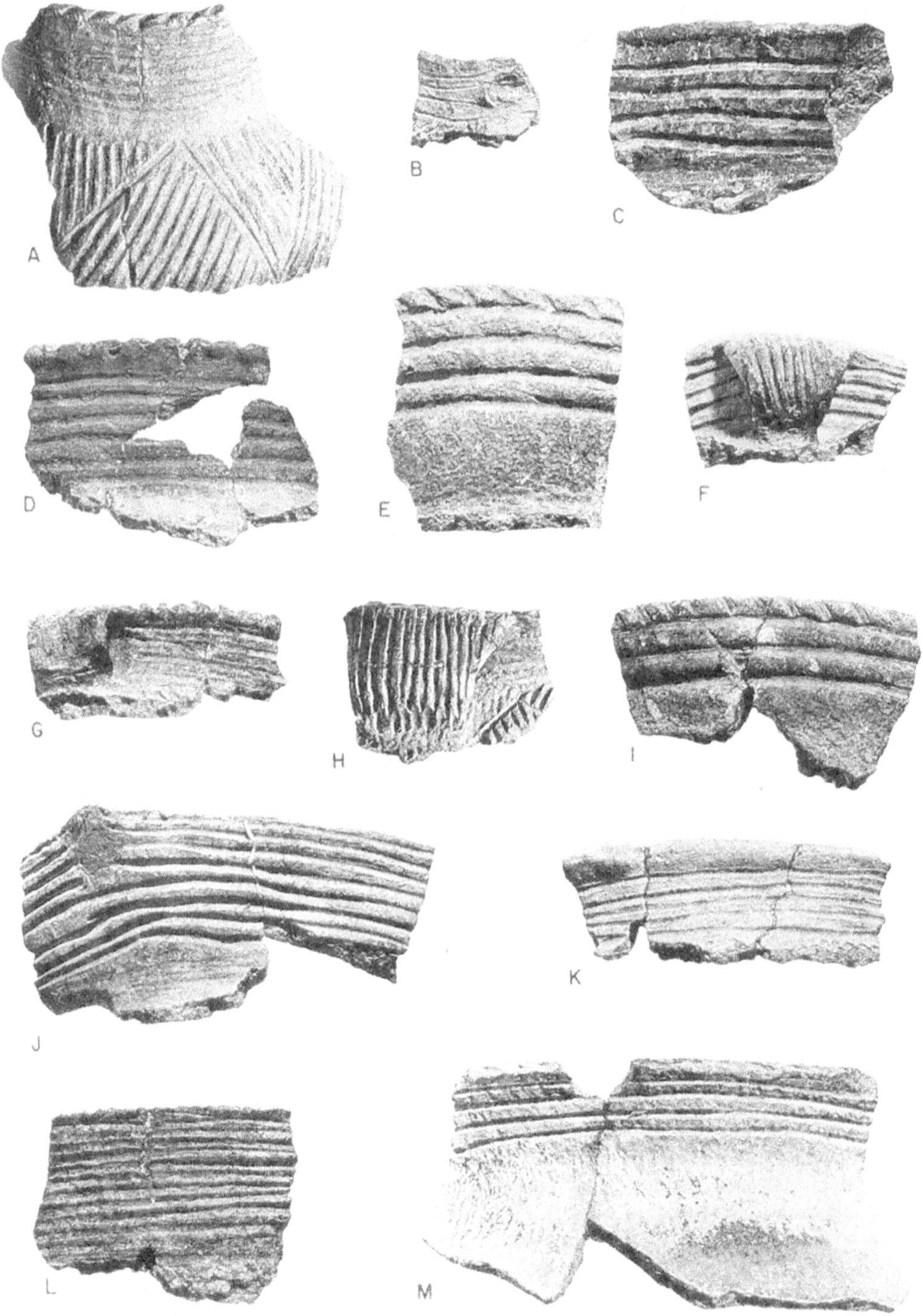

PLATE XII

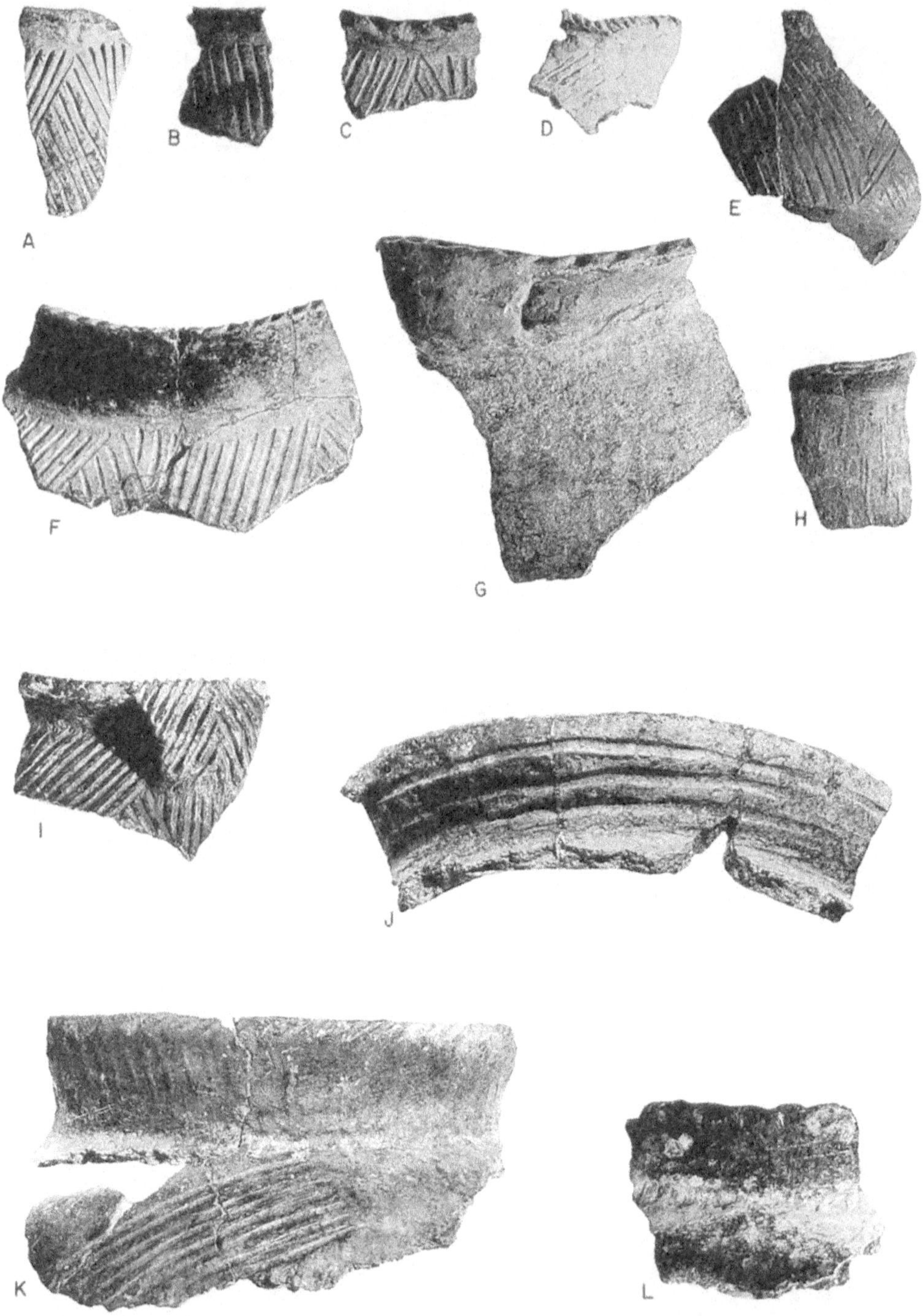

PLATE XII

Decorated and other noncollared vessels (Hughes Group).
(Reduced approx. ½.)

	Field Cat. No.	Provenience (H = House)	Est. Lip Diameter (in cm.)	Rim Form	Basic Surface Finish	Remarks
A	AI 1	H I, fill	10 x 12(?)	48		
B	AII(?)	H II	10 x 12(?)	47		
C	AIII 47	H III, entrance post mold	12 x 15(?)	46		
D	AIII 55	H III, Feature 3	8 x 10(?)	48		Crudely made, tempering nearly absent
E	AI 164	H I, Feature 6	10 x 12(?)	49	Grooved-paddle stamped(?)	
F	AI 198	H I, Feature 9	15 x 18(?)	27	Grooved-paddle stamped	
G	AI 71 UMMA 7750	H I, fill	18(?)	43	Grooved-paddle stamped	
H	AII 30	H II, fill	10 x 12(?)	46	Grooved-paddle stamped	
I	AI 244	H I, fill	18(?)	46		
J	AII 36	H II, fill	18	42		Fragment of strap handle present
K	AI 164	H I, Feature 6	18 x 20(?)	29	Grooved-paddle stamped	
L	AIV 44	H III, Feature 3	17(?)	28	Grooved-paddle stamped	

PLATE XIII

Various noncollared rim sherds (Hughes Group).
(Reduced approx. ½.)

	Field Cat. No.	Provenience (H=House)	Est. Lip Diameter (in cm.)	Rim Form	Basic Surface Finish	Remarks
A	AI 13	H I, fill	15(?)	46		Plain lip, decorated handle and shoulder area
B	AI 123	H I, fill	20(?)	43		Plain handle and lip
C	AIII 41	H III, fill	Orifice elliptical, axes about 8 x 10	48		From same vessel as E. Two strap handles
D	AI 9	H I, fill		29		Rim projection
E	AIII 41					From same vessel as C
F	AIV 14	H IV, fill		23(?)	Stamped with end of stick	
G	AII 36	H II, fill		27(?)	Cord-wrapped paddle-stamped	
H	AI 4	H I, fill		28	Cord-wrapped paddle-stamped	
I	AII 67	H II, Feature 3		42(?)		
J	AII 83	H II, Feature 5	3.5		Smoothed with brushing	Miniature vessel
K	AI 71 UMMA 7750	H I, fill	Orifice elliptical, axes about 19 x 23	28	Grooved-paddle stamped	
L	AI 22	H I, fill	Orifice probably not circular—about 15 on short axis	44	Grooved-paddle stamped	
M	AI 243	H I, fill		28	Probably grooved-paddle stamped	

PLATE XIII

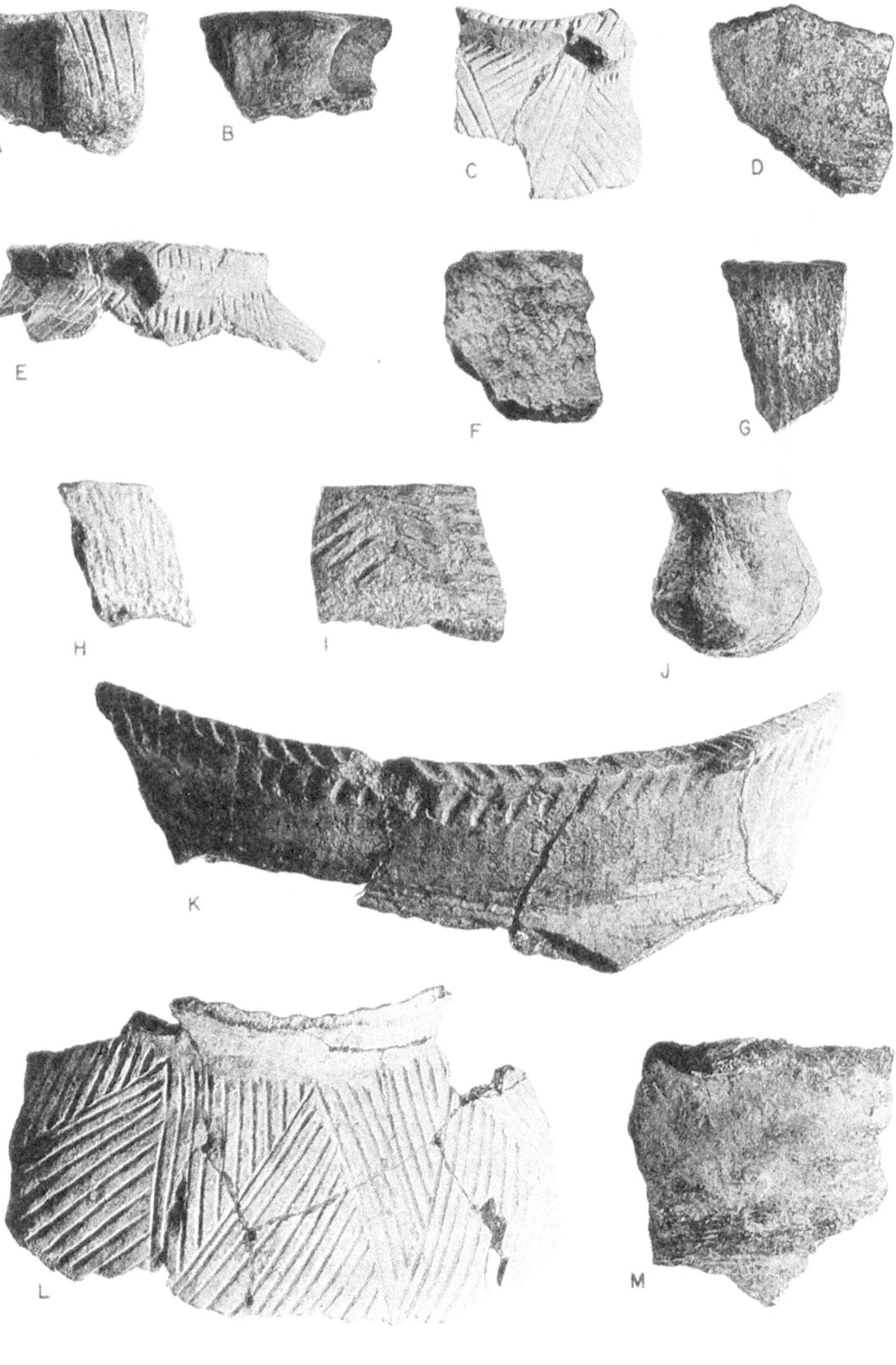

PLATE XIV

PLATE XIV

Hughes beveled sherds, lugs, and other rim sherds.
(Reduced approx. ½.)

	Field Cat. No.	Provenience (H = House)	Est. Lip Diameter (in cm.)	Rim Form	Basic Surface Finish	Remarks
A	AI 14	H I, fill				Cord-impressed decoration
B	AII 17	H II, fill				Cord-impressed decoration. Probably simple S-shaped rim "spout"
C	AI 159	H I, surface				Cord-impressed decoration
D	AI 203	H I, Feature 9				Cord-impressed decoration
E	AIV 44	H III, Feature 3				Cord-impressed decoration
F	AIII 4	H III, fill				Top view of small horizontally projecting lug
G	AI 6	H I, fill	Large vessel probably elliptical orifice	28	Probably grooved-paddle stamped	Top view of horizontally projecting lug
H	AIV 7	H IV, fill		25(?)	Cord-wrapped paddle-stamped	
I	AI 10	H I, fill		Unclass.		Smoothing striations or brushing on rim
J	AI 123	H I, fill		24	Cord-wrapped paddle-stamped	Slightly smoothed rim
K	AI 3	H I, fill	22	24	Probably cord-wrapped paddle-stamped	Paddle impressions nearly obliterated on rim by smoothing
L	AI 3	H I, fill	16	24	Cord-wrapped paddle-stamped	Cord impressions nearly obliterated on rim by smoothing
M	AIII 55	H III, Feature 3		24(?)	Cord-wrapped paddle-stamped	Rim smoothed, cord impressions show in a few places
N	AI 91	H I, fill		24		Vertical brushing immediately below punctations, perhaps surface finish before smoothing
O	AIII 55	H III, Feature 3	26	17	Grooved-paddle stamped	
P	AI 203	H I, Feature 9	25	24	Rim brushed and smoothed	Paste extremely friable with coarse tempering particles
Q	AII 35	H II, fill	16	29	Cord-wrapped paddle-stamped	Rim smoothed

PLATE XV

Handles, decorated body and rim sherds, and other pottery features. (Reduced approx. ½.)

	Field Cat. No.	Provenience (H = House)	Basic Surface Finish	Remarks
A	AII 7	H II, fill		
B	AI 57	H I, fill		
C	AIII 9	H III, fill		
D	AI 57	H I, fill		
E	AII 67	H II, Feature 3		
F	AI 111	H I, fill		
G	AI 11	H I, fill		
H	AI 11	H I, fill		Incised strap handle
I	AIV 7	H IV, fill		Painted sherd. See Pl. 17, C
J	AIII 5(?)	H III	Grooved-paddle stamped	Rim Form 27
K	AIII 4	H III, fill		Probably Rim Form 44
L	AI 76	H I, fill		Detached lug
M	AI 203	H I, Feature 9		See Pl. XIV, D
N	AI 14(?)	H I, fill		See Pl. XIV, A
O	AII 17	H II, fill		See Pl. XIV, B
P	AIII 25	H III, fill		Detached handle
Q	AII 30	H II, fill		Detached handle. See Pl. 10, A
R	AII 67	H II, Feature 3		Probably Rim Form 27. (See Pl. 13, I)

PLATE XV

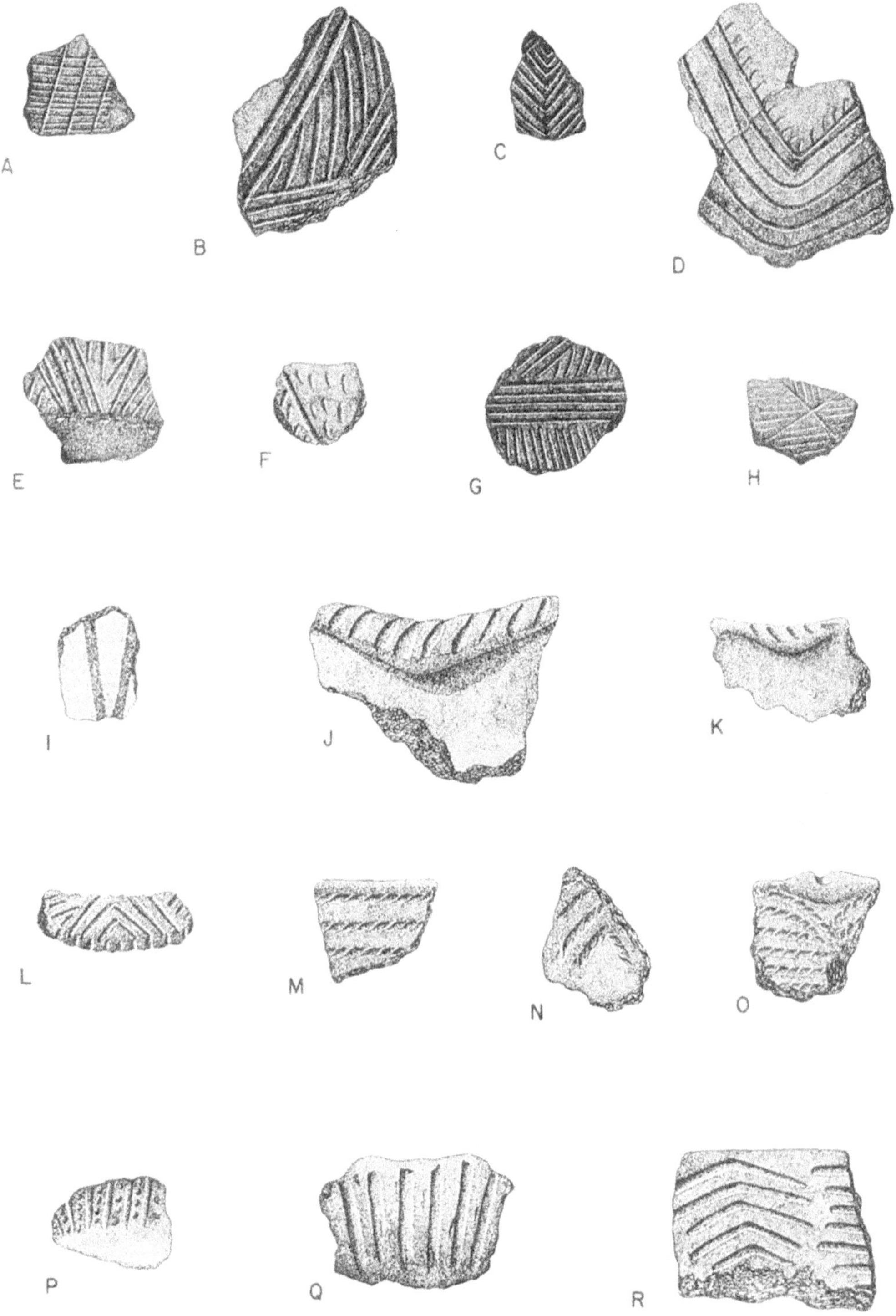

PLATE XVI

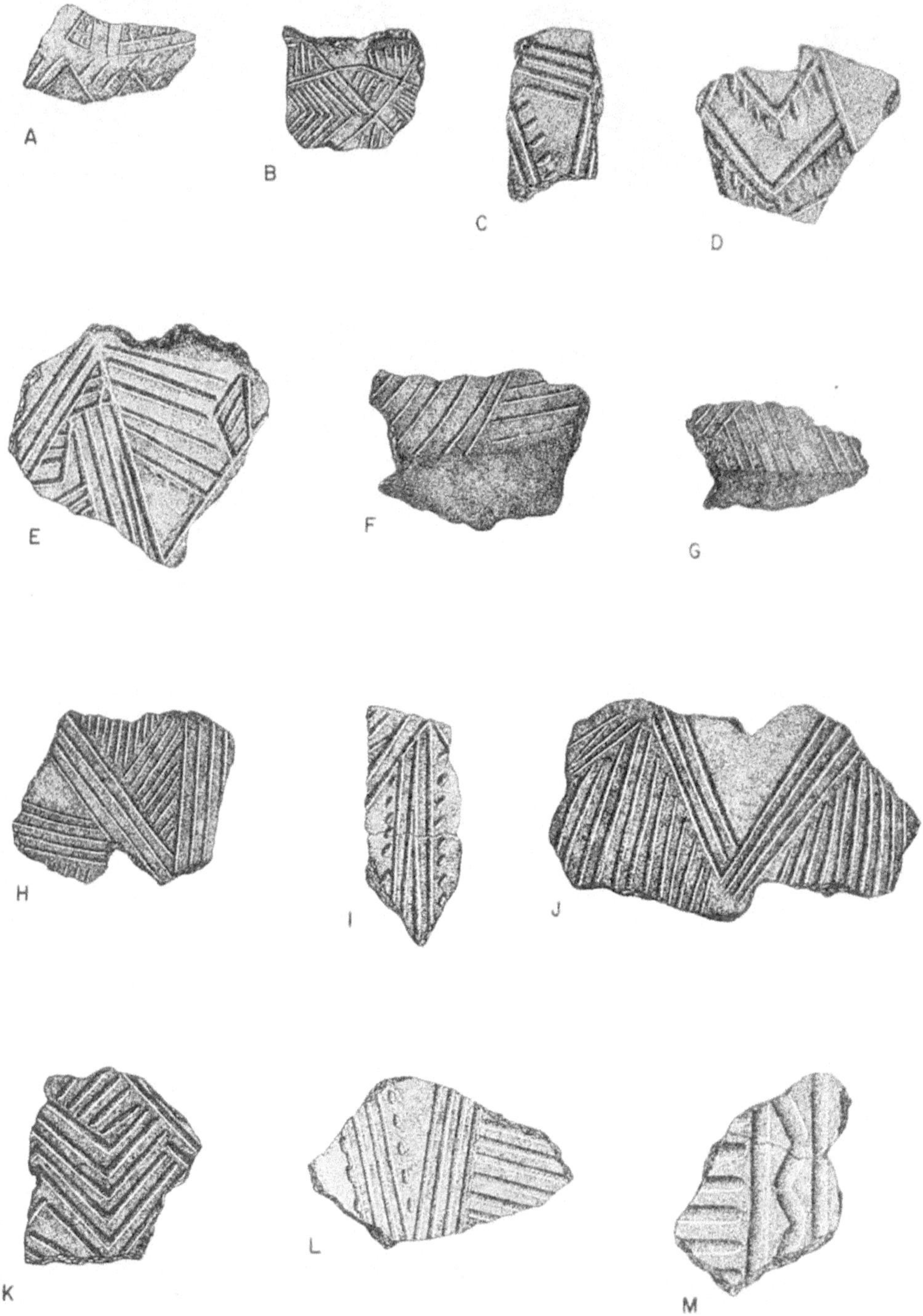

PLATE XVI

Decorated body sherds.
(Reduced approx. $\frac{1}{2}$.)

	Field Cat. No.	Provenience (H=House)
A	AI 19	H I, surface
B	AIII 24	H III, fill
C	AII 36	H II, fill
D	AI 14	H I, fill
E	AIII 4	H III, fill
F	AI 131	H I, Feature 3
G	AIII 4	H III, fill
H	AIII 43	H III, fill
I	AI 57	H I, fill
J	AI 19	H I, surface
K	AIV 6	H IV, fill
L	AI 1	H I, fill
M	AIII 62	H III, fill

PLATE XVII

Body sherds and handles.
(Reduced approx. ½.)

	Field Cat. No.	Provenience (H = House)	Surface Finish	Remarks
A	AII 30	H II, fill		Strap handle
B	AI 14	H I, fill		Strap handle
C	AIV 7	H IV, fill	Smoothed	Painted decoration on exterior
D	AII 17	H II, fill	Brushed (exterior and interior)	Angular shoulder, brushing horizontal
E	AIV 45	H IV, fill	Brushed (exterior and interior)	Angular shoulder, brushing approximately horizontal
F	Unknown		Cord-wrapped paddle-stamped	Angular shoulder, cord impressions approximately vertical
G	AI 4	H I, fill	Cord-wrapped paddle-stamped	
H	AII 30	H II, fill	Cord-wrapped paddle-stamped	Two sets of impressions at slight angle to each other
I	AIV 40	H IV, fill	Cord-wrapped paddle-stamped	Partial smoothing over cord impression
J	AIV 14	H IV, fill	Grooved-paddle stamped	
K	AIV 40	H IV, fill	Grooved-paddle stamped	
L	AIV 40	H IV, fill	Grooved-paddle stamped	
M	AI 10	H I, fill	Checked-paddle stamped	Smoothing over paddle impressions
N	AII 69	H II, Feature 2	Checked-paddle stamped	Smoothing over paddle impressions
O	AIII 59	H III, Feature 4	Checked-paddle stamped	Smoothing over paddle impressions

PLATE XVII

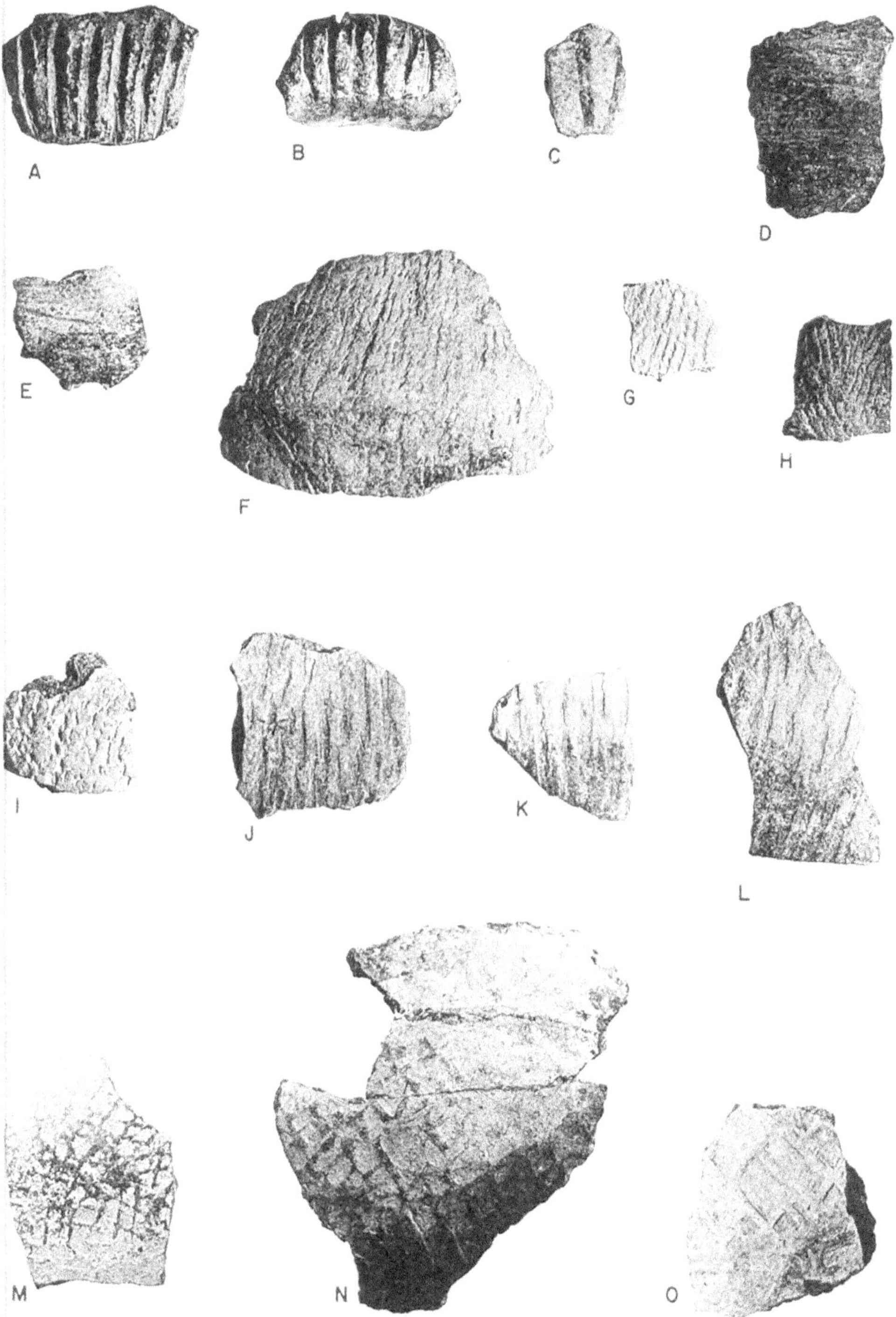

www.ingramcontent.com/pod-product-compliance
Lightning Source LLC
LaVergne TN
LVHW050021250826
846302LV00008B/45
* 9 7 8 1 9 4 9 0 9 8 4 9 5 *